BLACK OPS ADVERTISING

BLACK OPS
ADVERTISING

NATIVE ADS, CONTENT MARKETING,
AND THE COVERT WORLD OF THE DIGITAL SELL

MARA EINSTEIN

OR Books
New York · London

© 2016 Mara Einstein

Published for the book trade by OR Books in partnership with Counterpoint Press. Distributed to the trade by Publishers Group West

All rights information: rights@orbooks.com

First printing 2016

Cataloging-in-Publication data is available from the Library of Congress. A catalog record for this book is available from the British Library.

ISBN 978-1-94486-900-7

Text design by Under|Over. Typeset by AarkMany Media, Chennai, India.

10 9 8 7 8 5 4 3 2

"There is no need for advertisements to look like advertisements. If you make them look like editorial pages, you will attract about 50 percent more readers. You might think that the public would resent this trick, but there is no evidence to suggest that they do."

—David Ogilvy, founder, Ogilvy & Mather

"Nobody comes to Buzzfeed to look at the ads, but they'll come for the content. When the advertising is content—good content they're willing to click on and engage with, and share if it's good—that's the future for publishers."

—Jonah Peretti, founder, BuzzFeed

To David, for listening to me,
for believing in me, for loving me

TABLE OF CONTENTS

"Ads are baked into content like chocolate chips into a cookie. Except it's more like raisins into a cookie, because no one fucking wants them there."

—John Oliver

INTRODUCTION
WHY ADS DON'T LOOK LIKE ADS

On October 14, 2012, Felix Baumgartner attempted the impossible—to dive from outer space going faster than the speed of sound. Wearing what looked like a battery pack out of a 1950s sci-fi movie, millions of people watched as this Austrian jumped from a space pod surrounded by darkness to land safely in a sunlit field 128,000 feet below. Successfully traveling at 844 miles per hour, this leap was a triumph of technology and one man's fearlessness that became the talk of the world, a twenty-first-century version of Neil Armstrong's walk on the moon.

Years of planning had gone into this. Technologies were developed, test jumps executed, and millions of dollars spent. Numerous television networks were asked to be part of the project, and many turned it down. You can't really blame them. This project was dangerous. Weather conditions had to be perfect. The network and production crew had to be ready at a moment's notice. And there was the real possibility that the network would show, *live*, a man jumping to his death. Discovery Channel took on the challenge and aired this daredevil's plunge, creating one of the highest-rated programs in the network's history.

But this exceedingly risky endeavor wasn't a NASA mission or a physics experiment out of Carnegie Mellon. It was an extreme event called Stratos that had been developed and paid for by Red Bull, a producer of energy drinks popular with teens, young adults, and college students cramming for finals. Marketed with the tagline "Red Bull gives you wings," the product is all about communicating that the company is on the cutting edge of pop culture.[1] So cutting edge that the only clues to commercialization in the video are subtle displays of the Red Bull logo that fit seamlessly into the content—on the space pod, on Baumgartner's space suit, on t-shirts of people watching in the crowd below, and so on. The camera never lingers on these symbols and the viewer's attention is on the fantastic achievement about to occur, so unless you know to look for them they are easy to miss.

Incredibly, then, all this work, money, and even risk to a person's life were nothing more than an elaborate, exceptionally well-executed piece of advertising.[2]

• • •

Stunning events with arresting visuals like Stratos are part of a growing advertising phenomenon known as content marketing, a straightforward-sounding yet ultimately vague way to describe the means through which advertisers get people to spend time watching or reading "content" that the advertiser has paid for. The "content" masquerades as "news" (or entertainment) and, when executed to perfection, results in successful stunts like the Red Bull leap from space. This trend has become so pervasive that marketers are starting to proclaim that content marketing might soon become the only type of marketing left. Chances are, though, that you've never heard of content marketing, and that's exactly the point.

A key aspect of this marketing tool is to engage consumers without their realizing they've taken part in a promotional initiative. Red Bull did this brilliantly. In praising the Stratos jump as one of the best advertising campaigns of the twenty-first century, a senior executive noted in industry magazine *Advertising Age*: "The beauty of it was that it didn't feel like you were being sold something."[3]

Red Bull—and now almost every consumer marketer on the planet (close to 90 percent)—uses content marketing. They use it because it works. In this case, 37 million people watched a short YouTube video, while others viewed longer more detailed versions, or edits in different languages, or a documentary on Discovery, or as the lede news story in print or on television—free media for the brand that totaled in the tens of millions of dollars in the U.S. and conservative estimates suggest that this totaled more than six billion Euros worldwide in the first three days alone.[4] This space jump is a small part of the company's larger marketing plan in which traditional advertising is shunned in favor of sponsoring extreme sporting events, funding unknown musicians, and developing cutting-edge technology. Content about these experiences appear on the Red Bull YouTube channel, a site that in 2015 topped more than one billion views, and they are presented through documentaries, magazines, and reality series produced by Red Bull Media House. But the goal is not only viewership, it is sales. And the Red Bull content initiative paid off handsomely. In the first six months after the Stratos jump, sales rose seven percent to $1.6 billion.[5]

One small step for man . . . one giant leap for Red Bull.

CONTENT CONFUSION

Even with twenty-plus years of marketing experience, I didn't initially realize that this was an advertising ploy. I watched the jump as others had, and I never once thought that I was being sold an extreme energy drink. I thought I was watching news.

That Red Bull doesn't opt to use traditional advertising is their prerogative. But if the content is worthy of our attention, why doesn't the company attach its name to it? The answer is easy: Red Bull is well aware that if we knew an advertiser was involved, most of us would not watch it. Years of remote controls, DVRs, and now "banner blindness" and ad blockers have taught advertisers that consumers are utterly adept at circumventing advertising. In response, they have turned to new and improved forms of clandestine marketing.

Obscured persuasion, broadly known as stealth marketing, is defined as "the use of surreptitious marketing practices that fail to disclose or reveal the true relationship with the company that produces or sponsors the marketing message."[6] While not new, these hidden marketing practices have reached new heights and more devious methods in the age of social media. And with those methods have come a multitude of names—covert marketing, undercover marketing, embedded marketing, and more recently, content marketing, native advertising, buzz marketing, and brand journalism, among many, many others. There are few straightforward definitions for these strategies, but the goal is clear: find ways to get products in front of people subtly, so they don't realize they are being persuaded to purchase those products, as well as—the pièce de résistance—to push those products to their friends, creating a world where we are in a constant state of buying or selling.

Whatever the label, it comes down to the fact that advertisers can camouflage their sales message in only one of two ways: (1) hide the advertising within existing content environments, or (2) create the pitch themselves and make it look like something other than advertising. The first of these is native advertising, the second is content marketing.

Native advertising is designed to be seamlessly integrated into a website or social media feed such that visitors will click on the advertiser-sponsored content as readily as they do the nonsponsored editorial. The best example of this is BuzzFeed, a popular source for news and information online. Anyone who has spent time on the site or the app, or who's had BuzzFeed content forwarded through social media, has been privy to "listicles" like "51 Thoughts Every Lady Who Shaves Her Legs Has Had" or "12 Life Lessons We All Learned Our Freshman Year of College," as well as quizzes like "What Fraggle Rock Character Are You?" The difference with the middle article is that it is sponsored by Target, an advertiser promoting to students going back to school. How do you know this? Because of a teeny, tiny orange rectangle that says "promoted by" located on the article on top of an equally small logo. But native advertising isn't only on BuzzFeed. It's on Facebook and Twitter, and it's even on the *New York Times* website, which launched its in-house marketing group with a piece about women in prison that was sponsored by the Netflix series *Orange Is the New Black*.[7]

On the other hand, content marketing, according to the Content Marketing Institute, is made up of "valuable, relevant, and consistent content" that is used to appeal to a specific target audience. Red Bull creates content that communicates the idea of "extreme" using alternative music, exhilarating sports, or cutting-edge technology that appeal to its audience of over-caffeinated college students who dream of doing something extreme but probably never will. Chipotle created a three-minute, tear-jerking video with an accompanying website that included a downloadable game called "The Scarecrow," all of it meant to promote the negative aspects of processed food while presenting Chipotle as a healthier and more sustainable alternative. And Pennzoil produced a documentary called *Breaking Barriers* about breaking the speed limit. While the oil company's involvement with the venture was widely covered in the advertising trade press, Pennzoil does not appear on the consumer-focused *National Geographic* website or on the cable channel where the programming aired. Shrewder still are the sponsored tweets, blog posts, and Vines that never mention their corporate connections.

All of this advertising—and it is advertising, whether marketers call it native advertising or content marketing or anything else—is entertaining while appearing informative. We waste endless hours online reading this news clip or watching that video post, only to realize in the end that we haven't interacted with anything of depth, and we can't figure out why. Here's the reason: marketing is not meant to engage our intellect; it is structured to elicit emotions. In pursuit of those emotions—typically awe or anger or amusement—we willingly continue to watch or read. After all, what's one more cat video, especially when it's so cute that you just have to share it with your friends? The problem is that it's like eating potato chips; you can never have just one.

That's because user interfaces are designed to keep us enraptured and plugged in. We are glued to a screen in our pocket, on our desk, or by our bedside twenty-four hours a day. Mobile devices are electronic pacifiers, designed to be incredibly addictive. Notifications, while sometimes helpful, are designed as reward cues that give our brain little jolts of pleasure that tether us to the technology.[8] The techniques are so effective that a majority of eighteen to eighty-five-year-olds found that social media is harder to resist than smoking, drinking, spending money, sleeping, and sex.[9] More statistics: Facebook users are on the site 81 hours per year; office workers check their email 30-40 times per hour, and we switch between devices 21 times per hour.[10] In 2014, Americans on average spent 159 minutes per day on their computers, 163 minutes on tablets, and 134 minutes using smartphones for things other than voice. Only five years ago, those numbers were 184, 21, and 40 respectively.[11] Certainly much of this is due to the wide availability of broadband, the improved technology of smartphones, and the proliferation and addictive qualities of social media. However, that alone does not lead us to stare at our iPhones or Galaxys. It is the smartly crafted, data-driven advertising dressed up to look like an innocuous article or laugh-out-loud video.

As this affect-producing content mushrooms throughout the media pipeline, traditional news producers must compete against it and do so at a distinct disadvantage. While advertising sources create content with the express purpose of giving you something you want—advice, information, a coupon, a smile, a mindless break—news organizations are tasked with giving us information we need. To address that disadvantage, news producers reframe their stories to feel more like advertising, luring in readers (and advertisers) by using what one reporter called "whorebait." Whorebait—or more politely, clickbait—describes articles with headlines like "You Won't Believe What Happens Next" or "Here's The Problem with Self-Driving Cars Becoming a Mainstream Reality" or "Everyone poops, but 2.6 billion people do it in a really crappy way." More fundamentally, publishers and advertisers are in head-to-head competition with one another, because publishers *are* advertisers, advertisers *are* publishers, and the content both of them produce is an amalgamation of whatever they think will get you to "engage"—that is, spend time with them.

To be fair, to some extent the idea of clickbait is not new. Under the broadcast television model, we called it lowest common denominator programming. Think here of *The Bachelor* or *The Voice* or a myriad of other series—reality or otherwise—that are short on art and long on formula, but that are ultimately fun to watch, so many people do. The larger the audience, the more money a network makes through advertising, which leads networks to offer lots of "reality" and other mindless content while providing limited doses of news and PBS-like fare. In print, the corresponding example would be *People* magazine or a supermarket tabloid.

The difference today—and this is key—is that the race between advertisers and publishers centers on *creating content that grabs our attention while hiding its corporate sales pitch*. It is "black ops advertising," and it is the purposeful masking of corporate bias by either the advertiser or the publisher so that we can't discern the underlying perspective—is it an ad? Is it an article? Can it be both? This state of uncertainty is what I am calling "content confusion."

Content confusion occurs when advertising does not look like advertising, making it virtually impossible to separate hard news content from a soft sales pitch. The ultimate progression of this trajectory is a world where there is no real content: everything we experience is some form of sales pitch. While that extreme is unlikely to happen, it's already the case that more and more advertising blends in seamlessly with noncommercial content, overwhelming the media environment and pushing real news further and further to the margins. There is a simple reason for this: if the goal is profit, legitimate content must take a back seat to clickbait and quizzes and entertaining cat videos, items that get us to spend time online in the hopes that we'll purchase a product.

Getting us to click on content is only part of the equation. Once we read the "article" or watch the video, the hope is that we'll share it, causing the content to go viral: spreading from one consumer to another because of its entertainment value. Viral marketing is essential because it uses our social networks to sell products. We promote the brand, we tell our friends and family to watch the video or buy a product or "Like" a page, and because the endorsement is from a known and trusted commodity, our friends and family are more inclined to pay attention. This is word-of-mouth marketing (WOM), and it is the backbone of the new digital stealth marketing ecosystem. Marketers love word-of-mouth marketing because it is, and always has been, the most effective form of sales. Further: if the goal is to obscure the advertising message, word-of-mouth marketing is also the least suspect. After all, if a friend tells us they liked the latest *Jurassic Park* movie, there's no reason for us not to believe it. Unfortunately, what we also come to believe is that amassing friends on Facebook or followers on Twitter is ultimately about sharing with our compatriots. It is not: it is about creating an audience for advertisers. Our relationships, then, become means of facilitating market transactions, or in the parlance of the market: they have been monetized.[12]

Further complicating the distinctions between what is "real" and what is a marketing ploy is that we have taken on the tools of the marketer. We tweet, we post, we even add the corporate name. One example of this is #alexfromtarget. In November 2014, a teenage girl went into her local Target store and saw a cute guy bagging items at the cash register. She took a picture of Alex (his name was on his work badge), posted it on Twitter, and created the hashtag #alexfromtarget. Teens started retweeting his picture, and in twenty-four hours, Alex had more than 300,000 followers and was all over the news. This was not a PR stunt—it was an everyday teen acting as a marketer for the discount store. In another example, eight-year-old Evan, star of EvanTube, creates videos to review toys and videogames in a family-friendly format. This pint-sized pitchman rakes in over a million dollars a year and has more views than Katy Perry.[13] So are Evan and his YouTube channel advertisements for the products reviewed, ads for Evan personally, or legitimate consumer reviews? Hard to tell.

By now, you might wonder: was the article I read this morning paid for by Apple? Was that BuzzFeed quiz a promotion? Is that post on Facebook "organic," or did a marketer pay for me to see it? The newspaper article, maybe; BuzzFeed, almost definitely; and with Facebook, any content is increasingly likely to be advertising because the company continuously manipulates its algorithm to improve profitability by forcing marketers to pay for content. Most people have begun to suspect this, at least in the case of Facebook. We have also gotten savvier about how marketers use data to promote products to us. We know that at least a portion of online reviews are fake or paid for,[14] and Millennials, in particular, are not all that sensitive about giving up personal data for convenience if it means that they can get a discount or find out about the latest trend, lest they face the dreaded FOMO (fear of missing out).[15]

But what if you don't know that a blog post has a marketer behind it, or that the celebrity tweeting about a lip balm was paid $20,000 for those 140 characters, or that a newspaper article was sponsored by an online streaming video service, or that a documentary you watched on National Geographic was paid for by an oil company? If you knew it was advertising, chances are you'd speed by it the same way you zap past a commercial on your DVR or dump your junk mail in the recycle bin. Or if you did watch it, aware of the content's sponsorship, you might approach it with a more critical or cynical eye—something companies do not want you to do.

The line between unbiased content and commercials has gotten so blurred that even the language around these concepts has changed. Advertisers no longer think of themselves as producing commercials; they produce "films." Marketing departments are increasingly staffed by former journalists who labor not in a "bullpen," but in what are offensively called "newsrooms." Few of the former journalists I spoke with have an issue with creating this biased work because they claim that they wouldn't produce a piece that would offend a consumer. Unfortunately, that right there is part of the problem.

SOCIAL MEDIA: "FRIEND" AND FOE

Content confusion is exacerbated by social media, where native ads fit most indigenously into the noncorporate content. But creating engaging content is not enough. Marketers also need to create a relationship with us—they want to be our friend—so that we will feel indebted to them or inspired to share our information and experiences with others. This might be as simple as our posting the promotional video for the upcoming season of *Orange Is the New Black*, "Liking" a charity, or tweeting about the great service we got at our last stay at a Hilton.

To build these relationships, the company must get our attention. This is done through social media (and facilitated by data), which enables direct interaction between companies and consumers. Advertisers call this customer relationship marketing, or CRM. This relationship is important because the more time we spend with the product, the more likely we are to become a customer or a repeat customer. Having one-to-one connections with consumers is very new for marketers. Relationships, in contrast to yelling at someone to buy via a commercial, take time to build, and digital technologies allow for types of company-consumer interactions that traditional media technologies didn't. "Social is not for selling, it's for social," is the battle cry I heard over and over at the marketing events I attended. It frankly felt creepy, and if not creepy, sad.

Many of us buy into the attention from marketers because being seen online ties into our sense of self. "Like" something on Facebook, and it shows others who we are. Better still, if someone from the brand company we've "Liked" interacts with us via social media, we feel acknowledged, even appreciated. In one amusing example of social engagement, Groupon made a Facebook post about a product called the banana bunker, which protects the phallic-shaped fruit. Not surprisingly, people posted numerous sex jokes: "What do you do if your banana curves the other way?" and "Do they come with bananacidal lube?" In response, Groupon engaged in witty repartee: "Good News—the Bunker is Omni-directional!" and "Why would you commit bananacide?! Monster!"[16] Consumers were enthralled (12,000 comments, 18,000 Likes, and 43,000 shares), the event got press coverage, and the banana bunker sold out in less than two hours. In a more G-rated version of the same idea, the fast food restaurant Sonic ran a campaign called "Back-to-School Summaries" where they asked students to submit book titles from their summer reading list. The company then responded with a synopsis in ten words or less. These included *Hamlet*: "Wants revenge for his father's death, goes a little overboard"; *A Clockwork Orange*: "Futuristic totalitarian society. Violence, violence, violence," and finally, *Fifty Shades of Grey*: "Nice try. There's no way you're reading that for school." These examples are fun and fairly harmless, like watching a comedian, only in an asynchronous format.

Other sorts of relationship building via digital technologies, however, allow for extremely individualized interactions that are exceedingly invasive and border on stalking. For instance, Laura Spica—an average American dog owner—tweeted a picture of her dog looking out the window for squirrels. Purina tweeted back the dog's picture but with a twist: they had outfitted the dog by drawing in a hat, sunglasses, and a jacket. Purina had also drawn a badge in the upper left hand corner of the picture saying "Squirrel Patrol," and underneath the dog they had written, "starring HENRY the dog." The dog owner was so enthralled by the attention that she tweeted back:

> @Purina Oh-Em-Gee! You pimped my #PurinaDog! That's possibly the cutest thing I've ever seen!!! #SquirrelPatrol #HenryDog[17]

In under a minute, the company had reached out to someone and moved her from talking about her dog to promoting Purina. Just like #alexattarget, Laura didn't have to attach a brand name to her post, but she did, and Purina loved her for it.

Purina is able to engage with Laura and other consumers like her because they scan the Internet in real time looking for mentions of cats and dogs—an activity known as social listening—and determine how they can insert themselves into the conversation. Did Laura buy Purina? I don't know. But she did become a brand ambassador in response to some brief corporate attention. And it didn't feel like marketing, either to her or to the followers with whom she shared the tweet.

Undergirding all of this one-on-one interaction is big data—large stores of information made available by digital technologies—a topic we will cover at length in Chapter 5. For the moment, bear in mind that media and marketing companies track our every digital move. Put a pair of shoes in an online cart, decide not to buy them, and just wait for the image of those flats to follow you from website to website and from computer to cell phone to iPad and soon to your smart TV, a technique known as retargeting.[18] And by now, you likely know that the Google results you receive in response to searches are not the same as the ones your spouse or child or business associate sees. This is because as you roam the web, you leave trails of data for marketers to analyze—and to sell to others—in a never-ending attempt to persuade you to buy even more consumer goods. How you have moved around the web determines not only the ads that you see, but the types of sites that will make it to the top of the Google results. It isn't merely Google that uses your information to serve their business needs: Netflix created "House of Cards" using viewership data from their site (more on that later), Pinterest is the social media equivalent of a consumer focus group, and I could go on and on. The list of sites that use our information to garner information is virtually endless.

In the perhaps the most notorious case of marketing research, Facebook manipulated users' news feeds in the summer of 2014 to see if they could influence user emotions. The company increased the amount of negative content on the news feeds of 689,003 people to see if it would make them sadder, testing a theory known as emotional contagion. The question was: could Facebook use its algorithms to make an emotion spread like a virus from one person to another? In short, it worked: fewer positive posts in the news feed led to more negative posts being written, and vice versa.[19] Think about that: Facebook used their site to discover that they had the ability to stage-manage people's feelings. It sounds like something out of a sci-fi movie. Unfortunately, it isn't. Facebook claimed that this was legitimate product research and that they were protected by the legal notice that users agree to when they sign up for the site.[20]

Bottom line: the Internet is one giant marketing research experiment. The vast stores of data generated from spending time online enable marketers to tailor content to individualized wants and needs, to develop relationships with consumers, and through those relationships to compel us to engage with increasingly cloaked commercial content and to share it with our social groups.

DECLINING REVENUES = BLURRED LINES

Media and marketing have merged because the revenue models that buoy the production of noncommercial content are imploding. The long-term consequences of this are likely to be far worse than we can imagine, both in terms of the denigration of content and the amount of money we as individuals will all have to pay out of pocket for content that used to be free because it was advertising supported. In the short term, the "solution" is to hide the advertising—a choice that has far-ranging fallout.

In brief: media companies generate revenue either by selling advertising or via a hybrid model of selling advertising and subscriptions.[21] In its simplest form, for example, broadcast TV networks sell advertising, and magazines sell a combination of ads and subscriptions. Cable networks also work in this way: a network like MTV, say, gets money from advertising and a monthly fee from the local cable operator, such as Comcast or Time Warner.

The cost of an ad is determined by how many people see the ad (ratings) and by who those people are. The more people that watch a commercial, the more expensive it is. That is why commercials in the Super Bowl—the most watched program on television, with tens of millions of viewers—go for more than $3 million for a thirty-second spot. But cost is not just about tonnage. Advertisers want to reach some types of people more than others, and they will pay handsomely to reach those desirable consumer groups. Young men, for example, are a notoriously hard-to-reach but valuable target audience, and advertisers will pay up to twice as much money to reach them as they will to reach many female demographic groups, who tend to watch more television.

Obviously, companies with a combined revenue model have been better able to withstand the ups and downs of a volatile advertising market. MTV might lose advertising dollars in a down market, but the company retains a substantial monthly revenue stream from cable operators. In 2013, for example, MTV received a monthly average of 39 cents per subscriber and had 99 million subscribers, so their annual subscription fees totaled more than $463 million.[22] But any security that combined revenue models might have provided no longer exists. Digital technologies are threatening not only advertising revenues, but also hybrid revenue models.

In terms of television advertising, a combination of delayed viewership, reduced viewership, and the practice of viewing online has led to declining ratings and a concomitant decline in revenues.[23] Nielsen, the agency that determines the viewership of TV programs, counts C3: commercial ratings for live viewership, plus anyone who watches their DVR within three days of the broadcast. Thus people who record programs on DVRs but put off watching them for several days are lost in the ratings numbers. Ratings have declined further because people are simply shunning TV in favor of YouTube, Netflix, and other video outlets. More troubling still is the migration of TV viewing to tablets and mobile devices. That's because when you watch *Scandal* or *The Walking Dead* online, that viewership cannot be tracked by Nielsen.[24]

As the audience is moving from TV to online, so too is advertising spending, and this is happening at a faster and faster rate. Up to now, television has been immune to declines in advertising spending because of its ability to reach a large audience, something no other medium can do. In 2014, though, spending shifted for the first time away from traditional media to digital. Expectations are that those spending patterns will continue, particularly in light of the fact that in 2015, Procter & Gamble (P&G) and Unilever, two of the world's largest advertisers, planned to spend 30 to 35 percent of their budgets on digital, with some of those dollars being found at the expense of television.[25] These advertisers and others are shifting their spending to follow consumers, but they are also doing it because advertising online is significantly cheaper. This low cost advertising is great for marketers, not so good for media properties, whether offline or on.

In terms of subscriptions, cable companies are seeing declines as never before. More people (and particularly Millennials) are "cord cutters" or even "cord nevers," people who are either giving up their cable subscriptions or who've never bought one because they can receive all the programming they want online. Cable homes have dropped from 70 percent of American homes to 57 percent in the last fifteen years.[26] These "cordless" folks are the reason we are seeing more direct-to-consumer program options (called OTT, or over-the-top content, like HBO Now and CBS All Access), in addition to the propagation of streaming options from companies like Amazon, Hulu, and Netflix, a site which alone accounts for more than twenty-eight hours per month of viewing per subscriber.[27] According to Nielsen, more than 40 percent of U.S. households subscribe to at least one of these types of video streaming services.[28] Fewer subscribers mean not only less money for the cable operators, but also for the TV networks that they carry.

While broadcast and cable television, as well as newspapers and magazines, are struggling, Google—an organization that produces no content—generated $50 billion in ad income. That's more than twice that of all newspapers.[29] Think about that: the one company that spends absolutely nothing to create entertainment or news is blowing everyone else out of the water. And not surprisingly, the only media segment expected to experience increased advertising revenue is digital, which was predicted to grow by 19 percent in 2015 and to outpace TV spending by 2018.[30] Do you see how badly this could go?

From an economic viewpoint it is obvious why this is happening. In the 1980s, before cable took off, 90 percent of Americans watched one of the three major broadcast channels. Reaching prospective customers was easy: make a commercial and put it on network TV. After cable became ubiquitous, broadcasters could still reach a significant audience with its most popular shows. For example, during its run in the 1990s *Seinfeld* regularly reached more than 30 million viewers. Today, a major hit like *The Big Bang Theory* only reaches half that number, yet still commands a steep payment for a thirty-second commercial—close to $350,000. Since television networks continued to charge exorbitant prices yet could no longer accumulate large audiences, marketers began to think that producing their own content made more sense.

Crucially, it was not the mere existence of digital but rather the advent of social media that drove the rise of content marketing. Companies had been able to create blogs and websites for decades. What they had not been able to do was drive people to their sites, or better still, have people disseminate their message for them. With Facebook and Twitter, Tumblr, and Instagram, companies can get their brand messages in front of consumers at a fraction of what it costs to produce and broadcast a TV commercial. It's a no-brainer.

The importance of this decline in advertising dollars in TV and print cannot be overstated. As media companies have become increasingly desperate for revenues, the wall between church and state (editorial and advertising) has come crumbling down, enabling advertising to invade the editorial realm.

In the past, media organizations would work with advertisers to help them achieve their marketing objectives, while channeling those objectives within defined parameters. Marketers talked with the ad sales people at a magazine or TV network, and PR pros pitched the editorial staff or programming executives, trying to work their way into the editorial space. Yet editorial staff members fought tirelessly against bowing to the wishes of advertisers, particularly in the print realm. To do so was anathema to their journalistic integrity. The best an advertiser could hope for was that their ad would be placed next to content that related to their product. For instance, an ad for Dole Raisins might be placed in a magazine next to a recipe for oatmeal raisin cookies, or better yet, an article about how eating more raisins is good for your health.

Today, in pursuit of advertiser dollars, almost anything goes. A publication might produce a two-page spread of recipes, or a TV morning show might create a several-minute segment around how to integrate raisins into a healthy diet, both paid for by Dole. It's not as if executives in TV and print didn't see this change in the relationship between advertising and editorial coming. But still, no one seems to know how this will net out for legacy media, or what the ultimate consequences will be now that editorial integrity has been forced to utterly kowtow to the market.

Advertising and editorial become further conflated online, where advertising is allocated to one of three buckets: paid, owned, and earned media. Paid media is like traditional advertising, and might include display ads on a website, like a banner ad or a pre-roll on a video. Paid media also includes sponsorships, such as when a company's advertising overtakes a website, as well as paid search, like the ads you see on Google. In traditional marketing, paid media would be the foundation of an advertising campaign. Online, though, it only serves to support owned media and earned media.

Owned media typically refers to the marketer's website, but may also include blogs, mobile sites, and social media accounts like Facebook pages, Twitter accounts, or blogs on Tumblr. Websites supply information and give consumers a way to buy products; social, as we have seen, helps to create and sustain relationships. Both are meant to drive earned media.

Earned media is "when customers become the channel"[31]—that is, word of mouth. It can also include PR work performed through traditional media or bloggers. For example, in the case of the banana bunker, there was no paid advertising: Groupon's continuous posting on Facebook represented owned media, and the press attention and the tens of thousands of shares and Likes were earned media—that is, free advertising.

BLACK OPS ADVERTISING

Over the last two years, I have attended conferences, talked to industry insiders, and analyzed an endless number of surreptitious marketing campaigns across a wide range of media platforms. It turns out that the marketing prognosticators were only partly right. While content marketing has become pervasive, it is part of a larger overall trend of the muddying of advertising and editorial: that is, black ops advertising.

The correlation to combat is purposeful. Marketing has always been framed as contentious and militaristic. Marketers have objectives that they need to achieve: they use a variety of sophisticated strategies to achieve those objectives, and then they operationalize those strategies through the use of tactics. And of course, consumers—that is, you and I—are targets. On the ground, this might translate into setting sales goals (objective), stealing customers from competitors (strategy), and then offering coupons for anyone willing to switch brands (tactic). This is what T-Mobile did, for instance, when they got customers to switch from AT&T by paying early termination fees (ETFs), offering up to $300 in trade-in credit towards a new phone, and not requiring a long-term contract. Thus, by targeting young, budget-conscious consumers, the company was able to increase their sales by executing their strategy of stealing customers from their competition.

Just as technology has enabled today's military to move from obvious bombing assaults to covert actions and drone attacks launched from a distance, so too advertising has revised its strategies from loud and disruptive to subtle, camouflaged, and even subversive.[32] Red and white Coca-Cola signs, Nike "Just Do It" commercials, and McDonald's golden arches no longer cut it. Instead, news feeds and social media ads are barely noted as being "sponsored" or "promoted," disguising themselves as content from someone you know. As part of T-Mobile's strategy described above, the company provided customizable "Dear John" letters that people could post to Facebook via a specialized app to explain that they were moving to T-Mobile and to specify which cell carrier they were dumping. More than 80,000 people were willing to take the time to fill out the ad—and make no mistake that this was an ad—and post the letter to their news feeds, suggesting that by enabling them to vent their frustration with their existing cell phone carrier, the company had struck an emotional chord.

Gaming our emotions, tapping into needs, and using those to appear to befriend us is part and parcel of this "black ops" phenomenon. In fact, it has led to a *fundamental paradigm shift in advertising*: instead of telling us to buy, Buy, BUY, marketers "engage" with us so that we will share, Share, SHARE. It is the ultimate subtle sell.

Of course, T-Mobile is just one example. Do you share Jimmy Fallon videos or John Oliver's latest tirade? You are not alone. Millions of people do. Maybe you are a fan of Grumpy Cat. That brand reportedly earned $100 million in the last two years, no small thanks to people sending the furry creature's angry puss around the Internet.[33] And admit it, at least once you've read a listicle like "15 Animal Vines That Will Make You Laugh Every Time" or "13 Things Every Early Cell Phone User Remembers," or taken a quiz like "Which 'Peanuts' Character Is

Your Kid?" If you passed along these three items, then you promoted Geico, Best Buy, or All laundry detergent, respectively.

Detecting these and other types of corporate missives online is becoming increasingly difficult. Online there are no time or space limitations, no cues to let us know that we are watching a sponsored piece of content. Demonstration videos like Blendtec's "Will It Blend?" that show everything from marbles to magnets being whirled in a blender appear to be entertainment, not commercials. Similar demonstrations appear on blog posts or are recommended on Twitter. In their early incarnations, these might have both been legitimate endorsements. Now, however, whole industries have built up around getting bloggers and celebrities to promote products. Agencies like Izea and Ad.ly contact potential endorsers asking them to write or tweet about a product—perhaps a recipe with Tabasco or a celebrity endorsement of an insurance company—and pay them for doing so. Beauty bloggers are notorious for this practice, but it happens across a plethora of categories on sites and in social media. While these covert endorsers are legally required to say that a sponsor is paying them, the reality is that many of them do not, or they note it in the legal fine print where no one will ever read it.

In short, marketing has become about engagement, about getting us to spend increasing and inordinate amounts of time with a brand—often without our knowledge. To do that, companies create content that's made to look like news, made to look like entertainment, made to look and feel like anything but marketing.

The question to ask yourself is this: if you knew it was an advertisement, would you give it more than a split second of your time?

Black Ops Advertising shines a light on this increasingly widespread phenomenon so that we do not waste our time with advertising that has nothing to do with us or tries to sell us a point of view without acknowledging its underlying bias. We seem to be well on our way to an advertising-augmented world where our relationships are monetized and where news is not just entertainment but also full-blown corporate puffery. How many more times will we be enticed to watch what we think is a legitimate news event, only to find out that we've watched an ad? I suspect more than we can guess, especially since marketers are looking to Red Bull as their "best practices" prototype. And while we are watching fake news, real newspapers continue to fold and television revenues continue to decline, which in turn has led to advertising being inserted into all manner of content both on and off line. As the blending of church and state becomes status quo, we should not be surprised to see oil companies espousing environmental benefits and food companies suggesting that processed anything is good for you—all without an advertising disclaimer in sight.

But so what? After all, advertising has long been invasive and manipulative, even flat out trickery. Most practitioners argue that these new types of advertising are an improvement over other forms because they provide benefits for consumers. In theory, after all, we should only be receiving advertising for products and services we want or need, rather than seeing unnecessary commercial clutter. It is also less intrusive than traditional marketing messages because we do not have to stop to interact with it. It occurs in the natural flow of our day. And the ability to find out about a product and buy it immediately has become as simple as hitting a button on your mobile device.

But the costs, both for consumers and for society as a whole, far outweigh these benefits. First, the traditional line between church and state (editorial content and advertising) has virtually disappeared, and with it the symbolic cues that enable us to know when we are engaging with sponsored content. Second, word-of-mouth marketing (WOM), in putting the focus on individuals and personal relationships, is creating a world where marketers try to become our friends and monetize our existing friendships. Third, as companies become adept at data analytics, corporations control what information we see (and perhaps more importantly, what we don't) both in terms of content and in terms of the products and services we might want to buy. Fourth, the type of content produced is being driven by the tracking and manipulation of data, and thus popularity determines what gets published and supported. Rather than scientific achievement or artistic talent or information the electorate needs to fully function in a democracy, "Likes" and tweets and followers become the currency of importance. And finally, we—all of us—are being manipulated to spend time with technology, to interact with friends, and to always be "on," even when this is to our physical and mental detriment.

Media philosopher Neil Postman famously noted that any change in technology comes with a Faustian bargain. In explaining this rule, he said, "Technology giveth and technology taketh away, and not always in equal measure. A new technology sometimes creates more than it destroys. Sometimes, it destroys more than it creates. But it is never one-sided." As we increasingly live online, we give ever more power to the players behind its workings. We have traded privacy and identity for convenience. We have traded genuine face-to-face relationships for Twitter followers and Facebook "friends." We are lost in a corporate Neverland populated with pretty pictures and entertaining videos . . . and increasingly, we don't even know it.

1
FROM MASS TO MILLENNIALS

In a YouTube video called "Marc Ecko Tags Air Force One," two hooded graffiti artists spray paint the president's private plane with the words "Still Free." The video was shot at in the dark of night, and the images are shaky and grainy, suggesting that the camera is hand-held and shot by an amateur. Adding to the "authenticity" is the lack of audio save for periodic heavily-exerted breathing, coming either from the cameraperson or from the graffiti artists after they jump over a barbed wire fence and sprint to the plane to avoid detection from the military guards who protect the area. The video ends with an exhortation to find out more at stillfree.com.

Many who saw the video were appalled. Spraypaint the plane of the President of the United States? How utterly disrespectful. It could never happen . . . or could it? The responses on YouTube show people's confusion, with comments running the gamut from "it's a fake" to "this was a video game promotion" to "it was real moron." In fact, it was a fake. The video was produced by hot New York ad agency Droga5—it's been named agency of the year seven times—and as founder David Droga put it, the video "was done 100 percent to exploit news channels . . . I knew the average news network would want to believe it was real."[1] This is what cutting-edge marketing is today: a tool to get people talking by any means possible, be it confusing the consumer or junking up the news with over-the-top PR trickery.

Marc Ecko said he created the video and website to protest graffiti laws throughout the United States. Maybe he did, but that's hard to swallow, given that an advertising agency produced it. Rather than protest a policy, this short film portrayed the fashion designer as cutting-edge, hip, anti-establishment. These attributes marry well with his brand and with the new age of advertising, which puts products and brands into unexpected places doing unexpected things. In this new marketing model, social media, experiential marketing, stunts, and public relations take precedence over traditional, straightforward sales messages.

Marketers have turned to these types of murky tactics in response to advertising avoidance: consumers' ability to circumvent commercial messages, whether that involves flipping past a commercial or paying for subscriptions to services like Netflix or Amazon Prime. As more content goes online, we have increased our use of ad blockers, like Adblock Plus, Blur (formerly DoNotTrackMe), Disconnect, and Ghostery.[2] Already more than half of all Americans record TV shows so that they can skip past commercials, and the number of people watching online to avoid ads is rapidly increasing. We unsubscribe, unlike, or stop following brands that we once opted into 91 percent of the time.[3] "There's a growing realization that we're being trained to be blind to advertising," says Mark Popkiewicz, CEO of British-based advertising company Mirriad.[4] In fact, the term for that online is banner blindness. The ads are there, but we just don't see them.

Who can blame us? Advertising has invaded every corner of our lives. No longer limited to TV, radio, magazines or billboards, advertising now also covers buildings, cars, and even the floors of our local drugstore: what marketers call "ambient marketing." In a similar vein, theaters, parks, museums, and arenas sell naming rights to raise revenue, so we no longer go to places called Shea Stadium or the Helen Hayes, we go to CitiField or the American Airlines Theater. And as if real advertising were not invasive enough, marketers digitally insert ads into TV shows where they do not actually exist. You are likely most familiar with this in baseball games, where the billboard behind the batter is revised throughout the game. But this does not only happen in sports. CGI logos and products are also used in television dramas and sitcoms, which have the added benefit of enabling advertisers to insert products after the show has finished production. If Pepsi wants a can of soda inserted into a scene in your favorite show, no problem. Simply digitally incorporate it into the program. This capability also lets products be customized for individual markets around the world—a Bentley in the UK becomes a Mitsubishi in Brazil.[5]

It's not just that ads are everywhere. We are targets for promotion from day one. Companies use a cradle-to-grave marketing strategy, striving to get their products to us from the moment we are born until we go to the Great Beyond. Viacom is a good example of this. There is Nickelodeon for kids, Teen Nick and MTV for teens, VH1 for twenty-year-olds, TV Land for senior citizens, and Comedy Central for everybody. Another example is Disney. The company gives gifts to new mothers when they leave the hospital, markets to kids *ad nauseum* from toddlerhood into teen years, has created a line of bridal wear as well as a thriving business around theme park weddings, and instills guilt in grandparents if they do not take their offspring to Orlando as a rite of passage, like going to Mecca or Jerusalem. This strategy is not limited to entertainment companies. It pervades the corporate landscape and is used by Apple, McDonald's, Coca-Cola, and Target, to name just a few.

Until now, though, advertising has been obvious, and because of that you had the choice to interact with it or not. Recognizable configurations enabled you to readily distinguish advertising from programming content: TV ads are typically fifteen to thirty seconds in length, and there are only a handful of advertising formats, such as slice of life (Volkswagen's "Darth Vader" commercial or the Honey Maid "This is wholesome" ad), testimonials (someone endorses the product), or demonstrations (Wisk takes out "ring around the collar"). In print, there is typically a large main visual on the page, a headline, perhaps some body copy, and a "hero shot" of the product. While those traditional ads will continue to exist, they are becoming the exception. They are simply too easy to evade.

So marketers are concealing their messages. Yes, to combat ad avoidance, but that's not the only reason. As more and more advertising money moves out of television and newspapers and into digital, traditional media have had to come up with ways to replace that significant lost revenue. This has led to more and more advertising of the black ops variety—corporately sponsored content masquerading as news and entertainment.

Serving up those ads are social media, which is best suited to one-to-one, subtle communications rather than advertising that screams at you and begs you to buy a product. Remember: "Social media is for social, not for selling." Therefore, marketers have evolved from communicating with large undifferentiated masses to communicating with individuals whose behaviors are well known to them because the marketers have been stealthily listening in on their conversations and tracking their every digital move. Of particular interest to marketers are the demographic known as Millennials, because they have so willingly embraced these social spaces.

In this chapter, we will look at the progressive encroaching of advertising messages into media content. Product placement, also known as branded entertainment or more broadly as advertainment, has a long history in film and television.[6] Now, as this practice transitions into online spaces, it becomes far less recognizable.

FROM PRODUCT PLACEMENT TO IMMERSIVE SOCIAL EXPERIENCE

Product placement occurs when companies pay to have their brand included in media content, historically in movies and television shows, and today also in video games, music videos, and most forms of digital content. The technique has been used in film since the 1890s, but became broad standard practice after Reese's Pieces appeared in Steven Spielberg's *E.T.*, leading to a 66 percent increase in sales of the candy.[7] Since then, we have seen movies jammed full of products, from the James Bond series of movies (which are famous for having dozens of product tie-ins) to *Wayne's World* to *The Lego Movie*, which is in essence a two-hour commercial for a children's product, but which also found space to include family-friendly products from companies like Apple, DC Comics, the NBA, and Lucasfilm, among others. Morgan Spurlock, a documentarian famous for making *Super Size Me*, produced a documentary called *The Greatest Movie Ever Sold*, a film completely financed by product placement. (He also produced a film called *Mansome* about male grooming, which he claimed was independent. Later he admitted the film had corporate support after reviewers speculated that it had been underwritten by Gillette—a prime example of content confusion.) As film production costs increased to an average of $100 million, product placement became a go-to method to offset those expenses, either through payment by the product sponsor or through in-kind donations, such as Apple providing free iPhones and Airbooks to decorate a set.

On television, *Survivor* is typically noted as one of the first programs to propel the use of product placement in recent decades. Producer Mark Burnett had no choice: he wanted to get the show on the air, and CBS would only accept it if he could bring advertisers on board with him. At the time, CBS was struggling in the ratings and having a hard time getting advertisers for their traditional scripted programming. How were they going to sell an advertiser on an untested reality series, a format that was virtually unheard of at the time? Burnett took the network up on their offer and integrated a number of popular consumer brands into the program. Contestants who hadn't brushed their teeth in weeks would be given a challenge where the prize was a basket of Crest mouthwash, for which they were exceedingly grateful, or contestants won Doritos and Mountain Dew, which seemed like ambrosia after eating bugs or twigs or whatever else they could forage in the wilds of some exotic island.

Survivor was just the beginning. The show premiered in 2000, a year after TiVo was introduced. TiVo—and more broadly, digital video recorders—were slow to gain acceptance. By 2007, they were still in only 17 percent of U.S. households. Even so, television networks were concerned about what this technology might do to their business of getting eyeballs in front of advertising, because viewers could easily skip over commercials. While people had been able to do this using VCRs, DVRs simplified the recording process in a way that VCRs never could. Today, DVRs are in 48 percent of U.S. households. On the plus side for marketers, people who use DVRs watch more television; the downside is that they're less likely to watch the accompanying advertising, as 60 percent of DVR users skip commercials.[8] So if people are watching more TV but viewing fewer ads, the answer was obvious: put the product into the show itself.[9]

Product placement is now rampant. Global spending reached more than $10.5 billion in 2014, which was up 13.6 percent from the previous year.[10] *Modern Family* plugs Prius and iPads, *The Walking Dead* pushes Hyundai, and *30 Rock* shamelessly plugged everything from Verizon to Snapple, but does so with tongue-in-cheek. And who can forget the moment when Oprah Winfrey gave away cars—Pontiac G6s—to everyone in her audience, saying, "You get a car and you get a car and you get a car"? Somehow this seemed less offensive because every car recipient was presented as so deserving. Even online-only programs like *Orange Is the New Black* and *House of Cards* have bought into this, with the latter being so besieged with brand endorsements that the *LA Times* dubbed the show the "house of product placement."[11]

Most blatant are reality series, particularly contest-based programs. Starbucks cups sit in the armrests of the judges' chairs on *The Voice*, and Coke adorns the set of *American Idol*, whose contestants help to create Ford commercials: the making of these ads becomes a lengthy segment of the show. After *American Idol*, the biggest winner is *The Biggest Loser*, which has more than five hundred product occurrences per season. At approximately eighteen episodes per season, that equals thirty product mentions or product appearances per show.

To get an idea not only of how pervasive but of how embedded and subtle this has become, try this exercise I use with my students: watch one of the two-hour morning news programs and count how many times a product is being pitched to you. Do not count the commercials or the traditional marketing tools like billboards that say "This segment brought to you by Smuckers," but rather the less blatant forms of promotion. Is CBS doing a story about football because it is a news story, or because they have the rights to the NFL? And while you are at it, are they taking a less critical view of what is going on in the league than other news outlets? Is the athlete on "Good Morning America" talking about her sport, or about her new clothing line? If you do this sort of content analysis, you will find that very little of what appears on morning "news" contains anything of the sort.

Beyond building simple brand awareness in a way that's less intrusive and more economical than traditional advertising, marketers have good reason to use product placement.[12] Most people now watch television with another device present: 84 percent of Americans use mobile phones as a second screen while watching TV.[13] We may be checking email or posting to Facebook, but we also buy products: "Seventeen percent of consumers use secondary devices to purchase products featured on the programs they watch."[14]

But isn't this just like a commercial? Don't we know we're being pitched when we see the Coke can on the table or the lingering close-up on the car logo? Well, yes and no. Part of the reason why product placement is effective is that we tend to approach entertainment differently than we do advertising. Advertising is biased, so we look at it with our critical wits intact. Not so with entertainment. With product placement—and with all advertising to some extent—we don't have to consciously remember the product in order for it to influence our attitude toward the brand. This is particularly true if the product appears multiple times.[15] More important, according to Richard Heslin, professor of psychology at Purdue University, "When we watch a movie or something on television, our defenses are down and we become more receptive to the messages that are coming at us."[16] So if we see a product—say, GoPro cameras—used on sports programs, we might say to ourselves, "Wow! ABC Sports thinks these guys are great. Maybe I should get one." It doesn't work that way with an ad. If we see the product in a commercial, we are acutely aware of it, and we are more likely to think "that's cool." But before dropping hundreds of dollars for the camera, we'll go check other sources of trusted information for verification of its worth. If our favorite character in a show is casually using an iPhone or a celebrity nonchalantly wears a product, we do not think of it as an endorsement, and we tend to accept it, as we do editorial content or the TV show itself—an important idea to keep in mind when we look at content marketing.

Another place where this psychological mechanism plays out in untold measure is celebrity endorsements, particularly those made via social media. Public relations firms that have long worked with celebrities have added content integration to their toolkit. For example, Bang & Olufsen (B&O) wanted to introduce their high-end headphones

(BeoPlay H6) to the U.S. market, so they hired Kari Feinstein Public Relations (KFPR). This company is well known for their "Style Lounges," events held at major film festivals and award shows where companies pay to get their products in front of celebrities. For B&O, KFPR used a combination of their Style Lounge, editorial press, social media, and product seeding (aka product placement) to drive awareness of the headphones. They got the product into the hands of celebrities like Aaron Paul from *Breaking Bad*, who posted a picture of himself wearing the headphones on his Instagram account. Importantly, he does not mention the headphones; he is just casually wearing them around his neck. Dozens of other celebrities and online influencers did the same, until it appeared that the headphones were everywhere. According to KFPR's website, Bang & Olufsen ended up with 1.2 million "Likes," 450 million press impressions, and 120 million online impressions, for a total of 570 million impressions, or more than half a billion people being exposed to the headphones—all without traditional advertising.[17]

The practice of seeding products to generate press impressions is not new. What is new is the concerted effort to combine celebrity product endorsements with the ability to track the number of people engaging with the product. Oliver Luckett of theAudience Agency explained how this works to Douglas Rushkoff in his Frontline documentary *Generation Like*: "What we do is we basically run the social media on behalf of entertainers and artists and musicians and actors, and we help them express themselves inside of this medium."[18] (There are no statistics on this, but you can be pretty sure that your favorite celebrity is not writing his or her own content.) Not only do they manage the social component, but theAudience also produces content, like music videos, and then inserts products into that content. With Luckett's help, celebrities are reaching millions of fans and generating hundreds of thousands of pieces of content, which is something brands want to be attached to. Not only that, because of data analytics and "Likes," it is possible to determine the intersection between companies and celebrities, and that crossover can be exploited. As Luckett explained, "So if you're connected to Ian [Somerhalder of *Vampire Diaries*] and he likes the product, and then you like Ian and you like the product, then now you've got a double endorsement to your friends."[19] This, of course, should make us wonder why a celebrity "Likes" a particular brand and who's paying them to do so. Not only that: all those "Like" buttons you've been casually clicking are in truth not about demonstrating your interests, but are instead a deceptive means to update product placement in the digital age.

Marketers love all of this because it has made their lives easier. Tracking product placement used to be hard work, and few companies could account for the value of product insertions. Now marketers can have the information sent to their desktops, and return on their investment (ROI) can be assessed instantaneously. Not only is online content trackable, but the Internet provides for the perfect marriage of content and commerce: consumers are rarely more than a click away from what they might want to buy. If you see a celebrity wearing B&O headphones in your Facebook feed and you want to buy them, simply click a button.

Finally, there are immersive online environments that provide the perfect combination of product and entertainment. These are most common in advergames targeted at kids, websites that are created to engage rather than to sell outright (mostly because the target audience is too young to have a credit card), and they provide endless hours of entertainment.[20] Instances include sites like Barbie.com or Club Penguin, as well as the many food sites for kids such as Happymeal.com from McDonald's or cereal brand Luckycharms.com, which has a note at the bottom of the page that says, "Hey kids, this is advertising," a disclaimer that would be helpful if the site was targeted to kids of reading age, which it is not. Truly immersive experiences for kids exist in games like Neopets and Webkinz that encourage children to develop emotional attachments to virtual pets that "respond" with happiness when properly tended to, tending that usually requires buying either virtual or real products. The goal is to manipulate users' emotions to inspire consumer behavior that ranges from paying subscription fees to engaging in micropurchases for upgrades and new game levels.[21] While not specifically covert, I highlight these here because children under the age of eight cannot differentiate between advertising and editorial content, and because these websites are the type of advertising environments that Millennials grew up with: fun, engaging, online, and time consuming.

These examples show the significant and fundamental shift that is taking place: brands no longer merely place products in content; they actively create it. Put another way, the media environment we have today is populated by product placement in reverse: instead of putting products into content, content is inserted into advertising.

ADVERTISING: FROM MASS MARKETING TO SEGMENTED TARGETING

Advertising and marketing on a broad scale began in the 1950s with the advent of television. At that time, most people had access to a handful of national broadcast television networks plus a few local channels. Television programs targeted a broad audience, and advertisers spent the bulk of their budgets on these shows because there was really no other choice. The only competition in terms of getting a sales message in front of a large audience was radio, as well as perhaps newspapers and magazines, but these did not have the advantage of sight and sound, nor did they reach the millions of viewers that television provided.

In the nascent stage of television, producers and advertisers worked together to create television shows and then paid for an hour of time to air those programs on a network. These were shows like *Texaco Star Theater* or *The Colgate Comedy Hour.* The television and advertising industries were so intertwined, in fact, that the networks scheduled their programming based on when Detroit introduced their new cars: new car launches were in September, and so was the new fall television season. This was mass advertising through mass media.

By the early 1960s, networks created their own programming (or paid others to do so) and began to sell commercial space to advertisers, thus creating the advertising format we see today: television shows broken up with discrete commercial "pods" that include several commercials by different sponsors. This change was in response to the rising cost of television production, as well as to the game show scandals of the late 1950s. The most well-known of these cases involved a game show called *Twenty One*, where producers fed answers to more attractive contestants at the behest of their advertiser, Geritol. This became a notorious example of a trusted media source (TV) lying to its audience. We might even call it a fatal early misstep in content marketing. Even with these issues, sponsored programming like *The Hallmark Hall of Fame* continued, but it became the exception.

In terms of advertising messages themselves, starting as early as the 1920s marketers began to move beyond promoting products based on simple attributes (XYZ laundry detergent gets clothes cleaner because it has special ingredients, or ABC toothpaste gets your teeth whiter and brighter because it contains baking soda) to attaching a user benefit to the product (cleaner clothes will help you get a better job and whiter teeth will get you a husband or wife). Appealing to the psyche to sell products continues today, though the methods used have gone through several iterations over the decades. In the 1950s and into the 1960s, for example, there were two competing schools of thought about how best to get consumers to buy: the rational, or hard sell, versus the heart, or soft sell. The hard sell was based on differentiating products from their competitors by devising a Unique Selling Proposition (USP)—a simple phrase or tagline that would establish a brand as better than that of their competitors—a concept created by adman Rosser Reeves of the Ted Bates Agency. "M&Ms melt in your mouth, not in your hands" differentiated the candy as something that kids could eat without making a mess, and the line was used for decades. Key to this concept was to repeat the idea over and over *and over* until consumers could parrot the phrase back to the marketer, or more importantly, remember the sales message when they were standing in the aisle of their local store. USPs are still part of modern advertising, and we see this in taglines like "Expect More, Pay Less" for Target or "15 Minutes Could Save You 15 Percent or More on Car Insurance" for Geico. You might even be envisioning the little green gecko.

Alternatively, the soft sell, which was advocated by famous admen David Ogilvy and Chicago's Leo Burnett, sold products through emotional appeals. David Ogilvy is famous for Dove ("1/4 cleansing cream"), "Schweppervescence," and "The Man in the Hathaway Shirt," among many others. Leo Burnett is well known for his use of characters, like the Marlboro Man, the Pillsbury Dough Boy, and Charlie the Tuna. Burnett understood that people connect with a person—even a fictitious one—more than they do with a string bean or a can of tuna fish, and that this connection would lead to product sales. We see this idea continue today in products like Virgin, which built their brand around CEO Richard Branson, a character if there ever was one! Online, where engaging with the customer is a personalized one-on-one experience, brands-as-people and people-as-brands have multiplied. Think here of Steven Jobs and Apple, or Progressive Insurance and Flo, or Lady Gaga, Justin Bieber, or Beyonce. The difference in the early days of TV, however, was that whether the method used involved USP or cartoonish spokespeople, the appeal was designed to attract everyone: young, old; male, female; rich and not-so-rich.

The late 1960s and early 1970s brought the Creative Revolution in advertising. Commercials and print ads became more sophisticated, more tongue-in-cheek in order to appeal to an increasingly educated baby boomer audience. Rather than banging consumers over the head with the repetitious messages of the USP or seeing the Marlboro Man on yet another prairie, consumers were presented with ads like "Lemon" for Volkswagen and "You Don't Have to be Jewish to Love Levy's" for Levy's Rye Bread. At this time, psychologists became integrated into industry practices so that marketers could learn what emotional buttons to push in order to get us to buy. Focus groups, surveys, and personal interviews were used to ascertain the motivations behind consumer purchases. Today these methods have expanded to include ethnography, a technique whereby researchers trail consumers in their "natural habitat," often following them with video cameras to record every nuance. Researchers for Nickelodeon, for example, will move into a child's home for a few days and look in their closets to see what they actually buy and watch what media they interact with. Similarly, there are firms that specialize in marketing ethnography, such as ReD Associates, whose observers attend parties to learn consumers' vodka drinking behaviors or spend a day with consumers on behalf of sneaker brand Adidas, trying to understand the obstacles that keep them from working out.[22] This type of anthropological work is supported and expanded online through data analytics, which we will discuss later in the book.[23]

Understanding what motivates consumers to buy is useless, however, unless advertisers can connect that learning to their product and unless that product provides a corresponding emotional benefit. This is where branding comes in. Branding, quite simply, is the use of a recognizable logo, a tagline (though not always), and a mythology.[24] A sneaker isn't a running shoe; it is a Nike and the athletic excellence that embodies. Disney isn't a theme park; it is magic. Coca-Cola isn't a sugary carbonated beverage; it is happiness. For example, while in the past Coca-Cola would create a commercial and teach the world to sing in "perfect har-mon-y," today they convey the same essence through the "Happiness Machine," a video that shows college students being delighted and surprised by receiving not one but several bottles of Coke from a vending machine. As the video progresses, hands appear out of the machine to deliver first a bouquet of flowers, then balloon animals, and then a several-foot-long hero sandwich. One student even says about the vending machine, "I want to give it a hug," and "Thank you, Coke." Just like the earlier commercial, millions of people saw this video.

The connection of a commodity product to a story or an idea that will evoke emotion—"I want to give it a hug"—is what marketing is all about. These emotional connections become attached to a visual image that you immediately recognize—the swoosh, Cinderella's castle, a red and white logo—and as soon as you see the symbol, it instantly conjures up memories of your interactions with these products. This is particularly important in a media environment that has become overwhelmed with competing product messages. Estimates are that we see upwards of 5,000 marketing messages per day.[25] We are not conscious of all of these, for sure, but the ones that do make it through the mental clutter are those that have the most emotional and psychological relevance. I may remember Banana Republic and Fage and Chipotle, but Abercrombie and Dannon and McDonald's, not so much. You likely have a different experience. This is incredibly important for marketers because research has shown that as the media fragment and products proliferate, consumers reduce the number of brands they consider when buying a product. We are too busy to find something new, so we stay with what we know.[26]

As marketers moved toward a psychological understanding of consumer purchase behavior, the introduction of cable television into

American homes in the 1980s pushed marketing still further away from talking to a large homogeneous audience toward more divided and differentiated niches. Three broadcast networks morphed into dozens, and within a decade there were hundreds of television networks. Today the average American home has 189 channels to choose from, and each of us typically watches 17 different channels—more than five times what we watched in the 1980s.[27] Each of these cable networks appeals to discrete viewing tastes and lifestyles. There is MTV for teenagers and young adults, ESPN for men, and CNN for the news junky who was also likely a reader of *Time* or *Newsweek*. There are channels that appeal to women and ones that are devoted to kids. As time progressed and digital technology enabled cable systems to expand, there were channels not just for sports, but for single sports like tennis or golf, and even for individual sports teams like the Yankees and the Boston Red Sox.

These target audiences correspond to groups that advertisers are interested in reaching based on demographic characteristics (such as age, gender, income, education, and so on) or based on psychographics, which define people in terms of values, lifestyles, and personalities. For instance, a psychographic group called "Movers & Shakers" are adults between forty-five and sixty-four who shop at Nordstrom, play tennis, and drive a Land Rover while "Shotguns & Pickups" are adults between twenty-five and forty-four who order from Mary Kay, own their own horses, and drive a Dodge Ram Diesel.[28] Sorting the population in this way is known as segmentation, and it is used to fragment the marketplace into groups that will be most interested in a company's product. Once an advertiser has identified the audience segments that will be interested in their products, they become "the target audience" for the brand. So iPads might appeal to moms who want to use the tablet to find new twenty-minute recipes or to read books to their kids or to find apps that will help juggle their busy schedules. These tablets are also popular with businesspeople who want a streamlined piece of technology, particularly when they are traveling. They might also be of interest to older adults who want to connect with their grandchildren via Skype or FaceTime, or even to use the tablet to play virtual games with them. Moms and businesspeople and grandparents are different market segments. As a group, they (and many others, in the case of iPads) make up the target audience. Once the target audience is determined, marketers pick the appropriate media to reach these groups with their message. So if Apple wants to reach moms, they might put commercials on Nickelodeon, *Grey's Anatomy*, and *A Baby Story*, as well as print ads in *Parents* magazine and *Good Housekeeping*; if they want to reach grandparents, they might put ads on the evening news or in the local newspaper or sponsor a program on PBS. What we will see later is that because of digital tracking, connecting content to target audiences has become superfluous, meaning that advertisers have no motivation to support programming with substance, only content that attracts the target audience of interest.

Today, when it comes to target audiences, marketers are most interested in the cohort known as Millennials. This young adult group accounts for $1.3 trillion in annual spending, according to the Boston Consulting Group, and that figure will grow as this generation continues to mature and more fully enter the job force.[29] By 2015, there were more Millennials than baby boomers (83.1 million versus 75.4 million).[30] Millennials are also the primary users of online technologies, and they are the Influencers that marketers want to reach who will help promote their products both online and off.

THE DEMOGRAPHIC THAT STILL MATTERS: MILLENNIALS

Marketers talk about an age of post-demographic consumerism. According to marketing research firm Trendwatching, "people—of all ages and in all markets—are constructing their own identities more freely than ever. As a result, consumption patterns are no longer defined by 'traditional' demographic segments such as age, gender, location, income, family status and more."[31] To a certain extent that is true. Identities are more fluid. There are senior citizens interested in skateboarding, and in the UK there are more female than male video gamers, as well as more over forty-four than under eighteen. However, this idea misses the point. The Internet and its concomitant data will reduce—but not eliminate—the need to segment consumers in traditional ways. That is because while marketers need to get people to interact with them online, the way to get them there, for now, is mostly through traditional media. Because of this, marketers continue to categorize audiences by focusing on predictable life cycles. Those life stages—particularly the transition into adulthood—still and likely always will affect consumer purchases. Those transitioning now are part of a cohort known as Millennials.

Millennials—also known as Gen Y or Echo Boomers—are defined typically as those born between the early 1980s and the early 2000s.[32] The Pew Research Center describes this generation as "relatively unattached to organized politics and religion, linked by social media, burdened by debt, distrustful of people, in no rush to marry—and optimistic about the future."[33] They have been widely maligned as entitled, coddled, lazy, self-centered, and digitally addicted.

Societally, they have grown up in a time of instant gratification, abundance, and on-demand products. I have seen this in my own home. My daughter is a Millennial, and when she was young I got a video of *H.R. Pufnstuf* from the library. It was a TV show I loved as a child, and I wanted to share it with her. At the end of the program, one of the actors points at the viewer and says, "See you next week." It was then my daughter asked me, "Why wait until next week?" I had to explain that unlike her ability to watch *SpongeBob* whenever she wanted to, if

I wanted to watch my favorite TV show, I could only watch it once a week, and I had to be sitting in front of the television at the one and only single time during the week when it was on. She was horrified. The idea that she would not be able to watch what she wanted when she wanted was completely alien to her, as it is for others of her generation. On a personal level, Millennials grew up with helicopter parenting, being told they were special, and almost never hearing the word "no."[34] Most importantly for advertisers, they are the "digital natives"—a generation that has grown up with digital technologies and who fluidly move between their online and offline lives.[35]

Millennials are the largest generational cohort, accounting for just over 24 percent of the U.S. population.[36] In a wide-ranging research study, MTV found that their key concerns are getting a job, graduating college, and moving out of their parents' house: really no different from previous generations in that regard. Where they differ, however, is that they are "later to launch"—that is, they tend to postpone adulthood (and marriage) for as long as possible.

No group this large, however, is homogeneous. To better understand their concerns, marketers break up this demographic into psychographic segments. Ypulse, a research company dedicated to understanding Millennials, created these five groups: Muted Millennials (live at home, risk-averse), Supremes (socially high achievers, most well educated of the groups, more than half are influenced by word of mouth), Moralistic Middle (old-fashioned values, thrill-shy), Alt Idealists (cause oriented, value individuality), and Beta Dogs (very passionate, networkers, most open to advertising, and driven by appearance).[37] Interesting to note that two of the five groups (Supremes and Beta Dogs) are open to marketing and particularly to word of mouth. These segments are the Influencers that drive brand adoption by others.

They are a generation dripping in brand culture. Not only do they interact with brands, they spend time talking about brands and recommending them (or not!) to their friends and followers both online and off.[38] Millennials, and in particular younger Millennials (ages eighteen to twenty-four), are more likely than boomers to say "people seek me for knowledge and brand opinion" (52 percent vs 35 percent), and to say that they are willing to share their brand preferences on social media (57 percent versus from 31 percent).[39] According to MTV, a whopping 81 percent recommend brands to people by word of mouth, while research from Intel found that 74 percent believe they influence the purchase decisions of their peers.[40] This makes sense, as this group is used to crowdsourcing information, so they value the opinion of many others when making decisions.[41]

Moreover, they do not only influence each other. If you are the parent of a Millennial or a Gen Zer (the generation after Y), you know what I mean. We are on Facebook, we text, and we might even learn Snapchat, if for no other reason than to be connected to our offspring in the way they feel most comfortable in relating.

MARKETING AND THE MILLENNIAL MINDSET

Given the changes in technology and Millennials' propensity to interact with brands, marketers have changed how they interact with this group. While in the past, the goal was to know who the consumer was in order to craft a message that resonated with them, today the goal is to know who the consumer is so that you can get them to spend time with you. Consumer product companies want to be Millennials' friends.

Marketing campaigns therefore play to making Millennials feel good about themselves. Doritos inspires Millennials to create advertising for the brand in hopes of having their commercial appear on the Super Bowl—recognition on a grand scale—and convinces them to "be bold" by participating in adventurous missions, like jumping from a thirty-foot platform or participating in a roller derby with pro racers, an act which might lead to tickets to SXSW to see Lady Gaga. Doritos psychographically describes this group as "Young and Hungry," literally and figuratively, and their marketing reflects this attitude. In another example, Marlboro has an international campaign that uses the tagline "Don't be a Maybe." Their videos show young people having fun—driving in a car with their hair blowing in the breeze or jumping from a significant height onto an air-filled blob. Similar to Doritos, they play to the idea of living boldly. As they say in an internal promotional video:

> As a brand Marlboro was not resonating with adult smokers even though its values of freedom, authenticity and master of destiny were. Smokers missed the essence of the cowboy which led us to our opportunity. Eliminate the word MAYBE from our smokers' vocabulary to become the catalyst that inspires smokers from just thinking about life to taking the lead in life. To live the Marlboro values. To be True. Bold and forever forward.[42]

The communication to Millennials, then, is that Marlboro smokers don't sit back and watch; they take part in the action. But this is just an updated twist on the cowboy that represented freedom and individualism for past generations.

Another gimmick marketers have used with this group to considerable effect is asking young people if they can pick up and go away for a weekend—the ultimate expression of freedom. Anheuser-Busch asked Millennials if they were "up for whatever." One thousand lucky Millennials who submitted an audition video on Facebook and who promoted the brand on Twitter with the hashtag #upforwhatever were put on a plane and sent to an unknown destination. Once on the ground, they found themselves amidst a three-day party including celebrities, games, and lots of Bud Light.[43] This campaign was so successful that Anheuser-Busch has run it multiple times.[44]

Undergirding these youth-targeted campaigns is experiential marketing. It's not enough for consumers to see an ad; they have to experience it, interact with it, be immersed in it much in the same way as they're immersed in a videogame. This is why brands that never had a physical presence before are creating retail outlets. Of course, there's the Apple Store, but there are now shops for M&Ms and Asics, and there was even a pop-up store for Pop-Tarts in New York City.

A Millennial campaign with broader appeal was Coca-Cola's "Share a Coke," which combined a number of elements that work for engaging this age group. The heart of the campaign was to print bottles of Coke, Diet Coke, and Coke Zero with labels that bore 250 of the most common first names, as well as a few group titles like Mom and BFF. If someone's name was not available, they could request it at ShareaCoke.com for five dollars, or they could go to the site and send virtual versions of a personalized Coke bottle to friends. The availability of these specially marked bottles was promoted through in-store marketing, print ads, social media, experiential marketing, and a microsite, among other elements.

In one commercial for the campaign called "Share a Coke This Summer,"[45] a young woman wearing a necklace, "Jess," goes into a store and buys a personalized Coke for herself as well as one for her friend Alisha, whom she meets on a rooftop where they drink their sodas. Appropriately for this generation, Alisha is African American, which taps into the group's multiculturalism. Jess and Alisha go back and buy four Cokes—two more for themselves and two for friends (Alex and Maria). They go back again with still more friends to get sodas for a picnic at a park. In the final shots, hundreds of people are dancing and drinking Coca-Cola. Then, at nighttime, Jess goes back to the store where the clerk is closing down for the night. She hands the cashier a bottle that says "Chris," and they walk away holding hands.

Integral to the campaign was the hashtag #ShareaCoke, which consumers were meant to use when they posted pictures of themselves with their personalized bottle of Coke. Close to 600,000 pictures were posted to Instagram alone.[46] Millennials were encouraged to share with the promise that their picture might be featured online or on a national billboard. This campaign was so successful that it reversed Coca-Cola's ten year sales decline, a tough feat in light of concerns about obesity (and most particularly among teens).[47]

What makes all this messaging so interesting is that it is the exact opposite of how advertising traditionally worked. Ads would tell you that you had ring around the collar, so you needed to use Wisk. Or that you had halitosis, so if you didn't use Listerine, you would never get the guy or girl. Advertising was all about telling you what was wrong with you so that you would use the product. It was the very definition of problem-solution advertising. Now, it is all about entertaining you and telling you how great you can be so you will promote the product for them.

• • •

Moving from mass marketing to one-to-one interactions has changed how marketers communicate not only with Millennials, but with all of us. Unlike the thirty-second commercial that screamed at you to buy, Buy, BUY, these communications are subtle, friendly, and relationship-building. They don't appear to be a prelude to a monetary transaction. Because they are personal, they are effective: it's harder to say "no" to someone you have a connection with than to a nameless, faceless corporation.

These relationships are about getting us to share, as many women did with Dove's "Sketch Artist."[48] In this video, women describe themselves to a professional sketch artist who is behind a curtain and cannot see them. One after another, the women describe their flaws as they see them—their nose is too big, their lips are not full enough, their jaw protrudes, etc. Then, one by one, someone who has just met one of the women describes what they saw to the same sketch artist, and in case after case, they provide a gentler, more accepting description of the person they saw. The sketches are then placed side-by-side and shown to the woman depicted. The realization of how hard they are on themselves is sad and palpable. This video, like others we will look at throughout the book, manipulates our emotions to generate those strong feelings that move us to share content with others. "Sketch Artist" was viewed more than 65 million times. That's more than the number of people who typically watch a prime time television show, or the advertising in it. And this video is three minutes long—six times the length of a typical TV commercial. That's powerful marketing. But stop to think about it for just a minute and ask yourself: What does moisturizer have to do with feeling good about one's self? And if you passed it along, why did you help Unilever (Dove's parent company) promote their product?

There are any number of reasons why you might have shared the video, which we'll talk about in the next chapter. For now, be aware that marketers will increasingly provide you with motivation to pass along their messages. Campaigns will be designed to include participation and personalization. Participation means that we produce the content, whether that's creating an ad or voting for a favorite Starbucks holiday coffee with a hashtag (#VoteforJoy) so that we can get 50 percent off on the beverage. Technologies are allowing for increased personalization. For example, @AmericanExpress, which sponsored an "Unstaged" Pharrell Williams concert, sent tweets personalized and autographed to people who livestreamed the event.[49] Participation and personalization—combined with continuity, being continually in touch with consumers—are the tools marketers use to sustain long-term relationships, particularly with the ever-important Millennials whom they know are most likely to share, share, share.

2
WHAT WE SHARE & WHY WE SHARE

Marrying marketing messages to editorial content is not done because of some malicious plot by advertisers to fool us. To their minds, they are providing cost-effective, useful information and entertainment . . . that just happens to be produced by a marketer. And if you like it enough to share it with your friends and family, all the better.

In one fundamental way, this is not all that different from traditional forms of marketing. In the mass media model, the idea was to promote to a lot of people in hopes of finding the "Early Adopters"—who today are called "Influencers"—who would then tell their neighbors and friends about the promotion.[1] You might remember the commercial from Fabergé Organics shampoo, where a woman says that she tried the shampoo and loved it. She told two friends, and they told two friends, and so on and so on, with each "so on" leading to the screen being divided into more and more people. That is the idea behind word of mouth (WOM). One person tells a friend, who tells another friend, until the product becomes a topic of conversation and the latest must-have product. Alternatively, companies have used PR tactics to get trusted others to do the selling that advertising could not. For example, the father of PR, Edward Bernays, promoted Beech Nut bacon by coaxing doctors to recommend the benefits of the product to their patients,[2] and bartenders have long been an important component to selling alcoholic beverages. Now, with the rise of digital media—and in particular social media—a number of those discussions have moved online. Marketers amass tracking data based on our interactions and can use it to find Influencers, who might be professionals (like Bernays's doctors), celebrities, or simply fans of a brand. With this ability, messaging tends less toward mass advertising and more toward Bernays's one-to-one cloaked methodologies.

Talking about products and brands has become part of day-to-day conversation. In the past, we gave someone information about a product or service because we wanted to be helpful, or because we wanted to appear in the know. You might run into your neighbor and say, "Try Fabergé Organics," or more likely, "Sam the butcher will order special lamb chops for the weekend if you tell him by Tuesday," or "I just saw that the record store is having a sale starting on Friday. You better get there early." Today, you might tell a friend, "I just saw the new *Avengers* movie. You should really go see it," or, more likely, you post the movie's trailer on Facebook and tell your friends what you thought. Similarly, you might provide a link to a business article on Twitter or LinkedIn or post wedding dress ideas on Pinterest. Online, these communications are to be helpful, for sure. The difference, though, is that the technology has been created in such a way as to compel us to share information, and we are not sharing with one or two people, but more likely two or three hundred.[3] A few hundred may still not seem like a lot, but if just a handful of people share with their friends, it can scale to reach as many people as some television programming. According to social media company Lithium, if a brand conversation reaches more than a thousand people, it can "generate up to half a million conversations about your brand," which is the modern-day version of the so on and so on idea. To reach those numbers, marketers find (or pay for) "Superfans." These well-connected, digitally plugged in folks generate three to five times more word of mouth (WOM) messages, and those messages are four times more likely to have an impact on purchase decisions.[4] And most importantly, word-of-mouth recommendations are responsible for 20 to 50 percent of purchases, according to McKinsey & Company.[5] Bottom line: companies need to get people talking about their product, and the more the better. Luckily for them, because of digital technology we share more content with more people than we ever have, more quickly and more often.[6]

Perhaps unexpectedly, while it feels like we share an awful lot online, the vast majority of word of mouth happens in offline conversations. According to research from the Keller Fay Group, "91 percent of respondents' information about brands came as a result of face-to-face conversations or over the phone."[7] While this is true, those offline conversations are facilitated by *word of mouth marketing*, and that marketing more than likely happened online. Word of mouth marketing is defined as "the technique of promoting a product, service or business by soliciting positive comments from satisfied customers. Word of mouth marketing is an interactive process such that customers are collaborating with the business, product or service for which they have derived enough satisfaction that they are willing to speak out about it and even recommend it to others."[8] Word of mouth marketing, then, asks consumers to talk about products and services. More often than not this will include some remuneration for us, like a coupon or a prize for having participated in a contest, and for Influencers repayment is typically free products or cash payments—a form of paid endorsement that we do not see.

Marketers consider one person telling another about a product to be the most effective form of advertising because—not surprisingly—people trust their friends and family more than they trust an advertiser. According to Nielsen's *Trust in Advertising* report, word of mouth is the most influential form of advertising, with 84 percent of respondents saying it was the most trustworthy.[9] Word of mouth is integral to stealth forms of marketing because "peer group recommendation is the ultimate marketing weapon."[10] With WOM marketing, although the idea gets seeded by the marketer, consumers sell it to one another, and it doesn't feel like marketing.

WHAT WE SHARE

Marketers have traditionally used a combination of what are called push and pull strategies. For push strategies, think about a pushy salesperson. They push the product on you. That is like the old broadcast media model. The opposite of that is a pull strategy, where consumers like the product so much that they help pull it through the distribution channel. That is what word of mouth marketing is all about. To facilitate WOM, marketers use a number of different tools to get us to engage with and then ultimately talk about their products.

Marketing professor Colin Campbell and his colleagues developed a helpful way to categorize the types of messaging available, which is to delineate media based on two axes: (1) who created the content, and (2) whether the content was paid or unpaid.[11] Building on Campbell's work, I have revised the template to reflect current terminology, as well as to present it as a tool for thinking about how different methods facilitate sharing.

BRANDED CONTENT MESSAGING STRATEGIES

	CONTENT CREATOR			
	BRAND	**BRAND AND NEWS MEDIA**	**NEWS MEDIA**	**USER**
UNPAID	Viral Video	Publicity	Editorial Content	Word-of-Mouth Consumer Generated Marketing
PAID	Display Advertising Content Marketing	Native Advertising (Branded Content)	Native Advertising (Sponsored Content)	Sponsored WOM "Brand motivated" CG Marketing

Source: Based on Campbell et al (2014).

Starting on the top line, content creators can be the brand (Coca-Cola, for example), a combination of the brand and the news media (Coca-Cola and the *New York Times*), the news media alone, or the user—that is, you and me. Unpaid content, or earned media, is publicity—for example, when a product is mentioned on a news story or an author appears on *The Late Show*—and paid media is, of course, advertising. Editorial content is the only element in the chart that is not—or at least not necessarily—influenced by corporate bias.

Below, we will look at examples of word of mouth strategies, including viral videos, consumer-generated content, and sponsored word of mouth. Native advertising and content marketing, the most covert of the types, will be discussed in subsequent chapters. Bear in mind that the point of view, the bias of the content, changes based on the scenario. Given the example of Coke and the *New York Times*, imagine how different a story about Coke and obesity written by the newspaper would be from one that was paid for by the soda company.[12]

Some of these categories are more driven by stealth than others, and not all marketing will be covert. It cannot be: we have to have some familiarity with a product in order for covert methods to work. That is why these methods rarely exist as standalone communications, but rather as part of an overall campaign.

Procter & Gamble's "Thank You Mom" campaign provides a helpful case study to see how the integration of online and offline, as well as of stealth and visible methods, can make a marketing effort effective. As part of this initiative, P&G bought traditional television commercials. These ads were originally created for the 2012 Olympics, and creatively they pull at the heartstrings by showing mothers from around the world doing tireless work in support of their children's athletic careers. Prior to the TV advertising, the campaign started with unpaid media online in the form of a video called "Best Job," which introduced the campaign and which became "a digital sensation."

The commercials and video were followed by an integrated segment (paid product placement) on NBC's *The Today Show*. According to a document from P&G's advertising agency: "Throughout the broadcast, the cast referenced the online popularity of 'Best Job,' aired the full 2-minute version within programming and additionally aired the :60 version in the 'A' position during the commercial break. The pièce de résistance was a P&G executive appearing on the show to surprise moms of Olympians with a financial gift to help them get to London (based on the insight that many families couldn't afford the trip)."[13]

Throughout the Olympic Games, social media (unpaid) was used in the form of a Thank You Mom Facebook page, a Twitter handle (@ThankYouMom), and YouTube videos. P&G created Facebook and Twitter pages to give mothers around the world an opportunity to post pictures of themselves with their children, and thus to create an emotional connection with the brand. In addition, athletes from around the world—many with extensive followings—posted thanks to their mothers. YouTube videos presented winning athletes and their moms. Some footage for these videos came from NBC, which agreed as part of the sponsorship contract to capture shots of mothers reacting to their children's wins and losses.

This outlines just some of the paid and unpaid methods that P&G used to grab our attention by pulling on our emotions. Some of these methods were stealth (the *Today Show* mentions, the mom footage as part of the Olympics), and much of it depended on consumer word of mouth. In terms of consumer engagement, there were 17 million views on YouTube, Facebook fans increased by 65 percent, and Twitter followers increased by 20 percent. The "Best Job" video was shared during the Olympics more than any other advertising, making it the most viral.

In total, "Thank You Mom" became the most successful campaign in the company's 175-year history, leading to more than $200 million in incremental sales. Like many marketing campaigns, a mix of media types, both covert and obvious, worked in conjunction with one another to bolster awareness and promote sales. For example, showing mothers in the stands at the Olympics is not outright advertising. However, throughout a hundred-day period leading up to the Olympics, consumers were bombarded with messages connecting moms and P&G. It stands to reason that many would think of the marketer's advertising after seeing these images and then, once inspired, were led to talk about it or retweet it or post their own picture on Facebook in response to it.

WORD OF MOUTH STRATEGIES

VIRAL

VIRAL VIDEO:[14]	EXAMPLES:
Video created by the brand with the intent of entertaining, delighting, or in some way emotionally engaging the audience with the expectation that they will share the content through social media platforms, websites, and email.	Hey Minions Fans! (63 million+)
	The First Kiss (156 million+)
	Ice Bucket Challenge*

In *Contagious*, Wharton professor Jonah Berger outlines what causes a video—or any other content—to be passed from one person to another. According to Berger, content goes viral because of the acronym STEPPS: Social Currency, Triggers, Emotion, Public, Practical Value, and Stories. Much of this is not new. People like to share what they know in order to look cool or to become the go-to person for the latest info. That information is a form of social capital that gives one standing in a group, what we used to call "water cooler talk." It could be that you know what happened on The *Tonight Show Starring Jimmy*

Fallon last night, or that Prince played a live performance in a tiny venue in town. Triggers are reminders that lead us to talk about things around us. In the P&G case above, seeing moms react to their children winning an Olympic event is a trigger for us to think about the campaign. You likely know from your own experience that if something moves you in either a good or bad way, you comment on it or review it. It is emotions that drive these actions, and awe and anger are the emotions that are most likely to lead us to share content. Tied to triggers is the concept of making the private public. Bright yellow Livestrong bracelets, for example, made charity a public issue, and white earbuds made people using iPods visually stand out from the crowd. We might also share practical information like a recipe, or a video (maybe you've seen it) on how to correctly shuck an ear of corn. Finally, people share stories. Just as Leo Burnett knew that he needed to connect products to characters within a larger story, today marketers attach their products to a larger narrative that consumers can pass on to others.

There are many, many viral video examples that could have been used for this category. P&G's Always campaign called "Like a Girl," which also appeared as a commercial in the Super Bowl; "The Devil Baby" for the film *Devil's Due*; any of the many John Oliver videos that act as promotion for his weekly HBO show. Here I have selected "Hey Minions Fans!" for AMC Movie Theaters and "The First Kiss" to highlight Berger's thesis. In part, I've selected the latter because it takes the idea of obscuring who's behind the content to decidedly new levels.

Anyone with young children likely knows that "Minions" are the adorable animated characters from the *Despicable Me* movie franchise. In this video created for the holiday season, a group of Minions singing "Silent Night" are interrupted from their calm refrain by a more rambunctious Minion who leads the group in singing "Jingle Bells."

Connected to the video is the message that if you purchase a $30 gift card to AMC (presumably for a friend), you will receive free popcorn for yourself. This video was viewed more than 65 million times and shared on Facebook almost 4 million times, but it only had about a thousand Twitter shares. It was a no-brainer that families and friends would share this video among themselves, because passing this along to others gave kids and their parents social currency: it's an adorable piece of content and gave them something to talk about. The entertaining video evoked joy, as well as provided a practical incentive through the offer associated with it.

Even more viral was "First Kiss," the most viewed video advertising of 2014. In this beautifully shot black and white video, several couples—gay and straight, old and young—are introduced to each other for the very first time and asked to kiss while being filmed. The couples are understandably uneasy: they ask each other's names, they shake hands, they ponder how to start the process of locking lips with someone they've met only moments before. "First Kiss" does not present itself as advertising. The only indication that this is a piece of commercial content is a title on the screen in the upper left corner for about one second at the very beginning that says "WREN presents." This is followed by a screen that says, "FIRST KISS a film by Tatia Pilieva," language that suggests that this is an artistic work rather than an advertisement. Most people had never heard of the apparel company, Wren, so this did not initially register as advertising.

"First Kiss" has more than 156 million views on YouTube and spawned dozens of video parodies. The total number of Facebook shares for this video, at 1.5 million, was much lower than for the Minions video, but there were 74,000 shares on Twitter (a considerable number for that venue), with most of these happening within the first month of its release. Twitter tends to be a more adult and more business-oriented social media platform, and it is not surprising that marketers, for example, would share this with others as a form of social currency. The film itself is entertaining, and the concept is one that people have not seen before.

However, it was not just social media that led to this content's success. The film's creator sent copies to twenty-one friends, and by the end of the morning two million people had seen it. Then the *New York Times* did a story on this video in conjunction with the start of Fashion Week, as did other news outlets. The fact that this wasn't obviously advertising increased the content's appeal because people felt like they were watching an artfully produced, quirky film.

I would be remiss if I did not mention the Ice Bucket Challenge, a viral phenomenon that overtook the Internet during much of the summer of 2014. This initiative was a fundraiser to leverage social media and consumer-generated video to raise money for charity. Viewers were challenged to videotape themselves dumping a bucket of ice water on their heads or to donate money (most did both) and then challenge other people to do the same. Celebrities like Bill Gates and Martha Stewart, as well as thousands of everyday people, did just that. Most of the videos were fun to watch, with some evoking considerable pathos. What made this so successful is that social currency ("Did you see Lady Gaga's ice bucket challenge?" or "did you do the challenge?") and storytelling (why people chose to make their videos) are ingeniously embedded into the challenge itself. The Ice Bucket Challenge thus embodies the key elements that would lead people to share this content with others. That said, this example doesn't neatly fall into a single category. Yes, it went viral, but it was not produced by the ALS Association, an organization that raises money to help cure amyotrophic lateral sclerosis (Lou Gehrig's disease).[15] In that sense, this was consumer-generated marketing (discussed below). We all heard about the video challenge, in part from the mainstream media and in part by its online presence. However, it is difficult to quantify the success of this initiative because it is not based on a single video but on thousands of individual ones. Rather, the success of the campaign is evident in the funds raised for the organization: $115 million from July 29 to September 15, compared to $5 million raised in the same period the year before.

As is evident, not all elements are necessary for content to go viral. It can evoke emotion and be practical, but it does not have to contain a trigger or be made public. What I have found in using the STEPPS framework to analyze content is that emotions—the stronger the better— are what shape virality and social currency. We share content when we are moved by its message in the hopes that by doing so we will project a positive image of ourselves to the online world. And this ties in to what marketers are trying to achieve: the ever important customer-brand relationship. As Melissa Coker, Wren's founder and creative director, said about their video: "What we really wanted to do with this video is to generate lasting brand awareness and love, not just a quick hit sale."[16]

Static visuals can also be viral content, but these tend not to have the same emotional or widespread impact as videos. The most shared picture on Twitter, for example, is the Ellen DeGeneres/Samsung selfie at the 2014 Oscars, with 3.3 million retweets. This was achieved through a combination of product placement during the TV broadcast and from DeGeneres asking viewers to make it the most retweeted picture—an example of two stealth modes working in conjunction with one another.[17] To put this into context, the second most tweeted picture is President Obama hugging the first lady after he won his bid for a second term in 2012 (750,000+ retweets).

As marketers move away from written content in favor of visual formats, the practice of sharing video and visual content will increase. In just two years, video content is expected to make up 69 percent of online traffic.

WORD OF MOUTH AND SPONSORED WORD OF MOUTH

WORD OF MOUTH:	EXAMPLES:
Consumer generated information or content about a brand produced without payment from the product company. Editorial control is solely in the purview of the consumer. While this is typically positive, it does not have to be.	Social media shares and retweets Online reviews
SPONSORED WOM:	
Consumer or professionally generated information or content about a brand produced *with payment or other consideration* from the product company. Editorial control may or may not be in the purview of the producer, depending on the outlet. For example, compensated blog posts are at the discretion of the consumer, while compensated celebrity tweets are scrutinized by the brand.	Celebrity tweets & Vines Compensated blog posts Online brand pushers—BzzAgent, Amazon Vine, Vocalpoint/Tremor

We have already discussed word of mouth broadly as the communication of information from one person to another. More specifically, there are two types of word of mouth: unsponsored and sponsored. Unsponsored is what we have been discussing thus far: any natural or "organic" conversation about a product. Sponsored word of mouth, on the other hand, is far more stealth than its unpaid counterpart. These communications make it look like one person is simply making a recommendation to another, but in reality, there is a marketer behind the Influencer's message.

Word of mouth—sponsored or otherwise—is being driven by the ubiquitous use of mobile phones and the accompanying apps. These have enabled us to read, share, review, and retweet on the go when we have down time during our workday, or at night while we are engaging with other media. As of the third quarter of 2014, Americans spend more time on mobile devices than they do watching television. Most of that online time is spent with apps, and of that, 80 percent is spent with one of the following five sources: Facebook, YouTube, Pandora, Google Maps, and Gmail. Since advertising spending follows the eyeballs, spending on mobile has grown exponentially, with the expectation that it will reach $40 billion in 2016, more than doubling what it was in 2014.[18]

Talking about brands (unsponsored WOM) has become a part of everyday conversation. Here are the stats: on a typical day, 76 percent of Americans will talk about brands, ten brands will be discussed, and 70 percent of the time, those conversations will include a recommendation.[19] As noted above, many of these brand-based conversations are urged along with corporate intervention. This WOM marketing can also be called buzz marketing, viral marketing, and grassroots marketing.[20] Whatever it is called, the intention behind it is to drive consumer conversations without making it look like there's a marketer's hand in the mix.

Marketers generate brand conversations by finding Influencers (Millennials with followings or celebrities) who will positively promote a product in the hopes of it going viral, thus creating "buzz" around a product. According to the Word of Mouth Marketing Association (WOMMA), buzz marketing is "using high-profile entertainment or news to get people to talk about your brand."[21] There are several methods that can be used to do this. Sponsored celebrity tweets are used for a vast array of products, and the cost for those 140 characters can be substantial, depending on the celebrity and the size of their audience. The Kardashian sisters make more than $10,000 per tweet, and Kim is reported to have made double that to promote EOS lip balm.[22] Chinese actress Fan Bingbing combined her announcement of a new romance with three brands that she endorses.[23] Vine celebrities—people who have become online stars by making six-second videos—can also make a handsome sum by using these short snippets to promote consumer products. These "celebs" with anywhere from 300 thousand to 4 million followers have been known to promote everything from GE to Warner's Bras to Coke, and they can make as much as $30,000 for a Vine—which has no sponsor designation in sight.[24] There is now even an app called Cosign that enables individuals to make money when their friends purchase products based on their recommendation.

More controversial, and frankly illegal, is promoting products online without letting readers know that the blogger or Influencer received compensation for writing about the product.[25] A whole industry now exists to support connecting Influencers with products. Amazon, for instance, has the Amazon Vine program, which gives "trusted reviewers" products to sample so that they can write about them.[26] Beyond PR companies that connect Influencers to products, as we discussed in the previous chapter, there are now online companies, like Izea and Ad.ly, that match blogs and social media stars to products. Advertisers can go onto the Izea website, for example, and see how many followers a celebrity has and how much they charge for tweeting. The website then sends an email to the celebrity, who can accept the advertiser's offer of promotional money or not. If accepted, the cost gets charged to a credit card. It's that simple. Similarly, anyone who blogs, tweets, or uses Instagram can create an account on Izea and presumably be connected to advertisers. Their promotional video describes it in the following way:

> Say you're a blogger or a tweeter or a YouTuber or even an Instagramer, it doesn't matter. You're creating content online and people are eating it up. Guess what? You're a creator, and you can be making money. Top brands and local businesses will pay you to do what you love. The bigger your following, the more opportunity you have to earn. Now, say you're an advertiser that wants to get the word out about your product or service. Creators are eager to work with brands they love

and will produce engaging and shareable content in their own voice all while driving awareness of your brand. So, what are you waiting for? Sign up and get started today.[27]

The company began a major advertising campaign in December 2014, in part to find more "content producers." They have a series of videos on YouTube showing everyday people going about their lives and then stopping by a computer now and then to write a blog post or tweet to their followers, making this seem like a fast and easy way to make money.[28] While figures are not available, it is unlikely that many people—except perhaps the ones in their videos—are making a living wage from doing this. Given that there are now numerous YouTube videos explaining how to make money with Izea, and that the company now even produces a conference called IzeaFest to promote their services, we can assume that there are plenty of people hawking for companies under the guise of word of mouth. Similarly, Mylikes promotes the ability for "publishers" to make money through their services, and it even provides the content. Simply point and click, and you have content for your website.

And while website publishers are supposed to disclose that there was payment for promotional activities, this mostly does not happen. In a report by David Kamerer from Loyola University, fully three quarters of the fashion bloggers he studied did not disclose that they were being paid to promote their content. But it's not just fashion bloggers: celebrities have fan bloggers who follow them and the products they sponsor. For instance, when Bethenny Frankel of *Real Housewives* fame, owner of the Skinnygirl brand of food products, goes to an event, the brand company will line up food bloggers or cocktail bloggers or Bethenny bloggers for her to talk to and take pictures with. Who knows what the compensation structure is there, although at a minimum, they've been wined and dined and met their favorite celeb.[29] Perhaps even more deceptive are celebrities who promote companies in which they have a vested interest. Ashton Kutcher, who has invested in ventures from Airbnb to fab.com, often tweets about these companies without acknowledging his fiduciary connection.[30] And finally, there are increasing concerns about celebrities using social media to promote pharmaceutical drugs.[31]

Perhaps not surprisingly, paying for tweets (or at least attempting to) has moved into the political realm. TV sports host Jean Duverger claimed he was contacted multiple times with requests to tweet positive missives for Mexico's Green Party. He was offered 200,000 pesos for three tweets. While he did not take them up on the offer, according to *El Daily Post*, several prominent others may have put their public support behind this controversial party.[32]

A company that compensates with products rather than dollars is BzzAgent, one of the biggest and best known word-of-mouth marketing companies, which has been in existence for more than ten years and thus pre-dates social media. To learn how they work, I signed up to be one of the more than 600,000 BzzAgents and waited to see if I'd get picked. Most people don't. How it works: you go to the website (www .bzzagent.com) and answer a number of personal questions. The site also has a number of consumer product category surveys to fill out. The more you fill out, the more likely you will be picked to be an agent. Ostensibly, this is so the site can appropriately match you with products to review. The more you interact with the site, the higher your "BzzScore" will be, and the more likely it is that you'll be picked to be part of a Bzz campaign. The value to the participant is that you are given free stuff; the value to BzzAgent is lots of marketing research data.

After filling out numerous surveys and waiting several months, I was sent an email asking if I wanted to try a robotic vacuum. If I liked it, I could purchase it for the remarkably reduced price of $295. I took a pass. It was more than six months after I signed up that I was asked if I wanted to participate in a campaign for Crest HD whitening toothpaste. Not a high-end item, but okay. I tried the product and then was expected to talk about it on social media, preferably with a long written piece that included a picture of me using the product. BzzAgent provides incentives to post to social media through their site. When posts appear, a small BzzAgent bee icon is inserted on your post. This helps the company track social messages; it also represents a small level of disclosure. In comparison to the companies that connect paid Influencers, this site makes a point of telling people to be transparent about their postings, though this is no guarantee that their agents provide full disclosure.

Similar to BzzAgent were Tremor and Vocalpoint, which were both part of mega-conglomerate Procter & Gamble.[33] Tremor was started to integrate word of mouth into marketing efforts for teens.[34] It was created in 2001 to tap into the market of thirteen to nineteen-year-olds, who are now today's Millennials. That group was directly responsible for $120 billion in personal spending, as well as influencing an additional $485 billion in purchases, such as family computers and vacations. Within two years, the network included 280,000 teens who promoted a wide swath of products from movies to motor oil to their friends and family in exchange for coupons or free product samples. Said *Forbes*, "Their mission is to help companies plant information about their brands in living rooms, schools and other crevices that are difficult for corporate America to infiltrate. These kids deliver endorsements in school cafeterias, at sleepovers, by cell phone and by e-mail."[35] Teens were easily swayed by the offer of free goodies. The success was evident from the fact that Tremor's revenue for 2004 was projected to be $12 million.[36]

But there were problems with Tremor: teens are consumers of only a handful of P&G brands, and they aged out of the community fairly quickly. Thus P&G ultimately let the teen network fall away, while building on its initial success to create a women's and moms' network called Vocalpoint in 2006. Today, Vocalpoint is no longer part of P&G, but the company still uses the Vocalpoint name for a community of women who are given free products. Unlike BzzAgent, Vocalpoint does not push women to talk about the products online. They are aware that most product conversations happen offline, and therefore they do not feel compelled to force the issue among their members.[37] Yet here, too, a company is "facilitating" word of mouth.

The key benefit these companies bring to marketers is that they link their online information with shopper marketing. (This is called "onboarding," a topic I discuss in Chapter 5). This is incredibly important because 90 percent of shopping occurs offline. According to *Advertising Age*, "BzzAgent was acquired in May [2011] for $60 million by Dunnhumby, which has been a major force in loyalty programs for such retailers as Tesco, Macy's and Kroger Co." Vocalpoint, while still part of P&G, was integrated with the company's sales units.[38] Tellingly, Facebook in April of 2015 announced that Facebook Messenger users would be able to shop as well as chat with brands through the app— suggesting that talking is nice, but selling is better, at least from their advertising clients' point of view.[39]

These WOM methods perform at various levels of stealth. BzzAgents can be detected, but most other sponsored agents can't. It's rare for an agent to disclose that they are being compensated, and that's the whole point. The goal in all of this is to make it look like the celebrity or Influencer is providing unbiased reports in the same way that a friend would suggest a product.

The problem is that the real endorsement and the paid endorsement are indistinguishable. Here's an example. In the same Oscar show that brought us the selfie seen round the world, Ellen DeGeneres ordered in pizza for the audience. In order to tip the deliver guys, she grabbed Pharrell Williams's famous hat and began passing it around for money. The *12 Years a Slave* actress Lupita Nyong'o put not money but her lip balm into the hat. This ignited the hashtag #LupitasLipBalm, and consumers went crazy trying to figure out the brand. Once they did, Clarins HydraQuench Moisture Replenishing Lip Balm practically sold out around the country overnight.[40] To the best of my knowledge, this endorsement was not compensated. Either way, this simple act demonstrates and drives home for marketers the power of trusted endorsements, while at the same time leaving us wondering who we should trust.

CONSUMER GENERATED MARKETING

CONSUMER GENERATED MARKETING:	EXAMPLES:
Consumer generated brand content created because of an affinity toward the product. This typically does not conform to traditional advertising content, and it is produced at the consumer's discretion without compensation.[41] It can be positive or negative.	ChipotleFan.com Nutella
"BRAND-MOTIVATED" CONSUMER GENERATED ADVERTISING: "Brand- or product-related content created by consumers and which emulates the style and intention of advertising. Consideration in some form is provided by the brand as an incentive."[42] While editorial control rests with the consumer, it is prescribed by limits placed by the brand company.	Social media postings in response to brand prompts Doritos Super Bowl advertising

Consumer generated marketing is created out of people's genuine appreciation for a brand or product. You might think of these people as "brand fans" in the same way there are sports fans. Chipotle, for example, has long had a substantial fan following. Well before the company created its own advertising and content marketing, the brand was promoted primarily through PR and consumer word of mouth. One fan loved the product so much that he created a website called www.chipotlefan.com that introduces others to the wonders of this sustainable, organic food chain.

Perhaps the most extreme case of brand fandom is Nutella. Users of this chocolate hazelnut spread are wildly passionate about the product, so much so that they created a World Nutella Day—all managed by consumers—which has been in existence for almost a decade. Surprisingly, the brand was not initially happy with this event and tried to shut it down. Incredibly, they even presented cease and desist orders to fans who created Nutella fan sites.[43] Most companies would give their eye teeth to have consumers do this kind of unpaid marketing for them, but initially parent company Ferrero was not onboard. In the end, the company realized the value of consumer-driven promotion and allowed it to continue, in part by trying to incorporate some of the passion into the company-led Facebook page. To date, the Nutella Facebook page has more than 29 million "Likes," which makes them Number 15 on the list of top Facebook brands, a list that includes Coca-Cola, McDonald's, and Starbucks (all of which have considerably larger marketing budgets.)

Few brands generate this kind of unprovoked enthusiasm and loyalty. Rather, companies provide prompts to get consumers to show their support for a product, particularly through social media. The Bud Light #upforanything campaign from the previous chapter is a great example of motivating people to talk about their experience. A three-day vacation with celebrities and booze. Who wouldn't want others to know about that and toss in a mention of Bud Light, if only to thank them? Of course, the hashtag is built in as the reminder to do this. This is social currency par excellence, because it makes Millennials look better in the eyes of others—hipper, cooler, more exclusive. In a tamer example, Belkin and Lego produced a customizable iPhone case that was designed with studs on the back resembling LEGO blocks. Because of this design, people could connect their phone to LEGO constructions—build a person and let the iPhone be the face, create a picture on the back of the case, and so on. With a prompt from Belkin to demonstrate their creativity, people came up with all kinds of fascinating ways to integrate the phone with LEGO blocks and then posted pictures of themselves with their designs onto Instagram with the hashtag #LEGOxBelkin. From a marketing angle, this was brilliant word of mouth. Pictures of real consumers using the product became the company's product page. Thus, consumers did the selling for Belkin, showing other potential customers how cool the phone case was and giving the feeling that lots of people already had the product. What is particularly surprising about this is (1) there is no inherent enthusiasm for the product like Nutella, but rather an artificial one prompted by the brand, and (2) the consumer gets little out of the exchange, other than perhaps to demonstrate their creativity to others.

More typical are campaigns that give consumers something for their time and effort. Eyewear company Warby Parker sends five pairs of glasses to a prospect's home to try on before buying. Consumers are encouraged to take pictures of themselves in all five pairs, post them online with the hashtag #WarbyHomeTryOn, and ask their network of friends which they like most. This was really smart on the part of the company. They started this practice in 2012, early on in the time of social media. Consumers felt that they were getting assistance with the at-home service (the company started as online only), the brand got considerable social media exposure (aka free advertising), and the prospect got closer to buying the product because they received all kinds of positive feedback from friends and family. The T-Mobile campaign from the first chapter also provided these types of tangible benefits: fees paid for by T-Mobile, a new cell phone, and a public dumping of their current mobile service provider. Moreover, because the content had to be created through a Facebook app, the company was able to maintain control over the messaging while making it easy for consumers to post.[44]

Most extreme are when companies attempt to get consumers to spend time thinking about brands by getting them to create a commercial for the product—a time-consuming endeavor under the best of circumstances. The Doritos "Crash the Super Bowl" commercial contest has become a staple of this annual event. For almost a decade, the Doritos parent company Frito-Lay has offered the opportunity to compete to create an ad that will appear during the Super Bowl—the advertising event of the year. The win also comes with a cash prize, which last year totaled $1,000,000.

Through all of this, we are seeing the burden of spreading marketing content falling fully on the backs of consumers. Marketers may produce an interesting video, but the video only goes viral if we do that work. As the web becomes more and more reliant on visual content, we are being called on more and more to participate in campaigns that create a video or that ask us to take pictures of ourselves—with the product in hand and a smile on our face. And while one person may have won a million dollars from the Doritos ad, the company also got six thousand other creative ideas for free. Marketers frame these contests as empowering in order to get us to participate, but it is less empowering than they would have us believe.[45]

WHY DO WE "SHARE"?

A million dollars is certainly good motivation for willingly promoting a product, but that kind of prize money is, of course, the exception.

So why do we participate in word of mouth, either to promote a product or not?

We share because of personal motivations and gratifications. Key among these are that we want to create social bonds and stay connected with others, we want to be helpful, and we want to manage how others see us. Knowing this, marketers develop campaigns that will get us to engage with them. They create social media initiatives that allow for two-way conversation that communicates with us—rather than talks at us—in order to create a social bond; they create utility by offering coupons or by buying out our contracts so that we will share information; and they create a specific, defined brand so that we will communicate about it as part of managing our identity.[46] Moreover, as Berger and others have noted, we share feelings, especially heightened emotions and whatever provokes them. Passing feelings from one person to another is what is behind emotional contagion, what Facebook took advantage of when doing their online experiment. Because of this phenomenon, marketers are motivated to create content that generates strong feelings in order to get us to talk about their products. Manipulating our emotions combines with the ease of social media, creating the perfect formula for videos to go viral.[47]

All this interaction is great for marketers, but it comes with notable downsides for us. In his book, *Sharing our Lives Online: Risks & Exposure in Social Media*, communications scholar David R. Brake writes that posting online has considerable risks due to overexposure, yet we still do it even when other methods of social interaction are readily available. This is true in part because we find value in doing so—social connection, for example.[48]

Is this worth the trade off? At this point, it is hard to say. What we do know is that a confluence of cultural, technological, and commercial forces is "driving not only the adoption of SNSes [social networking sites], but also an increase in the breadth of information being shared on such services."[49]

The first element that drives us toward self-disclosure is the network effect. Quite simply, this means that the more people who use a service, the more valuable it becomes. Think about the adoption of cell-phones. Initially, you might not have felt you needed one, but as more people were texting rather than talking, the need for the mobile phone increased. It was also helped along by "friends and family plans" that utilized the concept of network effects to promote cell phone usage. The same idea applies to social. Every time one more friend joins a social site, the more we feel compelled to join as well. So much so that today Facebook has 1.44 billion users, Twitter 284 million, and Instagram, Pinterest, and LinkedIn have 300, 40, and 364 million respectively. As the number of people using social media increases, not being part of the site becomes difficult, even isolating. Recently, an older woman told me that she felt that she had to join Facebook because other people knew more about what her son was doing than she did because she wasn't on the site. It is just that sort of social pressure that drives us onto these social sites. Once there, notes Brake, "peer expectations may . . . pressure even reluctant users to share." According to Pew Research, 24 percent of American Facebook users feel pressured to share more information than they'd like.[50] And based on their own research, Facebook has found that newcomers see how much their friends share and emulate that. The company is capitalizing on social pressures to conform. What we see other people do affects what we choose to do and influences what we think we are supposed to do; this is called the Chameleon Effect.[51] This creates a cycle of ever increasing exposure, even if exposure isn't our personal preference.

Beyond network connectedness, sociological factors play into why we share. Sociologists have suggested that individual identity is defined reflexively, that is, "we come to know who and what we are through inter-action with others."[52] This helps explain social media's appeal. These sites are a stage wherein we can create who we are for ourselves and others. But the availability of these sites, combined with our need for per-sonal definition, did not lead to virtually unfiltered sharing. That, rather, was driven by the ideal of openness as a norm in the online community almost from its inception.[53] Today, this gets talked about as authenticity, an ethos of both online and advertising. Note, however, that this is counter to offline norms, in which we tend to think before we speak, have multiple identities (mom, employee, friend), and live in what sociologist Erving Goffman called on-stage and backstage spaces. Think *Downton Abbey*, where the maids and cooks act one way alone and another way when Lady Mary walks into the downstairs kitchen. The rejection of offline norms on Facebook is driven by the philosophy of its founder, Mark Zuckerberg, who fervently proclaims, "You have one identity," and that therefore there is no longer a "backstage" persona to hide. While this is interesting to think about in theory, the truth is that we do show one side online, and that tends to be a pretty rosy picture: it's the pictures of the beautiful trip to the Bahamas rather than the picture of an argument with your wife that ends up in the news feed. High school students take picture after picture to drive the number of "Likes" they receive, or alternatively take down posts that people don't respond to.[54] So whether or not we're unified or perfectionist about our identities, we use the online space to derive feedback about who we are or who we want to be.

Technology also helps propel disclosure and sharing. Most people do not effectively use privacy settings, and so they overshare without even knowing it. Facebook continually changes its privacy settings to test how far they can go with making information visible by default.[55] In addition, the sites are set up to create more and more activity online. Say you post a story to Facebook. That generates comments by other people in your network. You get a notification every time someone comments, leading you to head to the site so see what they said. This may also connect you to other "friends," or it simply gets you back online to check your news feed. Or apps like IFTTT ("If this, then that") enable content on one site to be reformatted to another: post on Facebook, and it also appears on Twitter. More broadly, Hootsuite allows users to visualize multiple social sites simultaneously in order to be better able to manage one's online presence.

Social networks profess to want to do good, which is why they claim to have set up the sites to aid in perpetuating communication. Facebook was built "to make the world more open and transparent."[56] Google famously claims to be committed to "do no evil." These are lovely ideas in the abstract. In the real world, however, these are companies with shareholders that demand continually increasing profits. Every fiscal quarter there is a headline about Google that reads something like this one that appeared in the *New York Times* in April 2015: "Google's Quarterly Revenue Rises, but Analysts Still Fret About Growth."[57] The headline for that same article online appears as "At $17.3 Billion, Google's Quarterly Revenue Rose 12 Percent." That's right: the company generated more than $17 billion in revenue, it is growing by 12 percent, and analysts still have concerns.

Advertising makes up the bulk of that revenue for Google. The same is true for Facebook, which in the first quarter of 2015 saw advertising revenue gains of 42 percent. Partially, this was achieved through restricting the number of ads (basic supply and demand), but the ability to exploit consumer data has also enabled Facebook to increase the price of its advertising. In the same quarter, the average price per ad rose 285 percent. This is because the more information we disclose, the more targeted the ad can be, and the more money the advertiser will be willing to pay for it.[58]

Social network sites, then, are becoming no different from their legacy media forbearers. They want to generate profits at obscene levels, and the way to do that is to get us not only to spend time with them, but also to spread their message—they want us to share. The choice of that word is not a fluke. Notes Israeli researcher Nicholas John in his article "Sharing and Web 2.0," "the spread of the notion of sharing lies in its positive connotations of equality, selflessness and giving, in combination with its resonance with what is viewed as the proper mode of communication between intimates. In brief, sharing is associated with positive social relations, as expressed through the popular phrase, 'sharing and caring', which has been appropriated by SNSs to infuse their services with the positive implications of that term."[59] He explains that this is easily seen in how Facebook discusses the share buttons thus: "the best and most interesting items get noticed by the people you care about."[60] But putting a positive spin on this activity hides what the button should really say: corporate sponsored WOM.

• • •

Marketers are increasingly social. Against our better judgment, we share our perfect selves and their sales missives. Some of what we share is noncommercial content and some is advertising. Some of what we share may be advertising, but we are unaware of it.

The most covert forms of marketing in this environment are native advertising and content marketing. The first puts ads in the content; the other is advertising made to look like editorial content or light-hearted entertainment. Some have called this a natural progression coming out of ad avoidance and changing media devices. It also stems from people not wanting to pay for news or entertainment anymore, whether that means getting free access to the *New York Times* or "stealing" video from a bit torrent. If we are not willing to pay for content, and if we don't want to consciously interact with advertising, then the blurring of church and state is the price we are paying. As we will see in upcoming chapters, marketers and publishers are still stumbling in trying to figure out the balance between hiding the advertising message and building brand awareness among consumers. For now, though, the trajectory is toward increasing levels of concealment.

3
NATIVE ADVERTISING: PUBLISHERS AS MARKETERS

On January 14, 2013, the home page of the *Atlantic* looked like it did on any other day—same typeface, same white background, same picture layout. But something was amiss. The lead story seemed somehow, well, off.

The headline read: "David Miscavige Leads Scientology to Milestone Year," with a subhead stating: "Under ecclesiastical leader David Miscavige, the Scientology religion expanded more in 2012 than in any 12 months of its 60-year history." Uncharacteristically, and in opposition to traditional journalistic standards, the piece effusively listed the institution's numerous global achievements with superlatives that proclaimed "unparalleled growth" and described the leader as a "driving force" and "unrelenting in his work." The pictures showcased church openings around the world and were captioned to note that thousands of people attended these events, though there was no verification of those numbers and no evidence in the pictures.

There are clues that this content was native advertising (a sales pitch disguised to be integral to the site) rather than typical *Atlantic* fare. Beyond writing that would undoubtedly not pass muster with the publication's editorial board, it was clearly marked with a bright yellow highlighted bar proclaiming "SPONSOR CONTENT." At the end of the piece, the Scientology logo and the text "Sponsor Content presented by The Church of Scientology" are clearly displayed.[1] The publication thought that was enough to designate this as advertorial content. It was not.

The problem wasn't that it was native advertising, which can be done without tricking the reader; the problem was that it was native advertising done badly. Let's break it down: native advertising doesn't look like advertising. It fits seamlessly into the flow of the publication. And it has symbols or text that label the article or posting as advertising. But this piece was too native, too *Atlantic*-ish. Visitors to the site got suckered into the content, and once they started reading, they knew fairly quickly that this was not a typical story. Readers were furious, and rightly so.[2]

The response to this trickery was palpable.[3] In a quite pointed tweet, one freelance journalist who writes for the *Atlantic* posted, "What the fuck is this shit?" and provided a link to the page. News coverage, from the *Washington Post* to *NBC Nightly News*, lambasted the *Atlantic* for providing Scientology with such prominent space in a well-respected publication.

Journalists were not only upset by the content itself but by the lack of ability to comment on it. Early commentary was unanimously positive, about as positive as the piece itself, yet critical voices could not get their negative commentary posted, which raised suspicions. They would come to learn that this was because the comments were being moderated by the marketing team—not the editorial staff—and their job, unlike editorial's, is to filter out comments that attack their client. A few negative comments did ultimately make it through the censors, such as "I guess money talks. You better hope people don't WALK away from your publication for allowing this ruse," and one of my personal favorites: "If the *Atlantic* wanted to do something degrading and pathetic for money, they should have tried scat porn. It would be less embarrassing to explain to their children."[4] By the time the nightly news broadcasts were over at 11:30 p.m., the content had been pulled.

The following morning, the *Atlantic* guiltily apologized:

> We screwed up. It shouldn't have taken a wave of constructive criticism—but it has—to alert us that we've made a mistake, possibly several mistakes. We now realize that as we explored new forms of digital advertising, we failed to update the policies that must govern the decisions we make along the way. It's safe to say that we are thinking a lot more about these policies after running this ad than we did beforehand. In the meantime, we have decided to withdraw the ad until we figure all of this out. We remain committed to and enthusiastic about innovation in digital advertising, but acknowledge—sheepishly—that we got ahead of ourselves. We are sorry, and we're working very hard to put things right.[5]

Nice try, but duplicitous. The publisher was pushing the limits to see how far native advertising would go, and they lost. Advertising is advertising, and this "article" was produced by the client like most advertising is. Before any ad is put into a publication, it is reviewed for content. If the ad is unacceptable, don't publish it. It's really hard to imagine that editorial or even the marketing staff thought this was acceptable—on any level.

"The Scientology ad" came up again and again as the worst-case scenario for native advertising. No one I spoke with could provide other egregious cases or anything more recent. That puzzled me. Why aren't there more examples? Have we become more accepting of native ads? Is it that marketers have gotten better at hiding them? Or is it that we just don't know the ads are there?

It seems to be a bit of all of the above. A few years ago, pieces like this got our shorts in a knot, and you could just hear fingers banging on keyboards demanding transparency in journalism. Today, not so much. Granted, the Scientology piece is effusive in its praise for an institution that most find deplorable or at least mildly offensive, which would explain the pushback. However, is this really any different from other native advertising we see now? There was no outcry when the *New York Times* ran a puff piece on urbanization and sustainability for Shell Oil. There was no angry public lambasting when Chevron had a piece about "changing energy needs" that was really about the competitive world market for energy.[6] Admittedly, there was some negative response to the same paper's piece for Goldman Sachs, a bit of puffery that was meant to improve the company's reputation after the financial crisis. That negative response, however, has become the exception.

The *Times* has gotten really clever at integrating advertising with editorial content, and so have other publishers. On mobile platforms especially, native ads can be extremely elusive—and this is important, because everything is moving toward mobile. In a particularly under-handed example, men attending the SXSW festival found themselves matched on the dating app Tinder with Ava, a stunningly beautiful twenty-five-year-old woman. After some short banter, the conversation turns to where the couple should meet in person. "If you could meet me anywhere, where would you choose?" asks Ava. "Considering we're both in Austin right now, I'd have to say Austin," responds the prospective date. Ava answers, "You are clever. You've passed my test. Take a look at my Instagram, and let me know if I've passed yours :). @mee-tava." Thing is, Ava's a robot, and the Instagram account was a native ad for the movie *Ex Machina*.[7]

Integrated content of a more serious nature can also appear offline. In 2015, CNN announced that they were forming an in-house studio to produce advertising that looks like news. Of course, they do not call it advertising. They call it Courageous. That's the name of their new marketing arm, which is made up of journalists and filmmakers and headed by a former creative director from OgilvyEntertainment, a division of advertising giant Ogilvy & Mather.[8] While Courageous hasn't produced anything to date (or at least they aren't promoting the fact that they have), you can get an idea of where this is heading by looking at case studies of what CNN has done overseas. "Leading Women" is an on-air segment, a monthly program consisting of interviews with influential women from Bobbi Brown to Oprah Winfrey to Sheryl Sandberg, as well as online content. It is used to promote high-end watchmaker Omega. Programs and interviews are done by CNN's on-air talent, and the segment looks analogous to soft news pieces the network would air. While the online content was obviously advertising, the pieces on CNN's air were not—or at least not that I could tell.[9]

Even as they pander to advertisers, CNN and other news organizations are twisting themselves in knots trying to maintain their credibility while producing camouflaged corporate content. Producers claim to be working toward transparency, but come on. Really? As an executive from Turner, CNN's parent company, said: "This isn't about confusing editorial with advertising . . . This is about telling advertisers' stories—telling similar stories but clearly labeling that and differentiating that." He even went on to say, "This is CNN. We're not here to blur the lines."[10] Does anyone believe that nonsense? What he and the advertising clients are counting on— and what they are paying for—is that the patina of trustworthiness associated with an unbiased news source with CNN's journalistic credentials will come to be associated with the products and services that appear within their content. As the no-nonsense, tell-it-like-it-is Janine Jackson of Fairness and Accuracy in Reporting (FAIR) told Al Jazeera: "Advertisers aren't stupid. When they pay money for something they expect to get money in return. With native advertising, [the advertiser's] ad seems to be a little bit more under the aegis of [a] respectable news organization. If it didn't work like an ad, they wouldn't pay for it like an ad. And that's the important thing to remember, whether it's called storytelling or content or co-branding. An ad is an ad is an ad."[11] This is at the heart of black ops advertising, including native: it only works if the content looks more like editorial than it does like advertising.

Publishers are caught between a rock and a hard place. They have to make money, most of the money is going into digital, and increasingly that money is funding native. In the case of the *Atlantic*, digital advertising at the time the Scientology ad appeared made up 59 percent of ad revenues for the company, and approximately half of that is attributable to native.[12] And they are not alone. Adoption of native advertising is widespread, with research suggesting that between 62 to 75 percent of publishers are offering this service, with another 16 percent having planned to jump on the native advertising bandwagon in 2015. That means that only about *10 percent* of publishers are not looking into offering a native advertising format.[13]

That said, native advertising has not, and likely will not, replace all other forms of online promotion. Ben Williams, editor for digital at *New York* magazine, noted that banner ads, display ads, and home page takeovers remain that publication's biggest revenue driver.[14] This is because as discussed in the last chapter, marketers still need to facilitate consumers' relationship with the brand, and simply seeing an ad is valuable, even if no one clicks on it. So while native is growing, for now it still constitutes only a small piece of marketers' budgets at five percent or less, while native makes up about 20 percent of publisher revenues.[15] However, spending is growing and growing rapidly as mobile becomes the go-to format and news feeds dominate. In November of 2014, eMarketer was predicting that native ads would reach $8.8 billion by 2018.[16] A mere three months later, *Business Insider* and the IAB were predicting spending to be $7.9 billion in 2015, with that figure almost tripling to $21 billion by 2018.[17]

It is easy to see why this has gained in popularity. No one reads banner ads, and full-screen takeover ads are appealing for advertisers, but they don't have the pass along factor. Native ads, on the other hand, circumvent clutter and grab our attention; we are "25 percent more likely to look at a native ad compared to a banner, and will view a native ad 53 percent more frequently."[18] Not only that, we are more likely to share this content, and we have higher purchase intent after viewing native content.[19] The stealth nature of these ads is what makes them particularly appealing. Being similar in tone with the publication makes it difficult to parse native advertisements from editorial content. According to Meredith Levien, executive vice president of advertising for the *New York Times*, readers spend similar amounts of time with sponsored posts (that is, advertising) as they spend with legitimate news stories. Some "paid posts" have even outpaced news stories. The question is, though: did readers know they were "paid posts"? We just don't know.

NATIVE ADVERTISING

If you are confused about what native advertising is and how to spot it, you are not alone. Marketers themselves are bamboozled. A survey noted: "respondents [marketers] commented about their lack of knowledge about native advertising, did not know what the term referred to, or had never heard it."[20] Even industry insider website Mashable asked the question, "What Is 'Native Advertising'? Depends Who You Ask."

The Internet Advertising Bureau (IAB) has this definition: "Paid ads that are so cohesive with the page content, assimilated into the design, and consistent with the platform behavior that the viewer simply feels that they belong." Better is that of GigaOm founder Om Malik: "a sales pitch that fits right into the flow of information." Or, more frankly:

native advertising is content camouflaged to look like other content in the hopes that we will read it and share it.

But that doesn't explain it all either, because examples can be wide ranging and ads are disguised in different ways. The Scientology ad looked like a magazine article. CNN's content looks like a celebrity interview segment. A humorous video on The Onion about a man obsessed with removing Internet Explorer from everyone's computer is actually an ad for Microsoft created by the website's creative agency, The Onion Labs.[21] In yet another example, Gawker did one better by creating a piece called "We've Disguised this Newcastle Ad as an Article to Get You to Click on It," which was an ad for beer and a commentary on native advertising all at the same time.[22] Finally, in one of the more offensive cases, *Wired* presented an article written by a widely respected scholar, MIT's Grant McCracken, about how TV viewing habits are changing. It says things like "people are not watching predicable shows with happy windups by the end of each episode. They are not watching junk TV. They are watching great TV: *House of Cards* and *Orange Is the New Black*." Why not say *Walking Dead* or *Breaking Bad* or *Game of Thrones*? Because the article was sponsored by Netflix, that's why.[23] Still worse, the "article" never addresses the social or economic consequences of binge watching, or the fact that we have to pay for Netflix while TV used to free.

This is all very interesting, but how are you supposed to tell what's news and what's not? What's reality and what's corporate puffery? How are you supposed to know? Truth is, sometimes you can't. But if you know what to look for, these ads can start to become more obvious. Let me break this down.

TYPES OF NATIVE ADVERTISING

The Internet Advertising Bureau (IAB)'s *Native Advertising Playbook* outlines six types of native advertising, including in-feed units, paid search units, recommendation widgets, promoted listings, and custom, or "can't be contained" formats.[24] You don't need to know all of these, and most of them we will dispense with quickly. First, paid search units and promoted listings are the ads that you see at the top of a search engine like Google, as well as the advertising that runs down the side of the search page. Most of us are familiar with these. On the other hand, you might be surprised to learn (as I was) that pictures with a headline at the bottom of a web page that say "from around the web" are also a form of native advertising called recommendation widgets. These sponsored links make suggestions for content based on what you've been looking at online. Produced by companies like Outbrain, Sharethrough, and Taboola, the ads look like the publisher's site, but they link to the advertiser's page. Both of these forms of native advertising are of less concern, as the promotional aspect is fairly obvious (or is quickly made so.)

Two types of native ads are more obscured and therefore of more interest. They are in-feed ads and custom ads. We will look at both in depth here.

IN-FEED AD UNITS

In-feed units appear within media news feeds (thus the name). As native advertising, they look similar to other content but contain some minimal labeling to denote that they're advertising. On Twitter, for example, commercial tweets have a (really) small gray arrow in a box next to the word "promoted" that appears at the bottom of the tweet. On Facebook, native ads say "Susie Smith likes Uber" or "suggested post" in ghosted type above the post, and "sponsored" in faded type appears below the company's logo. Or at least it was like that until July 2015, when Facebook tweaked the format to make it more subtle—adjustments of a kind I saw happen again and again. "Sponsored" is now under the company name, and the "thumbs up" button replaced the words "Like Page," making these sponsor indicators more obscure. On both sites, it is incredibly easy to miss these sponsor cues.

Beyond the major social sites, in-feed ads are becoming ubiquitous. They appear in everything from music sites like Pandora and iHeartMedia to respected news providers like Slate.com, Business Insider, Salon.com, Vox, and Talking Points Memo (TPM), to name just a few. The in-feed native advertising for most of these sites can be discerned if you know what to look for: words like "sponsored" and "promoted content" appear in a colored bar somewhere in the post—but you have to really look. Native ads are only part of these sites' arsenal. They also employ a variety of techniques, including product placement in their video content and custom content, which as we will see below is far more camouflaged.[25] Given all this, it is safe to assume that most sites you visit, particularly if you access the site via mobile, have native advertising on them.

There are a couple of different types of in-feed ads. Linked ads redirect you to an external site, much like the recommendation widgets do. If you have ever been on Facebook and clicked on Candy Crush by mistake, you've come face to face with this type of ad.[26] Alternatively, embedded ads don't require you to leave the site to view the ad—click on a video and you remain on Twitter. Finally, endemic in-feed units are the most widespread version of native advertising. These units are usually written by the publication to replicate the site's appearance and voice, sometimes in collaboration with the brand, and they appear in the feed with a label indicating that the content has a marketer behind it. Publishers creating ads for marketers has helped eliminate the possibility of another Scientology snafu, a situation that arose in part because the article was not written by *Atlantic* staff writers. Today, in-house advertising departments have become standard operating procedure. The model here is BuzzFeed (more below), where the publisher creates the content with input from the advertiser. Alternatively, Forbes's BrandVoice invites marketers to create content that appears on their site and in the print publication.[27] This is a bit more controversial in that this site allows marketers to write posts on "the same platform as *Forbes* writers and contributors," decimating the church/state wall.

In all of these cases, the content is labeled as promotion, though there is not a uniform term for it, which adds to content confusion. Google and YouTube use "advertisement" or "ad." Twitter uses "promoted" or "promoted by." Less obvious are Facebook, LinkedIn, and Yahoo, which use "sponsored" or "sponsored by [XYZ Company]" or "Sponsored Content" or "sponsored post," while BuzzFeed and Huffington Post favor "presented by [XYZ Company]" and "Featured Partner." *Forbes* uses their trademarked BrandVoice, which assumes the reader already knows they are looking at content that has been paid for. This conglomeration of terms belies publishers' claims to transparency; rather, transparency standards vary widely. As Bob Garfield—host of *On the Media*, former columnist for *Ad Age*, and vocal critic of native ads—has so aptly noted, if publishers really wanted to be transparent, they would label it advertising instead of using "weasel words" like those listed above. Moreover, consumers are confused by the labeling. A 2014 survey by the IAB and Edelman PR said that 41 percent of consumers said the ads were clearly identified. But that means that a far larger majority—59 percent—thought they were not.[28]

Indications are that this already subtly promoted content will get even more subtle. As mentioned, Facebook has been fine-tuning their layout, and so has Twitter. In April 2015, Twitter changed their yellow arrow icon next to the word "promoted" into the now faded gray one, so as to replicate other social sites.[29] This may cause some people to click on advertising by mistake, but you can avoid that by looking for the stray symbols and checking for whatever promotional language the site decides to use.

Until recently, no rules or guidelines existed for labeling these ads as there are for print advertorials.[30] That changed in December 2015 when the Federal Trade Commission came out with guidelines for native advertising which called for uniform labeling of sponsored content.[31] Not surprisingly, the IAB responded by saying the section of the guidelines called "Clarity of Meaning" (subtitled "disclosures must be understandable") was "overly prescriptive."[32] This response is a clear indication that advertisers are not as committed to transparency as they claim.

BUZZFEED

When it comes to endemic in-feed native advertising and social sharing, no one does it better than BuzzFeed. The numbers speak for themselves: BuzzFeed gets more than 200 million unique visitors per month.[33] Most of that comes via social media; 75 percent of people come to the site because of sharing. BuzzFeed dominates with Millennials; 50 percent of visitors are 18–34.[34]

At a marketing industry conference in 2014, Jonah Peretti, the company's founder and CEO, explained that a simple question drives everything BuzzFeed does: How do you make things that people love, and love to share? This is of paramount importance because so much of BuzzFeed's traffic comes from Millennials sharing their content.

Peretti learned the importance of sharing through experiences he had in the early 2000s. When Peretti was a student at the MIT Media Lab, Nike had just launched the Nike ID, which was a customizable sneaker. Peretti tried to order the shoes with the word "sweatshop" printed on the side. Given Nike's issues with international labor, it is not surprising that the company wrote back and said that the word was inappropriate, so they would not produce the shoe for him. Peretti's response was to ask if Nike could at least send him a picture of the young Vietnamese girl who was sewing up the Nike ID shoes overseas. Nike let it drop after that. Peretti did not. He forwarded the email exchange to friends, who sent it to other friends, who sent it to their friends, and so on. The Nike email was Peretti's initial foray into understanding the impact of viral content.

At the same time that Peretti was figuring out what makes content go viral, other future BuzzFeed executives were having similar experiences. Ze Frank, the head of BuzzFeed video, was creating visual content like the Atheist game (http://www.zefrank.com/atheist/) and its variation, the Buddhist game, as well as a site that showed friends how he wanted them to dance at a party he was having. Ze's web server company told him he had a bill in the tens of thousands of dollars because of all the traffic he was generating. For Ben Smith, the company's editor-in-chief, epiphany came while at a press event. He watched traditional reporters call in news stories to appear in the next day's papers. He figured out he could type the story on his Blackberry, post it on a blog, and beat the traditional reporters to the punch. All three, then, realized, "There's a way to reach people that's divorced from the way media works . . . it's not business . . . it felt cool and interesting so we began exploring it."[35]

All that learning was turned into BuzzFeed, an entertainment and news website that provides mostly short, "snackable" content—be it advertising or not. The site is known for its listicles and quizzes and just about anything to do with cute cats.[36] David Carr in the *New York Times* explained the site as reverse-engineering what Peretti had done as co-founder of HuffPo. "At The Huffington Post, [Peretti] used search optimization to create a gaudy funhouse behind a serious front page. At BuzzFeed, the funhouse was the point of it all. The main headers on the home page told the story: 'LOL,' 'cute,' 'win,' 'fail,' 'omg,' 'geeky,' 'trashy' and 'wtf?'"[37] So while the company is moving into hard news, few people consider the site for that content, given its origins as an "aggregator of memes and barrel-scraping viral content,"[38] even with Ben Smith's *Politico* credentials.

That "funhouse" content is fundamental to the mission of creating items that people will share. BuzzFeed relies on technology that seeks out viral Internet content, puts that through an editorial process, and feeds the content to visitors.[39] One of the first successful pieces of content on the site was something they call "disaster girl," which is a picture that had already had some traction on the Internet. An ominous looking little girl appears in the foreground of a picture in which a house is engulfed in flames. The odd smirk on her face made visitors wonder if she was somehow involved in this crime (she was not). People began Photoshopping her picture into the front of a number of different disaster shots, and BuzzFeed posted these mashups. Disaster girl appeared everywhere from Jesus' crucifixion to the invasion of Poland to the OJ trial. Popular posts like disaster girl are heavily promoted. As a former BuzzFeed executive put it, "We feed the winners and starve the losers."[40] The goal is to create a continuous circle of sharing and viewing and sharing again. To keep the cycle in perpetual motion, BuzzFeed constantly makes media and constantly learns from it. Creatives can keep posting content, and they can immediately see whether an idea connects with an audience, a technique now widely used by most content sites.

Humorous, mindless, irreverent content makes up the bulk of what appears on BuzzFeed. That and cats. This lightweight content is used to attract the "bored at work network," Millennials who are at their desk during lunch looking for a lift and a laugh that they can share with friends.

BuzzFeed's cycle of sharing, analyzing, creating, and re-creating goes for its native advertising as well. Advertising, like other content on the site, is meant to be shared. That's why BuzzFeed does not use banner ads. Rather, the site works with advertisers to create content that is entertaining, emotion-inducing, and easy to share.[41] Said Peretti, the company is "taking all the ways people consume media and extending that to solutions for brand partners. So we do lists and quizzes and animations and custom integrations and videos and whenever we develop a new format we will extend that format to branded content." A quiz for HBO, for example, was "How would you die in *Game of Thrones*?" and they created "Which Barbie doll are you?" for Mattel, both of which received more than 1 million views. They created videos called "The evolution of the burrito" for Taco Bell, "Why we get tattoos" for Spike TV, "What kind of thinker are you?" for GE, a promotion that included first a quiz to determine visitors' thinking style and then videos to explain each style in more detail—combining the best of both marketing worlds. Probably their most well-known sponsored video is, not surprisingly, about a cat. "Dear Kitten," which was created for Purina, has more than 21 million views just on YouTube and has been so successful that it spawned a series of spinoffs.[42] Sponsored content, then, sits seamlessly side by side with "news" stories, and like the news stories, sponsored content is meant to be shared. These pieces are marked as sponsored or say "promoted," but if you are reading these pieces on your mobile device—and most people do—these notations are easy to miss.

BuzzFeed's point of difference for now is that they have figured out what people share through their analytics and why people share through social listening, and they've transferred that to assist advertisers.[43] This explains BuzzFeed's appeal: they create content that will convert paid media to earned media. As Will Hayward, BuzzFeed's vice president in Europe, explained: "It's not about eyeballs on Buzzfeed.com. It's about creating content for brands and distributing that on Facebook, which has more than one billion users. That's a pretty huge audience we can deliver messages to."[44] It's all about the conversation—that's what BuzzFeed understood before anyone else.

Peretti claims that he intends BuzzFeed to become a legitimate news outlet. But it will be difficult for a site known as the list and kitten network to gain credibility, given advertising's vaunted place in the company and given their habit of blurring church and state—even while they take pains to proclaim loudly that they do nothing of the sort. The company stirred up commotion in early 2015 when it pulled an article about Dove products that poked fun at the brand. Dove is owned by Unilever, which is a major advertiser on the site. Gawker called them out on the deletion, saying, "[The reporter's] post was legitimate criticism of an exploitative marketing campaign underwritten by one of the largest and most powerful advertisers on the planet. In other words, the reason her post was necessary—in a way so many BuzzFeed posts are not—seems to be the very reason BuzzFeed deleted it."[45] News director Ben Smith did a mea culpa on Twitter and the article was restored. The reporter, however, left the company and did not return.

This is not the first time BuzzFeed has done this. In 2013, ad critic Mark Duffy was fired from BuzzFeed for attacking Axe, another Unilever product. He claimed he was asked to dial back his criticism and delete posts to appease advertisers.[46] We can only wonder at the critical content that never even makes it to the consideration stage because it does not fit the native advertising environment.

BuzzFeed claims there can be no qualms about its integrity because they distinctly mark sponsored content. Says Mark Frackt, CFO, "We do our best to label commercial content. If it's being promoted by a brand, we specifically say so . . . The other thing is that it's engaging—consumers are happy that they're reading a promoted item and the proof is that they share it on Facebook and Twitter. If they didn't like the content, they wouldn't be sharing it."[47] But do they know it is advertising? That's one bit of analytics the company hasn't done, or if they have, they have not made it public. Moreover, Peretti's attitude toward the blurred line is evident in a comment he made at *Advertising Age*'s digital conference in 2012: "People still worry about the line between editorial and advertising . . . the bigger distinction is now between advertising that sucks and ads that are engaging and are ripe for sharing."[48] And this is from a guy who claims he wants to get into hard news.

Perhaps most telling is that BuzzFeed is listed on Hoovers, the financial information company database, as an *advertising agency*. Not so their competitors. Facebook, Google, and Twitter are all listed as Internet Publishing, Broadcasting & Search, and Portals. Peretti claims a separation between church and state, but the company's reputation and history make it impossible to take him at face value. Whatever journalistic integrity they might have is fundamentally undermined.

As they are, BuzzFeed has influenced a number of other sites which have implemented similar strategies, not all of whom are hiding the advertising. A good example here is Thrillist, a site that caters to urban male Millennials, and the native advertising campaign they did for General Electric. As Paul Josephsen, VP of integrated marketing, told me, the problem that GE was facing was that they no longer have a consumer product division. They needed a way to connect with consumers, particularly young guys interested in tech, who might want to work for the company. Built around the forty-fifth anniversary of the moon landing, Thrillist wrote a series of articles à la BuzzFeed—"11 things you didn't know about the Apollo Missions," "10 Reasons Why The Apollo Astronauts Were Certified Badasses," etc.—highlighting GE's role in making this event happen. All this led up to a limited edition "moon sneaker" produced by GE, the company that had also produced the rubber for the boots and the helmets used in the moon landing. One hundred sneakers made to look like moon boots (selling at $196.90—or "1969") were sold on Thrillist's ecommerce site, JackThreads.com. They were a huge hit. "They sold out in seven minutes," claims Thrillist CEO Ben Lerer. In fact, the sneakers became so popular that they were selling on eBay for $2,000.[49] This advertising would not have worked for GE if their participation was hidden. It was not. GE logos were prominently displayed throughout.

I asked Josephsen who he considered his key competitors. I was surprised when he didn't say BuzzFeed. He explained why: unlike BuzzFeed, Thrillist is not primarily a media company. It is an ecommerce one—one might call it a "native shopping" experience. This economic structure and integration of buying within the content experience is what makes this so different from traditional media. The company derives between 70 and 80 percent of its revenue from JackThreads, making it far less dependent on advertising than their competitors. So while Peretti may be getting the buzz, Thrillist is better positioned as a company: not only do they have a business model that is difficult to reproduce (unlike BuzzFeed), but they also have email lists and local penetration, which would be difficult and costly to replicate.[50] Only the companies that are totally dependent on advertising have a vested interest in not flaunting their sponsorships.

CUSTOMIZED CONTENT

Customized content is created by the publisher to look like newspaper and online articles and, like the name suggests, it is specially produced. What makes this different from the work of BuzzFeed and others is that these ads do not appear within a news feed.

Like the *Atlantic*, most organizations stumbled with their first outings of custom content. A year after the Scientology ad, the *New York Times* ran a flatfooted piece about Millennials and computers sponsored and created by the computer company Dell. The online publication, Gawker, presented an uninspired fake article about how to be a "nerd babe" as a promotion for TBS's program *King of the Nerds*.

After these missteps, companies developed more formal in-house studios or "labs" devoted to creating native advertising content. Former journalists staff many of these in-house marketing departments, which explains why these ads are virtually identical to the editorial content.

The *Washington Post*, owned by Amazon's Jeff Bezos, took the lead in custom native by starting BrandConnect in 2013 and allowing posts on their home page. Like other traditional newspapers, they fervently state that the newsroom is not involved in the creation of this content. The *Washington Post* also offers "BrandConnect Perspective," a service similar to Forbes's BrandVoice that allows organizations to submit their own commentary to be featured on the *Post's* opinion section online.[51] Bayer provided a piece titled "Modern Agriculture is Based on Sound Science" that was written by a company executive. Across the top of the page it says "Perspectives," and the Bayer CropScience logo appears on the article, but the look and feel of the page is still very much that of the site's Op-ed space.[52] More obscured are the "news" pieces. "Keeping Road Cars in Formula One Shape" has all the identifying tags and logos we have come to expect, but the landing page is filled side-to-side and top-to-bottom with a picture of a spectacularly flashy sports car and a headline in ginormous type. The visual is so stunning and the type and colors so overwhelming that the sponsor mention is easily overlooked. In this case, the "story" about a partnership between Shell and Ferrari stresses the importance of changing a car's oil often. It is hard to imagine anyone being fooled by this content, as the sponsor is mentioned again and again . . . and again.

For now, this all seems innocuous. But we cannot trust that advertiser indicators will always be this obvious, especially when the team creating this content "sits in the marketing group but looks for inspiration in the newsroom," according to an article in *Adweek* entitled "The *Washington Post's* Native Ads Get Editorial Treatment: Borrowing from newsroom."[53] In the case of the *Washington Post*, there's also the Bezos connection, which tends to mean Machiavellian approaches to profit generation.

A year after the *Washington Post*, the *Wall Street Journal* launched an in-house team called WSJ Custom Studios. This group is housed within the newspaper's advertising department. Their website notes: "[the studio] crafts stories that engage consumers and elevate the conversation for brands. Its global team of award-winning editors, designers and interactive developers are all held to the high standards for which the *Wall Street Journal* is known, resulting in highly original and credible content that resonates with the client's target audience." Ugh! This group offers not only native advertising but custom infographics, research and white papers, and campaign measurement. What I found particularly interesting were the content hubs, which could be offered within wsj.com or on a client platform. The one I delved into was an elaborately produced online magazine called "Curiosity" that was created for a private bank—a fact that was utterly hidden in the magazine itself. There was ghosted text stating that the magazine was created "in collaboration with WSJ Custom Studios," and in one other place I saw "Content is provided by WSJ Custom Studios," but that was it. More bizarre, though, was that the bank was barely mentioned at all—a new level of hidden marketing. On the newspaper's site itself, though, the advertising aspect was clearly labeled. A heavy blue band containing the words "SPONSOR GENERATED CONTENT" runs across the top of the page, a fairly large sponsor logo is on the left, and the Custom Studio logo appears on the right. When you click on the blue bar, it states: "This content was paid for by an advertiser and created by the *Wall Street Journal* advertising department. The *Wall Street Journal* news organization was not involved in the creation of this content,"[54] making it more obvious than other sites.

As the paper of record, the *New York Times* is held to a higher standard, and the expectation is thus that they will be the most cautious when it comes to avoiding confusion around advertising and editorial. The reviews are decidedly mixed. To debut its new site for native advertising, the *New York Times* created content for Netflix in conjunction with the launch of the second season of its hit show *Orange Is the New Black*.[55] Across the top of the page is a light blue band that states "PAID POST." Under that is another band that includes the *Times* logo followed by "Brand Studio" (it stands for T Brand, the name of their in-house studio) on the left, and in the middle the Netflix and *Orange Is the New Black* logos appear. The URL, which likely few will look at, starts with "paidpost.nytimes.com." Beyond this, however, the page looks like a journalistic piece in the *Times*. There is a headline, "Women Inmates: Why the Male Model Doesn't Work," a subhead, and what looks like a reporter's byline on top of an illustration of women heading into prison, the type that would appear with a typical story in the paper. The copy is interrupted by a video of women in prison and includes a clip from Piper Kerman, on whom the series is based. There is also a line in the article that says, "In an August 2013 op-ed in the *New York Times*, Piper Kerman, author of the prison memoir *Orange Is the New Black*, which inspired the Netflix series of the same name, calls the distance between women prisoners and their families 'a second sentence.'"

This native advertising is not only fundamentally different from the in-feed content of BuzzFeed, but even from other newspapers. This is in-depth reporting with visuals, infographics, and video—all professionally done, all visually appealing—all produced by T Brand staff with both journalism and marketing credentials. That staff includes Adam Aston, a former *Businessweek* editor, who has ghostwritten for brands, Melanie Deziel, a former staffer at Huffington Post's branded content studio as well as BuzzFeed, and news video producer Kaylee King-Balentine.[56] And it is evident that the paper is looking to do more, as they have said they would like to increase their ranks to thirty-five in total. This is on par with the *Washington Post*, though about half the size of BuzzFeed's similar department.[57]

The piece on *Orange Is the New Black* was followed by similar multimedia pieces for Cole Hahn, Goldman Sachs, and Shell, and now there are as many as three pieces appearing in a single month. Interestingly, there is no website link to the T Brand Studio on the *Times* website. Rather, it is housed in the "Idea Lab."[58] Much of this content contains beautiful photography and some infographics, but is light on copy. Several, "The Surprising Cost of Not Taking a Vacation for MasterCard" and "Distracted Parent, Distracted Teen for Toyota," are similar to the Netflix piece and include video, copy, and graphics. In each case, the content is uniquely tailored to the advertiser, so there are recipes for yogurt company Chobani, while photography is used to sell Costa Rica as a vacation destination.

Like other traditional news organizations, there are disclaimers that the studio "is intentionally and completely separate from our newsroom team, such that no members of our news or editorial staffs play a role in the creation of our branded content . . . We've gone to great lengths to make sure our content is distinguished and clearly labelled as advertising that comes from a marketer. Native advertising is not about tricking readers into thinking what they are reading is created by the *New York Times* newsroom; rather it is about providing readers with insightful and valuable content." Again I turn to the astute analysis of FAIR's Janine Jackson, who believes they are being disingenuous, at best. "Native, shnative. The *New York Times* should not be in the business of managing people's opinion of Goldman Sachs. There is no way that I can take as seriously the *New York Times* reporting on Goldman Sachs knowing that they have just been on this content creation journey together. It very simply represents another example of news outlets doing pretty much the definition of 'selling out.' Native advertising is just an effort to confuse readers to think that they're getting something other than an ad."[59]

Now, the *Times* finds itself in a difficult balancing act as advertisers want proof that the native content works. T Brand did research in conjunction with Chartbeat, a real-time web analytics company. This research must be taken with a grain of salt, however, as part of Chartbeat's business is to prove "the monetizable value of quality content over clickbait." That said, the research found that the T Brand Studio content could go toe-to-toe with editorial in some cases. Looking at unique visitors, engagement (time on page), and visits via Facebook, Twitter, and Google, posts created by the newspaper performed better than those produced by the advertiser, which of course suggests that advertisers should use the *Times*' in-house services. "The research also shows that while traffic on median-performing Paid Posts does not outperform traffic on median-performing NYTimes.com editorial content, some high-performing T Brand Studio posts received enough traffic to generate as much engagement as some editorial content on NYTimes.com." Among these was the Netflix ad, which was among the top thousand articles in the *Times* during 2014.[60] This confirms what believers in native say over and over again: "great stories can come from anywhere, and certainly from brands . . . audiences will engage with great content regardless of its provenance, provided they have a sense of where it's coming from."[61]

Comments like that raise concerns among critics. The *New York Times* can create content that looks like news. While the *Orange Is the New Black* ad was not derided like the Scientology one, it did raise concerns, mostly because it is a serious piece of journalism. It was written by Melanie Deziel, who has legitimate news credentials. Now, however, she is editor and social media strategist of T Brand Studio, which ultimately means that she answers to an advertiser, whether that is consciously acknowledged or not. This makes native advertising problematic. It can lead to solid, well-researched content being produced. But is it journalism? It may also be content that the newspaper might not have produced without corporate support. If that's the case, we have to ask ourselves: why not? It might be simply a matter of economics. This came up as part of a conversation I had with Jeff Pundyk, the vice president of global integrated content solutions at the *Economist*. He noted that native advertising allows the publication to cover content they would not have been able to afford. That's a good thing on its face. However, journalistic principles exist for reportage that do not exist for advertising—the most important of those being that reporters are trained to present at least two sides of a story. This is not awkward for BuzzFeed or VICE, but it is for the *New York Times* and the *Economist* and the *Guardian,* which has a long-running "seven-figure deal" with Unilever around their sustainability initiatives.[62]

The full brunt of the kind of conflicts of interest that can arise came to light in the UK when Peter Oborne, the *Telegraph*'s chief political commentator, quit because he believed the newspaper was being soft on investigating questions related to tax evasion, rigged currency markets, and racism against Muslims by HSBC, one of their largest advertisers.[63] The collapsing wall of church and state led not only to simply inept reporting, but to an outright fraud on readers. Newspapers are scrambling for readers, particularly young readers, so this was no isolated incident. Native advertising, too, is a fraud if not properly labeled, yet there is no evidence that publishers are moving in the direction of being clear about labels on sponsored content. As further evidence that publishers will continue to slowly but surely cave to advertisers, the *Times* toned down the labeling on their sponsored posts just like Twitter did, and they did it in response to advertiser concerns that readers would not give the content a chance if they knew it was advertising.[64]

In-house ad agencies like these are not limited to the print stalwarts. New companies coming to native include CBS Interactive,[65] and online publications like Gawker, FastCompany, and Mashable (in addition to sites like Salon, Slate, and Vox, mentioned earlier) are fully immersed in native custom content. NBCU recently announced investments in both Vox and BuzzFeed, which is likely to create native mashups we haven't even begun to imagine.[66] Mashable and FastCompany I find to be already particularly opaque. It is often only when my AdDetector app kicks in that I know I'm looking at sponsored content. (More on ad blockers and ad detectors in Chapter 6.)

The most hidden ads are on one of Millennials' favorite sites, VICE. I spent hours trying to figure out what content on the VICE website was advertising. I knew it was there, because I knew VICE used almost exclusively native, but I couldn't find it. Is the article about a new documentary about Leon Russell an ad for the film, or simply an interview with the filmmakers? What about the article about Kanye West that conveniently includes an Adidas video that shows the $200 sneaker he designed (and which sold out in hours)? It's hard to tell for sure. Here, there are no labels of sponsorship of any kind. I did finally find an area where they provide case studies of past campaigns, which included video content (a one-off or a series) and devoted websites, known as verticals. For hair company Garnier Fructis, for example, VICE placed the product on its music channel, Noisey. Bringing together style, hair, and music, VICE created "Style Stage," which included video and written content focusing on music talent appealing to a young target audience. This initiative included a series called Style Files about "emerging artists with amazing hair, including product integrations and styling" and music videos with product integration. The campaign also featured a launch party at SXSW with styling stations and sampling opportunities, a college bus tour, and both online and offline auditions for the host of the original series *Headhunter*. Separately, VICE ran a venture with Intel called the Creators Project, which explores the juncture between art and technology and for which Intel has reportedly paid tens of millions of dollars.[67] More typically, VICE creates videos for marketers that begin with "presented by XYZ company," much as feature films begin with producer logos. In all, the corporate sponsorship is as obscured as possible. Because VICE has tentacles in a number of media properties, including digital, print, and television (new cable network), the company has multiple ways to drive traffic from one platform to another (with considerable assistance from their Millennial admirers).[68]

Another example of a company that is very much in this mode is Refinery29, a one-time fashion and style hyperlocal blog that has now expanded into news and political content targeted to a Millennial female audience.[69] Founded in 2005, the site has become so successful in attracting this audience (and advertisers) that it is often considered to be an equal player with print stalwarts *Vogue* and *InStyle*. With ambitions to expand globally, the company recently announced that they had received investment funding from media company Scripps Networks Interactive and the advertising giant WPP. Like other sites, the company is looking to expand its video content and to push video distribution through social and mobile, as well as (like VICE) through television.[70] In praising this site, content marketer Sachin Kamdar of Parse.ly said that "their content is excellent. Sometimes, it's hard to distinguish between Refinery29's editorial content and its branded content, meaning that they're both equally engaging."[71] Starting to sound familiar? According to the company's website, "people around the world spent more than 3.6MM hours on the site, which is more than 150,000 days or 411 years. And, what were people reading in all that time? Everything. Stories ranging from runway trends and beauty DIYs to dating disaster stories and articles featuring the latest world news—all with our signature Refinery29 wink, of course."[72] Yes, and how much of that engaging content was advertising? That, they do not say.

The blurred lines between editorial and content are becoming fuzzier by the day. Condé Nast, publishers of notable magazines like *GQ*, *Vanity Fair*, and *The New Yorker*, among many others, is not even pretending to keep editorial and advertising separate. With their studio, called "23 stories by Condé Nast," the publisher is having magazine editors work directly with marketers. Perhaps they feel emboldened to do this because of one of the key arguments for native advertising: if the advertising is good enough, people will enjoy it as much as they appreciate editorial content. The next sentence is usually: "Just look at *Vogue.* Women read it for the ads as much as the articles." By integrating the work, Condé Nast can offer advertisers seamless content across platforms.[73]

This seems to be a bellwether of things to come. Already the *Daily Mail* uses reporters to write both news and branded content for its website. On the other side of the equation, marketing guru Seth Godin recommends that companies hire editors instead of brand managers—advice I hope they do not heed. A recent article called "What Content Marketers Can Learn from Journalists" touts the growing trend of journalists becoming content marketers and how they bring their storytelling and writing skills to marketing.[74] As this trend continues, readers need to be suspicious about any and all editorial content—whether it is labeled or not.

VALUE TO ADVERTISERS & PUBLISHERS/ PROBLEMS FOR CONSUMERS

As we have seen, proponents of native ads (and there are many) say that companies and their marketing allies can create content as interesting as anything published in a newspaper. Further, these companies are also experts in their field, so they can provide better information on that field than someone outside the industry might. Since display ads are becoming less and less effective, publishers have to make money somehow, and native ads can help fill the void.

Critics, including me, have said that if the content is that good, companies should be proud to put their name on it. Misleading readers will only come back to hurt the publisher and the advertiser. And in the case of the advertiser, if consumers don't realize that there's a brand associated with some engaging and interesting content, what is the advertiser actually buying? A number of advertisers have begun to realize this, and they have been discussing it with publishers—advertisers want the ad to be native, but not too native. Unfortunately, that conflicts with publishers' desire for native to be ultra-camouflaged.

Bottom line: native advertising is about making money for publishers and advertisers. The way to do that is to get us to read and engage with content for longer periods of time. They claim they are giving us what we want, but I'm not convinced that's true. Do we really want one-sided presentations like Scientology? No, and I doubt we want that sort of content from Shell or Unilever either. But far worse: do we want that sort of content produced in a way that's indistinguishable from legitimate journalism?

If we believe what publishers say, they really have drunk the Kool-Aid. Jay Lauf, the publisher of the *Atlantic*, has said, "A lot of people worry about crossing editorial and advertising lines, but I think it respects readers more. . . . It's saying, 'You know what you're interested in.' It's more respectful of the reader that way."[75] Paul Rossi, managing editor of the *Economist*, put it a bit differently: "The opportunity for media companies is to create content that's compelling for users on behalf of advertisers. . . . The real issue is how do you make content that's compelling to a reader that doesn't feel like an ad? That's the real challenge."[76] And Time Inc.'s CEO, Joe Ripp, told Bloomberg TV: "Not are we violating church and state? Whatever that was. We ask, are we violating our trust with our consumers?"[77] Certainly it was not so long ago that he would have referred to his audience as readers, not consumers.

Behind closed doors, it is hard to imagine that these publishers are not conflicted. On the one hand, they need to provide sponsored content that consumers will click. On the other, they need to make sure people don't become irritated when they realize they've been click-baited into reading advertising. And publishers have to do this all while maintaining some semblance of journalistic integrity. This is certainly worse for what was a venerable institution like Time, Inc., than it is for a digital newbie like BuzzFeed.[78]

The concern I heard from most people in the field was the issue of transparency. And that fear is not unfounded. Recent research by the Association of National Advertisers found that transparency was the single biggest issue for advertisers using native, and two-thirds said that the advertising needs appropriate disclosure information.[79] But what one says on a survey is not necessarily what happens in practice. "Especially on the Internet . . . there's a long tradition of new media companies being willing to blur edit/ad boundaries," says Ben Williams, digital editor at *New York* magazine.[80] VICE is the perfect example here. In April 2014, they ran an "article" with the title "Talking to Girls About the Good Ol' Number-Two Taboo." As only VICE will do, the piece was accompanied by young women pulling up their underwear while walking out of a bathroom or sitting on a toilet with their underwear around their ankles. Below these pictures were captions noting what they were wearing, mostly from American Apparel (an advertiser known for presenting scantily clad nubile models) as well as Dr. Martens, Reebok, and a few others. While the site said that no money exchanged hands, there was an in-kind donation of apparel, and nowhere was the piece marked as sponsored.[81]

Traditional publishers, however, cannot—or should not—stray too far, or they risk alienating advertisers who want to be associated with a venerable reputation. Dell and Netflix and Shell get the patina of authority on a site like newyorktimes.com that they can't get from an online-only publisher, even if they do have to pay for it.[82] These companies want to be sure that consumers are not being bamboozled. And while the sites I looked at did show that the content was sponsored, I have serious concerns about whether readers absorb that information, particularly on sites where the sponsor information disappears once you scroll down the page.

Native advertising is so new that there is limited good independent research as to what consumers know or don't know about it. What exists, however, is telling. In December 2015, Bartosz W. Wojdynski and Nathaniel J. Evans from the University of Georgia published research which found that only eight percent of participants were able to recognize content as advertising. In a smaller study out of Berkeley's Law and Technology Center, Chris Jay Hoofnagle and Eduard Meleshinsky demonstrated that even when content was labeled "sponsored by," more than half the participants either thought it was written by a journalist or were unclear about who was behind that content.[83] In writing about this study, Amar Bakshi notes that the Berkeley research likely underestimates consumer confusion, because subjects were alerted to pay attention and evaluate an article with specific instructions to decide if it had been written by a reporter. In the real world, readers easily overlook textual cues in the rush of typical web behavior.[84] The Georgia study concludes by mirroring what I have been suggesting throughout this book, "the growth [in native advertising] might not be because the customers find it intrinsically compelling but because many of them do not recognize it well enough to apply the avoidance and defense strategies they have developed for other types of online ads."[85]

In 2013, corporate research demonstrated similar findings in that eighty-five percent of consumers had never heard of native ads.[86] Today, though, people are more aware of this type of sponsored content, even if they cannot put a name on it. We know they are more aware because they protest that it is misleading. They feel most deceived by sponsored video ads: 86 percent report that they find those ads misleading, while 57 percent feel similarly about Facebook Sponsored Stories and 45 percent about Twitter Promoted Tweets.[87]

Until recently, most people have not been aware of the various forms these ads take. Once the truth fully comes to light, the value of native advertising will diminish. When that happens, native advertising may simply become another place where ad avoidance will occur—and if that happens, advertisers will need to obscure the sponsor mention still further.

4
CONTENT MARKETING: MARKETERS AS PUBLISHERS

Native advertising involves advertisers placing sponsored messages within publishers' websites: publishers as advertisers. Content marketing involves advertisers creating messages for their owned media, which are made to look like something other than advertising: advertisers as publishers.

Most people in the industry would probably say that this definition is oversimplified, that content marketing is a strategy and that messages themselves are branded content. As with native advertising, however, the definition is up for grabs.

In trying to secure a grasp on content marketing, I interviewed a number of people and asked each person I interviewed for their definition. This was the best explanation I received: "Content marketing is much longer term [than native advertising]. When it's done right, it should be completely devoid of solicitation. It's about adding value and giving, not receiving. The strategy is, 'I'm going to keep adding value to your life and proving that I'm an expert on this topic that you care about, and when it comes time for you to buy and you decide that you need something we might have, hopefully we'll be top of mind.'"[1] The components of content marketing, then, are: (1) it presents information or entertainment to the consumer that they find useful, (2) it does this over a sustained period of time, and (3) it is done without selling and without interrupting consumers as they go about their lives.

MTV, in its original incarnation, could be thought of as content marketing. Here was an entire TV channel devoted to nothing but promotional videos that looked and felt like entertainment. We watched and sang and danced along, and after hearing a video a half dozen times, we might go out and buy the CD, never once having thought that we've been sold to.

Here is today's digital update on that model:

Four guys dressed in simple black suits, skinny black ties, and white button-down shirts who look like rock stars from the 1970s walk into frame in front of a stark white backdrop and sit down on what look like futuristic black and white stools. They sit in a straight line, one behind the other, facing the camera. The group, the alternative rock band OK Go, is actually sitting on motorized unicycles. While atop these vehicles, they execute an intricate dance number, gliding and sliding and moving in rhythm across the screen; they dip side to side, ride forward and back, and execute perfectly choreographed pirouettes. As the music video progresses, the group rolls smoothly outside the studio until they are in an open area, where they are joined by a large group of young female dancers dressed like Catholic school girls who proceed to perform an elaborate Busby Berkeley-style dance routine while OK Go weaves in and out among them.[2] (Don't try this at home: the video was shot at half speed, so while the guys of OK Go seem to effortlessly glide around at top speeds, no one in the real world is going to be achieving that feat any time soon.)

This video for the song "I Won't Let You Down" is the epitome of content marketing. It is product placement, yes, but it's more than that. The video is built around the functionality of Honda's Uni-Cub (a so-called "personal mobility device") as much as it is around the song and OK Go. In terms of fulfilling the mandate of content marketing, it is spot on. It is video, it is entertaining, it is visually absorbing, and the product is integrated into the content without screaming "look at me" (or worse yet, "buy me").

A very different video starts with water streaming toward the camera from a showerhead. Someone turns the water off, and the video cuts to a tea kettle whistling, followed by the unseen protagonist bringing a mug to their mouth while looking through a small window that frames a vista of snowcapped mountains. The screen goes black, and "Candide Thovex" appears in white type. We then see the protagonist for the first time as he faces a mirror and puts on his ski goggles. From this point forward, we will see the world through the eyes of the skier/video-maker. He picks up his skis and his poles, looks up to see a flock of birds flying overhead, and begins his downhill travels.

Throughout the five-minute video, we see—or, because of the point of view, almost feel—the jumps, twists, and turns down the mountain. We speed down the slopes until we begin to lift into the air, at which point the video changes to slow motion to give the full effect of the 360-degree rotation, only to speed up when we hit the ground. The run ends with the camera (and the videographer) traversing the ski resort building, much to the surprise of those having their morning coffee or waiting for the ski lift. Throughout, there is no sound other than the whooshing of the skis on the snow. It is both exhilarating and exhausting.

If you saw this video (titled "One of Those Days 2") or had it sent to you via social media, you wouldn't guess that it was commercial content. There are no logos or brand names evident anywhere. It is very likely, however, that you associated this content with GoPro, the professional camera originally designed for surfers to be able to film their athletic exploits within the breathtakingly beautiful curls of an ocean wave. The camera and the type of video it produces are so iconic that the brand identification seems secondary.

Finally, "What Lives Inside" is a film in four parts directed by Oscar winner Robert Stromberg and starring Oscar winner J. K. Simmons, as well as Catherine O'Hara and Colin Hanks. The story is one of self-discovery. After a famous puppeteer dies, his son (Hanks) journeys into the magical world his father left behind. In the first segment, we see the son in his straitlaced, gray, dull working environment. Once he discovers his father's hidden world, the images transform into a magical wonderland that evoke a combination of Willy Wonka, with bright colors and oversized candy canes, and a Tim Burton movie, with dragons and mysterious adventures. Through exploring this enchanted world, the son comes to find his own creativity and takes over his father's show. The film ends with words of wisdom from the old puppeteer: "It's the magic inside that creates the magic outside."

This film was the fourth in a series by Intel, this one done in conjunction with Dell while the first three were in association with Toshiba. The first, called "Inside," was presented in the summer of 2011. It was a mystery about where and why a girl was trapped inside an unknown room (with a Toshiba laptop), and social media helped people solve the whodunit through clues provided on Twitter and Facebook. This was followed in 2012 by "The Beauty Inside," a series of six films in which a man named Alex wakes up as a different person everyday: same on the inside, different on the outside. This becomes problematic when he falls in love yet knows that his love interest will never see him again. Fans were asked to audition for the lead role of Alex. More than four thousand people—male and female—auditioned on Facebook, with twenty-six being cast as the lead and another fifty being featured via Facebook in a clever plot device through which Alex chronicled his/her daily experience and which integrated the Toshiba computer into the story. The third series, "The Power Inside," employed similar techniques—an online audition, a series of films presented over the summer, and big name talent (Harvey Keitel).

Strategically, this is brilliant. The marketer faced the problem of making a processor interesting. Really, what could be more boring? Yet by combining stunning visuals, top-level talent, and a heartwarming story, they have created a piece worthy of a theatrical release. And the content marries well with the message of the brand—it is what is inside that matters, and by using our products you can explore your imagination, that important part inside of you. Consumers learn this not by being whacked on the head, but by being entertained seamlessly within the context of their day.

CONTENT MARKETING: HOW TO SPOT IT

These three examples highlight the elements to look for in the not-always-obvious form of advertising known as content marketing.[3]

First: content marketing is all about the video. Initially, the favored content was infographics. As Matt Cooper, CEO of content marketing company Visually, told me, "Infographics are great and they are still going strong. The death of the infographic has been a little overdone, because when they are done well . . . they transfer information very well." He went on to explain, however, that as our attention spans have shrunk to eight seconds—one second less than a goldfish—marketers have less time to "set the hook." So rather than use infographics, content marketers now start by attracting us with Vines and other short, social-optimized videos, and then they present long-form videos like the ones above.[4] Importantly, videos cannot be avoided via ad blockers, which increases their appeal for marketers.

We can get a sense of just how important video is when we look at the competition heating up among major media companies. While YouTube is the undisputed leader, Facebook has begun to take them on, as have traditional media players like Comcast, which recently announced a new Internet TV service that will stream content from

BuzzFeed, VICE, and Refinery29, among others.[5] True, not all content marketing involves video, but almost every marketer I spoke with said that video was the direction digital marketing was going. The only thing holding them back thus far was the ability to track video on mobile devices (which is quickly becoming a nonissue, as we will see in the next chapter). Text-based content like white papers, ebooks, and infographics still exist, but these tend to be more in use in business-to-business fields.[6]

Second: while much content marketing appears effortless, don't let that fool you. These campaigns have been highly thought out and expertly executed to drive their appeal. It's just like your mother told you: "If it looks too good to be true, it probably is." The OK Go music video took a month to produce. It was created in conjunction with Mori, Honda's advertising agency in Japan, with lots of bells and whistles attached including intricate choreography and special video effects.

In the case of GoPro, the company has created a successful strategy that enables them to reach prospective consumers simply by providing a YouTube environment where people can share their "epic" moments.[7] This is really smart: it presents content that others are likely to be interested in, provides ideas about how to use the product, gives the sense that anyone can use it to produce fun and exciting content that could go viral, and plays on what academics call "hope labor" or "aspirational labor": the expectation that we might be able to earn a living by participating in activities like this. Moreover, we become complicit in creating branded content, unwittingly making that content more palatable to other consumers than if GoPro had simply released the content themselves. It feels like this strategy is seamlessly built into the product. It is not. Think about it: how many videos do you have taking up space on your cell phone?[8]

Finally, the Intel films/ads appear as straightforward entertainment, but have important strategic marketing embedded into them. According to Billie Goldman of Intel and Josh Brandau of ad agency Pereira & O'Dell, the goal of the Toshiba films was to reach eighteen to thirty-four-year-olds (i.e., Millennials) and to "deliver an unexpected experience that exceeded their expectations and drove an emotional connection for the Intel and Toshiba brands." Their challenge was that Intel was irrelevant to this target audience, while they thought of Toshiba as a brand for their dads. The strategy was to make the product a "character in the film" while making the story "as much about the audience as it was about the brands,"[9] and with each iteration they have progressively succeeded in combining story with product while integrating consumers.

This leads us to the third element: content marketing is often about creating stories that present the customer as the hero, not the product—even to the point of taking the brand out of the story altogether. This is the paradigm shift I've been talking about: marketers want to be friends with us so that we will do the work of sharing their content. OK Go simply tries to entertain us, but the other campaigns present customers as heroes in more complex ways. GoPro started like Red Bull, presenting primarily extreme content, but today, in addition to their videos devoted to surfing and skateboarding, speed, and sports, they have added general categories such as Life's Moments, Furry Friends, and Music. Anyone can submit content to the GoPro YouTube page in hopes that GoPro will upload it. (GoPro does not upload every video submitted to them, so getting on the site becomes a badge of honor.) One of the most popular GoPro videos is "Fireman saves Kitten," a video taken by a real-life fireman who revives a lifeless kitten by placing an oxygen mask over his face and pouring water over him. This video has more than 26 million YouTube views, was shared more than 600,000 times on Facebook, and received an *Ad Age* award for "Best User-Created Viral Ad." The video is the very definition of making the user the hero. The company drives this point home still further by the product name (Hero) and the company tagline ("This is your life. Be a Hero"). Intel also makes customers into heroes by incorporating them into the films, either directly through auditions or by including their artwork in the story, as was done with the most recent film series. Making us the hero of the content has an important advantage for marketers: we become more emotionally invested, which in turn makes us more willing to interact with the content, whether that involves submitting a piece of artwork to be included in a film, submitting our own "epic" video, or even taking a picture of a Coke with our name on it.

Making the consumer a hero means that the content is only tangentially related to the product. GoPro never shows the camera, only what the camera does. MasterCard (in an example we'll look at below) doesn't show you looking over your mounting credit card bills at the end of the month; they show how you can have undeniably meaningful (i.e., "priceless") experiences using the card. Intel doesn't demonstrate the power of their processor; they tell you a story about how computers bring families together. Commercials told stories, true, but in a very short, specific format. Also, unlike traditional advertising, content marketing does not communicate the attributes or benefits of the product. There are no mentions of how to use a camera or how fast the processor is. There is no "call to action," like "buy now" or "call today." Rather, marketers create humorous videos ("Dear Kitten"), or videos that evoke empathy ("Fireman Rescues Kitten"), or content that will in some way delight or amuse us while evoking the essences of the brand yet without mentioning the product (or, if the product is mentioned, doing so as an integrated part of the narrative). In these cases, we know who the corporate sponsor is, but as the trend to focus on the consumer continues, we can expect products to become further obscured.

This leads to the fourth and final point: make an emotional connection. Narrative is incredibly important to content marketing because stories engage us while remaining memorable. In order to be memorable, stories need two key factors: they must capture our attention (as any good advertising has always needed to do), and they must bring us into the characters' world—a phenomenon social scientists call transportation. The way to do this is by increasing the tension throughout the narrative.[10] Narrative studies and film studies discuss the concept of a universal story structure: The story starts with a surprise; tensions increase as the story's hero faces obstacles to overcome; these obstacles build to a climax, during which the protagonist must look within to overcome adversity; and then the story resolves itself. You might recognize this structure from the work of Joseph Campbell, or as the basis for the American Dream or the Horatio Alger stories. It is a structure that many companies use to frame their brand stories. This makes good sense from a marketing perspective, because as we become invested in the narrative, we want to know what will happen next. The longer we stay with the story, the more likely that we will become connected to the characters and that the story will resonate with us emotionally. These feelings induce a neurochemical response in the brain, causing it to emit oxytocin, also known as the "moral molecule" or even "the love hormone." Current research has determined that video content leads to oxytocin production in the brain, just as face-to-face interactions do.[11]

BECOMING MORE SUBVERSIVE

As the word "content" is becoming overused to the point of being meaningless, marketers are instead using "story"—a warm and friendly word, like "sharing"—and are creating their content with this concept in mind. In the case of GoPro, many of their videos are self-contained stories like "Fireman Saves Kitten." If a video is not a self-contained story, GoPro provides a background narrative to increase its appeal. This same technique is what makes *Monday Night Football* and the Olympics so compelling. The athleticism is wonderful, but it's the presentation of the heroic efforts, the struggles and the triumphs, that a single, dedicated person undertakes that keeps us coming back again and again.

The blender company Blendtec is another example of a company that combines storytelling with real people while pulling at the heartstrings. Moving on from an earlier campaign involving videos of iPads in blenders, the company has now embarked on a campaign called "Feed Your Passion," which contains three categories of videos made by Influencers: fuel (focusing on athletes and nutrition), nurture (taps into moms and kids), and create (for chefs and business owners). In the nurture category, for example, a mother tells a story about using her blender to prepare food for her child, who must use a feeding tube.[12] In a similar vein, Microsoft has a whole campaign called "Microsoft Stories" in which technology subtly plays the hero.[13] In one video, a boy who is missing an arm and is a huge superhero fan meets with Robert Downey Jr., the actor who plays Iron Man in a number of Marvel feature films. The boy is led down the hall of a hotel to a room where he is surprised by the presence of one of his superhero idols. Together they put on their bionic arms, while Downey charms the boy by saying that the boy's arm, which has been produced with new 3D technology, is better than his. This heart-warming story has close to 50 million views and more than 2 million Facebook shares.[14]

Whether the character involved is an athlete, a mom, a made-up hero, or even a magical puppeteer, marketers use this structure so that the content will stay with us. As the creative chief PJ Pereira notes about the Intel films, "characters are what the audience will remember and love months after the campaign is gone." We remember the stories: they induce a love response from us, and that positive impression gets transferred (marketers hope) to the product.

Are these examples any different from more traditional product placement? Yes and no. Integrating brands into music videos has become commonplace (particularly hip-hop videos, which have become notorious for promoting alcoholic brands to urban audiences.) This OK Go video, however, is built around demonstrating the functionality of the Uni-Cub product, not simply putting a bottle of Jack Daniels on a table or in the lyrics. We see computers in movies and television programming, and in that way Intel is no different. Where the Intel movies differ is that the producer of the product controls the storytelling to put a better light on the product, whether that product is front and center or not. In reality, you will never be able to ride the Uni-Cub the way OK Go does, GoPro cameras are harder to use than they look (the company just announced a smaller, *simpler* camera), and unless you are already artistically inclined, no computer will help you to create a Tim Burtonesque imaginary world.

Like native advertising, content marketing is not completely or always stealth, at least not yet. But it is not screaming its status as "advertising," either. "Microsoft Stories," for example, is promoted as #CollectiveProject and posted on YouTube as "officevideos," but unless you happen to know this content is from Microsoft, it is unlikely you would be aware of the sponsorship. And yes, it is housed on the Microsoft site, but it is through social media that people connect to this material, same as with native ads.[15]

As more video content is produced, it becomes commodified—no one thing is any different from another. To ratchet up engagement, content is likely to look more like original online series. The video service Hulu has become a hotbed for this. Subway has a series called "4 to 9ers" that follows the escapades of teens and young adults, including scenes that often take place in the fast food establishment. Chipotle produced "Farmed and Dangerous" about the detrimental impact of corporate farming, an issue at the heart of the company's business. To promote this content and add journalistic credibility, Chipotle paid *The Huffington Post* to create an area on its site called "Food for Thought" that covered topics related to farming and sustainability. While Chipotle determined the subject matter, they reportedly did not have editorial control.[16] Today, these practices have expanded into *Transparent* and *Alpha House* as marketing for Amazon Prime and *Orange Is the New Black* and *House of Cards* selling Netflix.

If you don't think this is advertising, think again. *House of Cards* was developed based on data analytics from Netflix viewership. Films starring Kevin Spacey are popular, as was the British version of the TV show. Add to this the fact that movies by David Fincher, the director of *The Social Network*, tend to be viewed to completion, and the streaming service, by combining these three elements, had the closest thing possible to a guaranteed hit. It is just this type of market analysis that is used to develop content and target consumers through the use of vast quantities of data, a topic we will address in the following chapter.

In shorter formats, content marketing looks more like Wren's "First Kiss" than a traditional Coca-Cola or Nike ad. Moreover, it will not only exist online. In light of Pennzoil's successful experience with National Geographic and Red Bull's Stratos appearing on Discovery, marketers are exploring corporate-backed documentaries. GE recently bankrolled a six-part documentary series called *Breakthrough*, which was produced with Imagine Entertainment (producer of films like *Apollo 13* and *A Beautiful Mind*) and which ran on the National Geographic Channel in late 2015. The series highlighted science and technology and featured scientists who work for or with GE.[17]

Marketers are increasing their use of content marketing because content marketing works, both to save money and to drive sales. For GoPro, the economics of this are astonishing. In 2011, GoPro's net income reached more than $24 million, double what it was the year before, while the company's marketing costs only increased by $50,000. The following year, marketing costs increased a mere $41,000, but net income was up by $28 million.[18] That's because GoPro can provide unending user-generated content that costs them exactly nothing. That content gets distributed via YouTube, where GoPro's three million subscribers see it and share it with their friends, again costing Go Pro next to nothing.[19] Intel's first film generated 50 million views (with the average age of the viewer being twenty-three), more than 7 million Facebook interactions, and a 43-percent increase in sales. "The Beauty Inside" was one of the top ten most-watched campaigns in 2012, had 70 million views and 17 million social interactions, contributed to a 300-percent sales increase, and even won a Daytime Emmy Award. "The Power Inside" generated similar numbers and led to the product being sold out at Best Buy.[20] As for *The Lego Movie* (which isn't stealth to you, but which is to your eight-year-old), the film grossed nearly $500 million worldwide, and sales from toys related to the film increased the company's earnings so much that they became the world's largest toy maker, beating out long-time leader Mattel, maker of Barbie.

Forget about thirty-second commercials, standard print ads, or online banners. Marketers can produce advertising that doesn't look or feel like advertising, increase consumer engagement, and do most of it at a fraction of the cost.

MARKETERS AS PUBLISHERS

Not every company can or should create a feature film or a TV series around a product. After all, who wants to see a movie about Saran Wrap or toothpaste? What these companies might do instead is publish a website with tips on how to keep food fresh longer, thereby helping consumers save money, or provide a list of ten ways that consumers have never thought of using toothpaste, including cleaning jewelry or creating art (yes, that article really exists.)

Today, it seems like every marketer—from Target to Chobani, from Purina to Mountain Dew to Totino's Pizza Rolls—has become a publisher. If they are not one now, they will be within the next year. This makes perfect sense from an economic perspective. After decades of turning to traditional media outlets to disseminate their message, marketers now can create their own content for their owned outlets and disseminate that content via social media.

These companies may or may not make their identities obvious on product websites. Some content presents a small logo. Some websites have a banner across the top that moves with the content as you scroll down the page, so you are consistently aware of the advertiser, while for others the banner disappears, so that once you are immersed in the entertainment, you might forget who's behind it. Some include the name of the company, while for others the sponsor is almost impossible to discern. It is this imbalance that makes it so difficult to know whether content is sponsored or not. Moreover, as with native advertising, most people don't initially encounter the content on the official website but rather through social media, where sponsor indicators are nonexistent or obscured.

To get a sense of the spectrum of brand visibility and some insights into the direction it is headed, let's look at some examples.

One of the most cloaked sites is for Van Winkle's, a digital magazine about all things related to sleep. Their tagline is: exploring the science, culture, and curiosities of sleep. The site is designed to look like FastCoExist, and it presents leading news stories like "For Our Returning Troops, Post-Traumatic Sleep Disorders are the New PTSD." Across the top of the site are links to sections on science, health, home, travel, culture, products, and resources. In travel, there is information about managing jetlag. In culture, there's a story about Michelle Obama inviting Girl Scouts to a sleepover at the White House. In health, there are stories about postpartum depression, sleeping pills, and why New York City school students should have breakfast during first period. Under the "products" section are articles about fitness trackers, sleeping bags, and Oyster, the reading app that allows you to borrow books the way Netflix distributes movies. The content is written by award-winning journalists. The content is brought to you by . . . wait for it . . . Casper. Who? That's what I said.

Casper turns out to be a mattress company that is doing to this market segment what Warby Parker did for glasses—cut out the middle man and sell directly to consumers online. The only indication that this is a marketing site is the phrase "Published by Casper" under the website name at the bottom of the page. Hiding corporate affiliation at the bottom of the page is a popular technique. General Mills has a site called Tablespoon.com that features a wealth of recipes under the tag-line "food that's fun." The only indication of the corporate sponsorship is a copyright line at the bottom of the site.

Other online magazines aren't quite this opaque about who is behind the content. However, magazine style websites are increasing in popularity, and their format is becoming decidedly similar—a pho-tograph that fills the entire screen, a small logo in the upper left hand corner, and a number of links across the top. Alternatively, sites contain a number of boxes surrounded by white space with photographs and short headlines, a look and feel that mimics Pinterest. Net-a-Porter, a high-end fashion retailer, has designed its website to look like a fashion magazine with this Pinterest-like layout.[21] Similarly, Marriott Traveler's site looks like a magazine rather than e-commerce. There is a band across the top of the page, so you know that the site is run by Marriott, but the content is heavy on visuals and all about local culture, fashion, food & drink, and so on.

Another trend involves corporate sites being reconfigured for broad consumer audiences. Target's content platform is the Bullseye View website. This started in 2011 as a catchall site for corporate infor-mation, but it has morphed into a more consumer-focused site that features not only how-tos and corporate sell, but also articles on issues like firearms and marriage equality. There is a large Target logo at the top and a subhead that says "Behind the scenes at Target," but beyond that, it looks like most other sites. Combined with this site is Target's skillful use of social media, notably Pinterest and Instagram. Tying in with designers like Joy Cho (13 million followers) and Jan & Earl of Poppytalk (eight million followers), Target can provide entertaining style and cooking tips to the followers of these social Influencers, who then help drive visitors back to the Bullseye site. This type of interaction between content marketing and social media is key to the success of this marketing strategy.

Similar to Target, Coca-Cola has changed their corporate website to a digital magazine called Coca-Cola's Journey. Evidence of their commitment to the narrative structure is their tagline: "Refreshing the world, one story at a time." Anyone going to the site would definitely know that this is a Coke venture, and the layout is of the boxes-with-photos variety. But when you dip further into the content, the connection to the brand becomes less distinct. That's because "about 60 percent of Journey's content has a connection to the company or brand. The rest—pieces on music, style, innovation, careers, and sports—aligns with the company's values."[22] Those nonbranded pieces are written by a network of bloggers whose work is housed under the name "The Opener," which includes content about "the best food, travel, career, lifestyle, culture and innovation." Thus articles about the best food in Brooklyn sit beside ones about a Coca-Cola and coffee Granita recipe, as well as a story about "5 Great U.S. National Parks" to visit this year. These ideas tie into the brand's long-running identification with happiness. Coke is spending more money to create this content than it is on TV advertising. That's a big shift. And, remember again, it doesn't matter where the content is on the site; once it gets disseminated through social media, no one will ever know that content from "The Opener" was housed on the Cola-Cola website.

More and more content being produced means more advertiser-provided information at various levels of obscurity. Here's why this might be an issue. According to the company's Mission 2020 agenda, Coca-Cola has the goal to be water neutral. The website has presented a number of pieces about reducing water usage, which is not only good promotion for them, but which achieves search engine optimization (SEO)—that is, their content appears organically at the top of the Google search. At the same time that the company was promoting conservation, one of its plants in India had to be shut down because its overuse of water was affecting local farmers.[23] This is no small issue, and water availability is becoming an increasingly important problem around the globe. Yet if Coke can keep churning out the positive content, it forces the reality of its role in water overuse further and further down the search.

This is a strategy that the Mormon Church has used with incredible success, so much so that corporations turned to the church to learn how to replicate their online strategies.[24] In 2011, the church ran an advertising campaign called "I'm a Mormon." In response, ex-church members created a campaign called "I'm not a Mormon." The church was able to quash the negative publicity—and quickly—in part through overwhelming the Internet with pro-Mormon content. The Mormons have been so good at SEO that at one time, when you typed "church" into Google, you didn't get the Vatican or the Conference of Southern Baptists, you got the Mormons.[25] Manipulating data in this way is part and parcel of content marketing, as we will see in the next chapter.

Two companies that pander to Millennials through their websites are Mountain Dew and Totino's Pizza Rolls. Mountain Dew, the over-caffeinated, over-sweetened soft drink owned by Pepsi, has an online magazine called Green Label (www.greenlabel.com). It covers the worlds of music, gaming, skateboarding, style, and other content that associates the product with exhilaration and intense experiences, much like Red Bull and GoPro. Their primary target is "urban" males in their twenties, though the site suggests that they are looking to appeal to younger targets, as well as a broader ethnic audience that includes whites and Hispanics. They are moving into film production, having released a movie about skateboarding called *We Are Blood* in August 2015. The only indication that Green Label has a corporate sponsor is a small note at the top of the homepage saying "A Mountain Dew (designed as mtn dew) Venture." Totino's is more obviously associated with the brand, but the association is made in such an over-the-top way as to almost make you forget that Totino's pizza rolls are a product. Part of that has to do with the name of the site, "Totino's Living," which contains no mention of the product itself (though the product appears here and there in videos throughout the site.) The other part has to do with the content on the site, which is base-level college humor that's meant to appeal to a "party" audience, just as the product does. The site is just silly, and it is meant to be. There are videos of the adventures of the "Pizza Human" (a person dressed head-to-toe as a slice of pizza), tie-ins with Comic Con, and other material featuring Comedy Central presenter Chris Hardwick. As with all branded content, the focus is on information and entertainment that's of interest to the target, without a hint of actual selling.[26]

Next to Red Bull, Purina is the company getting the most attention for implementing a successful all-encompassing content marketing strategy. The company has successfully integrated its commitment to pet lovers across social media, in native advertising, and through the content it creates for their own sites. In fact, they do so much publishing that some have said it is now the largest media company in St. Louis.

In "The Wolf at the Door," senior writer for *Columbia Journalism Review* Michael Meyer describes his visit to Purina headquarters, where he proceeds to deconstruct the tentacles that make up the newsroom that creates and interacts with pet lovers through the web. Constant content production is a priority, but real time engagement is the most important element of Purina's strategy.[27] Purina takes engagement and personal connection to consumers to the extreme. Stacy Schultz, a former reporter, writes upwards of 150 short pieces for the company per month. But what she also does is interact with consumers. She told Meyer: "If I know their dog had surgery, or was sick, or had a birthday, it's my responsibility to be checking back in, calling that dog by name . . . It's really my role to build a relationship with that consumer. It goes way beyond one two-minute tweet." It is that kind of one-to-one interaction that content marketing is aiming to get at. It is CRM taken to a whole new level, and one I find disturbing.

Beyond blogs or magazines, owned content—content published by the marketer—includes social media platforms, sites that by definition facilitate sharing. YouTube, which is both a social media site and the number two search engine behind Google, is an obvious outlet for most marketers to create their own channels. Of course, there's Red Bull, but companies like AT&T have taken to this site, creating a series called *Summer Break* (@summerbreak), which is in its third season (it also exists on Tumblr and Twitter.) Maybelline has a series called *Vanity*, identified on the site as "Style Haul" without reference to the company's brand name.

But companies do not need to create a series to raise awareness for their product or service. One of the most popular branded YouTube videos was a public service campaign called "Dumb Ways to Die" that uses humor and cartoon characters to reduce train-related deaths in Melbourne, Australia.[28] Research from ad buying and video marketing platform Pixability found in 2014 that "the top 100 global brands have nearly 1,400 YouTube channels." This constitutes more than 360,000 videos, with more than 19 billion views, representing an increase of 39 percent in just one year.[29] In 2015, Google (owner of YouTube) is hoping to augment those numbers by helping marketers in their content marketing efforts by providing information on best practices with a video series of their own called *Behind the Scenes*.[30]

YouTube is not the only social platform used by marketers. The "Daily Twist" by Oreo cookies used a variety of social media. This campaign was created to celebrate the cookie's hundredth anniversary. The company put together a creative team to execute a new ad tied to popular culture every day for a hundred days, which they posted to social media—Facebook, Tumblr, and Pinterest—as well as their own dedicated site. The first ad was an Oreo with six layers of different colors representing the stripes of the gay flag with the word "Pride" below it. This led to major press and mentions on *The Colbert Report* and *Jimmy Kimmel*. Other redesigned Oreos followed, including one for Comic Con, an Elvis Oreo, and a bat-shaped Oreo tied to the opening of the latest Batman movie. The Oreo ad that generated the most attention was created after the lights went out at the Superdome during Super Bowl XLVII. While other marketers sat on their hands, Oreo—who was still in the midst of tying into pop culture, and who had a staff to create an ad in real time—tweeted their now-famous picture of an Oreo in a darkened space with the line "you can still dunk in the dark." There was no sales pitch to these pieces of content, and they were clever and entertaining, so people readily shared them with their friends to the tune of hundreds of millions of impressions. In so doing, they reinvigorated a stodgy, little-thought-of sandwich cookie.[31]

This initiative was presented at numerous conferences as a "best practices" example of content marketing. Almost as many people say that this campaign is simply really good, clever traditional marketing. I fall into this latter camp. What Oreo did was put a new spin on the famous Absolut advertising campaign, the one which took the now iconic vodka bottle and tied it to multiple pop culture events. These ads were seen as works of art, and many college students posted them to their dorm room walls, a young adult version of sharing in the pre-

Millennial, pre-social media age. Oreo simply updated that campaign idea for a new media platform, and it is too blatantly advertising a product to be content marketing.

The Oreo campaign was from 2012, and since that time, content marketing has evolved to become more video driven and more covert. The most popular obscuring technique used by content marketers is slipping a logo well into the video, typically placing it at the end. Delaying brand notification is not a new advertising technique any more than the Oreo campaign is, but it is increasing in the digital space. The issue here is that because there are no limitations, we invest much more time with longer form videos before we find out we've been watching a commercial. A few examples here prove the point. An Android commercial called "Friends Furever" shows a number of different mismatched pairs of animals—an orangutan and a dog, a kitten and a chick, an elephant and a sheep—playing together while we hear a catchy ditty called "Robin Hood and Little John," a song from Disney's *Robin Hood* animated movie.[32] The video ends with "Be together. Not the same." For a few seconds, the name "Android" comes up on the screen, as does the cartoon robot man that is their logo.[33] Another video is the widely shared, much-awarded "#LikeaGirl" from Always. In this film, which runs for more than three minutes, adults were asked to run like a girl or fight like a girl or throw like a girl. The adults each enact stereotypical depictions of what those thing might be. Next, girls were asked to do the same things. Running like a girl, to actual girls, was simply running, as were fighting and throwing. When the director went back to the adults and asked if they would like to change their interpretations, they sheepishly did. More than halfway through the video, a title card appears, saying "Always wants to change that," meaning they want to change the negative connotations around "like a girl." At the end, too, the Always logo appears. Both of these commercials—and they are commercials—were shared tens of millions of times. This is most likely due to their entertainment value, with little attention paid to the corporate entity behind it. That's that point.

LIFESTYLE BRANDING

None of these brands, from Mountain Dew to Target to Purina, would be successful in creating branded content if they could not articulate how their brand fits into their audience's lifestyle beyond the actual use of their product. Mountain Dew and Red Bull are not about overcaffeinated beverages; they are all about the high-energy experiences you can participate in (or think you can participate in). Target is not merely a retail outlet; it is a destination for entertaining and design advice on a budget. REI is not about buying camping goods and hiking gear; it is about an outdoor lifestyle.

As discussed earlier, branding is a concept that marketers have used for more than a hundred years. Traditionally, branding has entailed a logo, a tagline, and a mythology or story. See the Starbucks logo and you think of strong brewed coffee from the streets of Seattle. See the Apple logo and you think of Steve Jobs, sleek design, or "think different." Even at this basic level, branding has been successfully integrated into our lives and our identity creation. We are Apple users or PC users. We drink Starbucks or Dunkin. This marriage of product to identity has become so immersed in marketing ideology that the phrase "I am" is often used in promoting products from Apple to FedEx to women's bag designer Vera Bradley.

Lifestyle branding takes this one step further by demonstrating for consumers, through stories, how brands connect with their values and way of life. Lifestyle branding has filled a void in cultures now that we are no longer defined by our family or religion or our jobs, which tend to be more fragile and more freelance.[34] Now, consumers turn to brands to help communicate their values. Laurence Vincent of strategic branding company Siegel + Gale noted: "We use brands to validate our lives. A lot of our consumption activities are becoming more sacred because we attach meaning to them."[35] This is why products like TOMS Shoes, which created the buy-one-give-one strategy, has been so popular. It taps into Millennials' sense of philanthropy and their self-perceptions related to caring and giving. Other companies using a similar strategy have also been successful, including eyewear company Warby Parker and headphone producer LSTN (pronounced "listen"). These products and others like them have an innately compelling story that drive consumer purchases while enabling Millennials to express who they are or want to be. They tap into the narrative needs of this younger generation.

Tied into lifestyle branding is the notion that experiences rather than physical goods drive happiness. This is why companies that can tie adventure into their products, either through storytelling or by directly providing adventures, do particularly well at content marketing. Companies with embedded experiences include REI or Harley Davidson. Other companies, like Apple and Ralph Lauren, create an adventurous experience through their retail environments (Lauren also embeds lifestyle in his advertising). As for creating experiences, remember Budweiser and its #upforanything promotion, or Jeep's Jeep Jamborees: family-friendly weekend events where people can experience the Jeep lifestyle by learning how to drive off road.

MasterCard has embraced a lifestyle perspective through its "priceless" campaign. Started as an advertising campaign in the late 1990s, the commercials and print ads had copy that said things like: "Two tickets: $28. Two hot dogs, two popcorn, two sodas: $18. One autographed baseball: $45. Real conversation with 11-year-old son: priceless. There are some things money can't buy. For everything else, there's MasterCard." Today, MasterCard's experiences are a bit more high-end than that trip to the ballpark, and MasterCard is branded through two different content platforms: "Priceless Cities," which showcases experiences in cities throughout the world (like the New York Food Festival, where tickets go for hundreds of dollars) and "Priceless Surprises," which includes sponsored music events from Gwen Stefani and Justin Timberlake. This is experiential marketing made manifest. MasterCard's marketing, both then and now, doesn't focus on benefits like interest rates or cash rebates from using the card. Rather, it expands the conversation to be about how MasterCard can help customers experience new adventures—usually by charging their credit card, but that is of course secondary. Like other content producers, this enables MasterCard to focus on stories, particularly ones that will evoke emotion.

A good example here is a video Mastercard produced of Hugh Jackman surprising one of his former acting teachers, saying how much that teacher meant to his career (and that MasterCard was creating a scholarship in the teacher's name, which appears as an afterthought). Jill Cress, Group Head and SVP of Global Consumer Marketing, says of the campaign: "We're focused on deep human passion points" and on creating "consumer moments of happiness."[36] Priceless surprises are about creating experiences that consumers would not ordinarily have access to, like Justin Timberlake and Gwen Stefani delivering cupcakes to you while you wait online for an iPhone 6. These moments of "happiness" and surprise are shared on social media, often with hashtags like #Mastercard #PricelessSurprises #GwenStefani. In all of this, then, we see the elements of content marketing: focus on the consumer as hero, stories that evoke emotion, tapping into existing cultural moments, and so on.

Under Armour is another lifestyle brand company. In the last few years, the company has made a few strategic steps beyond being a male-targeted athletic brand to being a lifestyle brand that embraces women's empowerment, while simultaneously becoming a tech company through the acquisition of fitness apps. This strategy has led to

Under Armour becoming the number two player in its category, just behind Nike and surpassing Adidas. Instrumental to this surge is its "I will what I want" campaign, which highlights the personal strength and athleticism of a number of celebrities. This campaign has multiple marketing tentacles from content platform to product integrations. Part of "I will what I want" is a commercial featuring Misty Copeland, a ballet dancer who moves gracefully and powerfully across an empty stage while the voiceover reads a rejection letter from a ballet school that she had received as a child. This ad appeared in the year leading up to Ms. Copeland learning that she would be the first African-American principal dancer with the American Ballet Theater. Other elements to this campaign were an ad and a microsite about supermodel Gisele Bundchen. The ad shows Bundchen in a spare gym room demonstrating her athleticism while social media commentary appears on the walls around her. Similar "creative content" was put onto a microsite (willbeatsnoise .com), which included an ever-changing wall of commentary scraped from social media around the web. Using a sentiment scale that showed negative comments in red, white neutral, and blue positive, the site demonstrated that more people were in support of the supermodel than against. The site was hugely successful, racking up "1.5 billion media impressions, $15 million in earned media, an average of four minutes spent on the site at the campaign's peak, a 42 percent increase in visits to UA.com and a 28 percent sales increase for the brand."[37] At the same time the company was developing these campaigns, they were also acquiring tech companies, which would enable them to tap into two growing trends: the Internet of Things and fitness tracking. Under Armour purchased MyFitnessPal and Endomondo, giving them access to the fitness and nutrition rituals of 100 million users. Combining access to personal workout and diet data with marketing that expands the perception of the brand to include women has turned this young, male dominated brand into a ubiquitous lifestyle brand.

Lifestyle branding is the immersive, all-encompassing evolution of connecting consumers and products through stories. Figuring out how to relate numerous topics to a brand—no matter how tangential those topics may be to the brand's core product—is a strategic imperative for marketers. Red Bull and GoPro have done it brilliantly. I mean, really, what does a kitten have to do with a camera? But GoPro has created a setup in which it does. Companies will keep pushing the envelope in terms of tying popular culture and special life moments to a brand, making everything we see a trigger for a moment of consumption.

THE BUSINESS OF CONTENT MARKETING

In the past, advertising was produced by agencies or in-house marketing and design groups. Typically, the account people would work with the marketing client to develop a creative strategy based on qualitative and quantitative research. Then art directors and copywriters would devise creative concepts that would go through several iterations before being presented to the client. After the client was happy with it, the concept would be tested in focus groups to ensure that it communicated the ideas appropriately for the target audience. Once the concept was tested and the script approved, the production process would begin, which would entail finding the right director, scouting locations, casting, and so on. The commercial would have to be edited and approved (again) and might even be shown to a focus group before going to air to make sure that it was perfect. This process took months and months of work.

Today, the process has been turned on its head. Marketers produce something in a few days or even a few hours, not a few months, and revise it on the fly depending on what data analytics say their consumers are attracted to. Real-time content with cultural relevance, as we have seen, is what drives the need to shorten the process. One marketer commented that now they do about 20 percent of the work up front, while 80 percent of the revising and testing happens online. Whereas in the past, we might have concept tested two different campaigns in a focus group, today that process happens online. Take two pieces of content, maybe with different pictures or a different headline, and post them on Pinterest. Based on which one gets more traction, the marketer revises and pushes the higher performing content through social media. It's testing in a real-life laboratory, and we're in the Petri dish.

The demands of SEO, needing to increase levels of engagement, and producing for owned media all drive the constant need for content. Producing one well-thought-out, meticulously constructed and researched ad just doesn't cut it. In order to keep the pipeline filled, marketers rely on a compendium of freelancers and others to help get their message out. While most companies still work with an agency of record (AOR), they are less dependent on them as the single producer of their content.

More often marketers now work with content marketing firms, like Newscred, Contently, Maker's Studio, or Scripted. These companies can have thousands—in the case of Contently, tens of thousands—of freelance writers, producers, designers, videographers, and photographers available to match up with corporate clients for content creation, both written and video. Newscred maintains relationships with a smaller number of creators because instead of creating new content, they repurpose existing content through licensing agreements with more than five thousand publishers. Say you are Pepsi and you want to make sure that the company is providing interesting content on an ongoing basis. Being a subscriber to the Newscred service, you could pick any article that the company has licensed. The demo I saw was an article about sports from a major news outlet. After that, it is a matter of cutting and pasting, as you would on any blog—copy the article, pick a picture that Newscred also has a license to (perhaps from Getty), create a headline, and presto: in less than a minute, you have "new" content for your site.

Content creation also involves processes for workflow (getting the content through the system quickly), distribution (getting the content to the appropriate outlets), and analytics (understanding what consumers engaged with). Companies work on all or part of this process. Companies involved from beginning to end include stalwarts HubSpot and Percolate—a name that came up often in research as a company to watch. Sharethrough, as the name suggests, is focused on distribution. Marketo specializes in email marketing, still recognized as the most effective form of digital marketing.[38] These companies provide slightly different services, but the premise is the same: provide ways to produce or license content, distribute it, analyze it, and curate it—that is, push what works and dump what doesn't.

Moving from slow methodical content to constant production changed marketing departments into newsrooms. A content marketer or editor typically oversees this. This person is responsible for strategy, writing and overseeing the content for consistency of message, much like a creative director would have done in the past. Supporting the editor are designers and contributors. Two new roles in this setup are the SEO/paid specialist and the community manager. As the name suggests, the paid specialist oversees content that is paid to be distributed, i.e., advertising. This is tied to search engine optimization (SEO) in that a combination of paid and organic content is what helps keep brands at the top of the Google list. The community manager learns to understand who engages with the brand, and based on that they distribute content in the appropriate social channels and interact with community members. This is the "Social's not for selling, it's for social" made manifest. This person becomes the "face"—one might even say the heart—of the brand.

Content creation companies and those with analytic skills are popping up every day to help marketers fill the nonexistent void. Almost 70 percent of marketers said that they're creating more content than a year ago, 48 percent post content either daily or several times per week, and on average, companies were working on thirteen content marketing initiatives. They are moving away from blogs and toward increased use of social media (averaging seven different platforms). The most popular social sites are Facebook, Twitter, YouTube, LinkedIn, Google+, Pinterest, and Instagram. Others used at a lower rate include Tumblr, Foursquare, Vimeo, Flickr, Vine, SlideShare, StumbleUpon, and SnapChat. Given all this, it is not surprising that 59 percent said that they would be increasing their content marketing budget in the coming year. The number one goal with this work is to "convert visitors on the website"—that is, turn us into customers.[39]

WHY SHOULD YOU CARE?

Because the digital calculus requires continually producing new content, marketers have bought into the rhetoric of consumers wanting more content. They talk about "feeding the beast" and consumers gobbling up content at a "blistering pace." In order to fulfill that perceived need, marketers churn out emails, tweets, posts, blogs, videos, Vines; the list seems almost endless. And it's not just advertising; it's also the content that supports it. As Craig Heimbuch, a former journalist and now content strategist and associate director of insights and planning at Barefoot Proximity/BBDO, explained it: "Publishing sites are designed to get eyeballs on i-media and they're going to do everything they can to put eyeballs on i-media which is why the Huffington Post publishes two thousand times a day. Is it because their journalism is that good? No, they get paid every time someone sees one of those ads."[40] Beyond this, there is the consumer-generated content, some of which becomes particularly salacious—a teenage boy sexually harassing women on the streets, girls wearing skimpy outfits to "make it"—when the imperative is to generate audiences for advertisers. This is particularly pernicious and exploitative when it involves kids and teens from underprivileged backgrounds.[41] With all of these factions fighting for our attention, there is no possible way to keep up with this medium that every minute produces more than 200,000 picture posts on Facebook, 100 hours of video on YouTube, and 278,000 tweets. No one wants that much content. But it's there, and so we get drawn in by the most entertaining material produced by some of the most creative minds in the world. In truth, we're all stuck on the hamster wheel.

What is of concern about this sort of content is not the entertaining and even inspiring videos from Intel. Rather, it is that companies get into the business of politics and news reporting. After Oreo posted its gay pride ad, an article in *Adweek* noted: "While there's likely to be plenty of fallout for Oreo over this simple photo post, at least the brand has shown it's not afraid to tackle a thornier issue than 'Do you ever think of Oreo cookies when drinking milk?'"[42] The question to ask is: why *should* the company tackle these issues? Shouldn't advertisers limit themselves to promoting their product? Or if they do step into these waters, shouldn't it be because they have done something newsworthy related to gay rights? What sort of partner policy does Mondelez, the maker of Oreos, have for its workers? What is its track record in terms of diversity hiring, particularly among the LGBT community? Comparatively, Home Depot has been quite open about its commitment to the LGBT community, to the point of being boycotted and targeted by anti-gay groups. In 2013, a video entitled "Spencer's Home Depot Marriage Proposal" went viral. This presented a flash mob dance in the lumber aisle of Home Depot that ended with a gay marriage proposal. While I do not know whether Home Depot sponsored this beyond providing the location, what I do know is that this was in line with the company's strategy, and no one was confused about who was behind the communication or why they were doing it.

Beyond companies attaching themselves to issues where they have no business, what about all the content that is being overlooked or pushed to the side because of this tidal wave of entertaining and "informative" content—not just online but across media platforms? According to Rebecca Lieb, VP of content marketing for analytics and integrated marketing company Teradata Applications, companies are churning out content all the time. "Large brands like GE and IBM are publishing more content per week now than *TIME* magazine did in its heyday."[43] Multiply that by hundreds or even thousands of companies and you can begin to see how editorial content doesn't stand a chance.

Why this is important: at the same time that Purina was making all of its popular cute, fuzzy cat videos and direct tweets to pet lovers, the pet food company was being sued because their product has been found to be allegedly killing dogs around the globe.[44] Ditto with Coke and the water access issue, Goldman Sachs glossing over their financial misdeeds, and Shell Oil giving advice on sustainability.

Content confusion exists because mobile in-feed ads, custom native, content marketing, and journalism all operate on a level playing field. It's just as we saw in the early days of the Internet, when the Church of the Blind Chihuahua had equal footing with the Vatican. With no physical structure or designation to tell us the difference between advertising and editorial content, there is no way to decide which article should get precedence over another for our attention.

Marketers have repeatedly said that no one cares where the content comes from. I'm not convinced of that. I have not seen any research to support it, and the limited research that has been done has been done by people with a vested interest in the outcome. What research does exist says that Millennials know when they are interacting with advertising and they believe that marketers can't influence them. They are wrong. Marketing critics have been fighting this notion for decades. It's not that they are not influenced; it's that they don't understand how influenced they are. It's called the third-person effect. It works like this: "I know advertising exists, and I'm sure it influences other people, but it has no effect on me." Just ask anyone sporting a pair of TOMS shoes or Under Armour. The truth is that this content exists to get us to buy more products. It is informing and entertaining, yet with an ulterior motive.

Edward Snowden has said this about surveillance: "Arguing that you don't care about the right to privacy because you have nothing to hide is no different than saying you don't care about free speech because you have nothing to say." I would tweak that slightly: arguing that you don't care where content comes from is no different than saying you don't care about truth.

5
THE DIGITAL SELL: BIG DATA, PROGRAMMATIC BUYING, AND LIVING BY THE NUMBERS

Four years ago, I met my fiancé through an online dating service. I had been divorced for six years and had been on half a dozen dating sites from Match.com to FitnessSingles.com when a colleague suggested I try OkCupid. Not only did the site have more intelligent prospects, she said, but it was free. That sounded great to me, as I'd already dropped thousands of dollars to meet, well, no one. I decided to make yet another attempt at baring my soul in the hope of finding long-term love.

Like other sites, OkCupid asks a number of questions to probe likes and dislikes about a potential mate. But OkCupid's questions are direct and often a bit salacious. Questions like: "Do you want your partner to be kinkier than you?" and "Say you've started seeing someone you really like. As far as you're concerned, how long will it take before you have sex?" were mixed with more typical queries such as "Are you Christian?" Unlike other sites, OkCupid asks how important these things are to me as they relate to being in a relationship. So I might answer "no" to "Are you a Christian?" and then say that I don't place much importance on that question, thus letting potential mates know that religion is not a make-or-break issue for me.

The site implores users to answer more and more questions. "Mara, your profile is only 73 percent complete," claiming that the more questions I answered, the better the match the system would be able to find. The idea is that there is a magic number of questions (at least 100) that you need to answer in order for the site to come up with a correct match.

Making this process seem scientific is part of OkCupid's sales pitch. Based on the questions answered, the computer assigns other users percentages based on how much of a match they are for you, and how much of an "enemy" they are. For example, someone could be a 91 percent match and a 27 percent enemy. Even the fact that these "statistics" are not given in round numbers provides an air of authenticity and scientific validity to them.

Whatever the trappings involved, OkCupid's algorithm is simply hocus-pocus. Based on their computer analysis, I was not a good match for my fiancé, but I was lucky enough to find him in spite of this. Since then, others, including the founders of the company,[1] have demonstrated that the numbers are virtually useless—or at least useless when it comes to helping someone find a partner. When it comes to advertising purposes, that's a whole other matter.

What future daters do not know is that the questions are marketing research—for OkCupid, yes, but also for the advertisers that they are selling the information to. Of course I understood that the site was advertising based, but given the usual type of person who is looking to date, I assumed that advertisers were marketing to a cohort of men and women from twenty to fifty years of age, as they had done with media in the past. At the time, it never occurred to me that the intimate questions I was answering might be used to sell me to advertisers.

So OkCupid was not actually free after all. I did not pay with cash. I paid with my very personal, and what I thought was very private, information.[2] I might have realized this at the time, but I was not thinking about whether or not I was being sold; I was thinking that I wanted to be back in a long-term relationship. This is what marketers—and magicians—count on, that we will concentrate on one thing so that we don't think about another.

Not only does OkCupid use this information for advertisers and themselves, but they also manipulate information to "improve their product." In one reported example, the company changed evaluations (a 30 percent match was revised to be 90 percent) and then watched the results (as measured in the number of interactions between "matched" users.) Turns out that people liked their matches after having been influenced with the idea that the other person was a good match—even if they weren't. This type of experimentation, called priming, is not new, and it is widely used in psychology and marketing. However, it is not typically used in this unscrupulous way. OkCupid's founder, Christian Rudder, seems to think that everyone is aware that this type of manipulation is happening. As he sardonically states: "Guess what, everybody: if you use the Internet, you're the subject of hundreds of experiments at any given time, on every site. That's how websites work."[3]

I was not convinced, and when there was widespread public outcry following Facebook's negative manipulation of people's emotions in 2014, my suspicion was confirmed.

These experiments, though, are a small part of data collection and research. Most of the information is derived from our everyday use of the Internet. Each time you go online or use your smart phone, you leave a trail of information—that is, data. What you click, what you type and delete, and how much time you spend on a page is all information that marketers can use to better understand who you are and how you shop. As we saw earlier, marketers are also gathering information through real-time listening, and more recently they have begun to analyze the photographs we post to see what products we interact with: for example, they may look at what beverage we're sipping with our Kraft macaroni and cheese.[4] Based on this data, specially targeted ads are sent to your computer or digital device, or marketers may use your data to improve their advertising by testing one version of an ad against another in order to see which one we are more likely to click on.

Not all uses of data are nefarious. However, as more data becomes available, companies are finding more ways to use and abuse it. And when it comes to data, we generate a ton: there are more than one trillion Google searches per year.[5] Google-owned YouTube has more than 1 billion users, all of whom collectively upload 300 hours of video per minute and generate 4 billion views per day. Facebook has similar video usage numbers. That translates to 8 billion video views per day on just two social sites![6] More broadly, there are 1.44 billion Facebook users, and they generate 4.5 billion "Likes" a day.[7] Instagram (owned by Facebook) now reaches 300 million users, making it bigger than Twitter (284 million) in terms of active users, and it is growing while Twitter has stagnated.[8] Instagram users send 70 million photos and videos per day. Looking at some less well-known and smaller companies: Qzone in China has 639 million users, Snapchat has 100 million monthly users, and Whatsapp has 600 million, to name a few.[9] But those are just social media statistics. Information is created every time you shop on Amazon or Apple, listen to Spotify or Pandora, or read the New York Times or your favorite magazine, and on and on it goes.

There are more than 100 million Internet users each in China, India, Japan, and Brazil, and other countries like Russia, Germany, Nigeria, the United Kingdom, France, and Mexico each have more than 50 million Internet users.[10] In the United States, while young people (aged eighteen to twenty-nine) are the demography with the highest percentage of users at 96 percent, it is not only Millennials who create data streams. According to Pew Research, 84 percent of American adults are online.[11] And we are all leaving a never-ending trail of data behind us.

In the wake of Edward Snowden releasing NSA documents about government surveillance, we have become acutely aware of being spied on through digital technology. A number of books and articles have been written that delineate the ways that we are tracked and how the information we provide is not as anonymous as we might think.[12] A few examples prove the point. In 2006, two reporters from the *New York Times* determined the identity of a sixty-two-year old Georgia woman based on anonymous search data from AOL.[13] Two years later, researchers from the University of Texas were able to "de-anonymize" information (i.e., identify someone by name) based on information from Netflix's database. Through that, they were able to uncover users' "apparent political preferences and other potentially sensitive information."[14] Julia Angwin—author of *Dragnet Nation*, former tech writer for the *Wall Street Journal*, and now with ProPublica—outlines a number of privacy abuses in her book. For example, seventy of the most popular websites unintentionally release private information, such as names and email addresses, to ad-tracking companies 25 percent of the time; major dating sites have released information on drug use and sexual orientation, and "75 percent of the top one thousand websites included code from social networks that could match people's names with their web-browsing habits."[15] In the case of Facebook, for example, this means that if you don't sign out of Facebook, whenever you go to a different site that has a Facebook "Like" button somewhere on it, Facebook knows you have been to the site, even if you don't click the link. The same is true for other social media sites. Finally, in a 2013 study Microsoft and Cambridge University researchers analyzed the Facebook "Likes" of 58,466 Americans. With this limited data, the researchers could accurately "predict a range of highly sensitive personal attributes including: sexual orientation, ethnicity, religious and political views, personality traits, intelligence, happiness, use of addictive substances, parental separation, age, and gender."[16]

Privacy is an important issue, and these few examples merely scratch the surface. However, they are not my focus here *per se*. Rather, the goal is to reveal how we are unwittingly and unthinkingly giving away our information. What most people may not have fully grasped is how and why marketers—perhaps even more so than governments—track our every move. They know what we search, where we search, and how we move from site to site; they know how much time we spend on a page, on a site, or on an article; they know if we watched an entire video or simply a few seconds of it. Amazon even knows what we read on our Kindle, how much we read, and what we highlight. All of this data is then used to pitch us products that marketers believe we are most likely to want. They can even fully customize the pitch to the prospect. For example, if the consumer is a woman in her fifties with a college-aged daughter, the ad she sees online will include a twenty-something female and a storyline that reflects her lifestyle.

All of this information—so-called Big Data[17]—intersects with marketing in two key ways. First, marketers can now assess where we are in the buying process so that they can micro-target sales pitches based on whether we're just beginning our product search or whether we're ready to push the "buy" button. Second, marketers have access to thousands of data points on millions of people, which they use to make educated guesses about what products and services we will want. Helping marketers to do this are the growing number of companies that amass huge quantities of information about us. Still other companies help marketers to analyze that data and coordinate their workflow, which has become increasingly complex and abundant. Together, these companies work to target the appropriate messages to us, over and over. We've seen this with OkCupid and Facebook, but they are by no means the only ones. What we post, retweet, like, and share are all used to tell marketers who we are and what we intend to buy. In all these ways, marketers use our interactions online to sell products back to us, even though we might not be aware of it.

CONSUMER DECISION MAKING AND THE SALES FUNNEL

It is easy to lose sight of the fact that while branded content from Intel and GE and BuzzFeed and all the rest may be entertaining and engaging and relevant, it is also—and foremost—about increasing sales. And over time, technology has changed when and how marketers insert themselves into a consumer's purchase decision.

The consumer decision-making process has five stages: need recognition, information gathering, evaluation of alternatives, purchase, and post-purchase behavior. Emotionally important and more expensive purchases, like a car or a computer, are called high-involvement purchases. Alternatively, a low-involvement purchase might be anything from a bottle of water to a bar of soap: anything that takes little thought or emotional investment. Given this, low-involvement purchases do not require any information gathering.

If we go through the process for a car, for example, the "need recognition" might be that you realize you have to get to work, pick up your kids, and maybe get to school, and public transportation does not enable you to do that. You begin to gather information about different options, thinking in terms of what you can afford, what gets good gas mileage, and what carmaker has the best safety record. During the evaluation phase, you go for test drives, talk to friends, read *Consumer Reports*, and visit a number of online sites to read reviews. You might also recall your past experiences with the product or with their customer service representatives. After narrowing down your choices, you think about where you want to buy the car, whether you can get the model you like in the color you want, and whether you really need an SUV or if a hatchback will do. You make your decision, you buy the car, and the marketer hopes you will love it so much you will tell your friends and family.[18]

The sales funnel is a metaphor to describe the process of moving from many choices to a limited number of real alternatives from which you will make your purchase decision, and it parallels the consumer decision-making process (see chart below). The first step is awareness: when consumers find out about a product. This is where traditional advertising has existed: loud, abrasive, in-your-face ads that made you aware of a brand's existence. The next step is consideration: when consumers have a group of products that they are deciding among. Do I get the iPhone or a Samsung Galaxy? The Nikes or the Adidas? The Sony TV or the LG? Salespeople want to move us from consideration—"this might be good for me"—to product or brand preference—"I have to have an iPhone 6!" Traditionally, moving us from consideration to preference is where a salesperson in the store could have the most influence. This can still be true today, such as when you go to your local mobile phone store. Yet inducing brand preference is highly influenced by what happens online, as we saw with word-of-mouth marketing in earlier chapters. More often than not, you will research your phone, talk to your friends, and comparison shop online, at which point you come into the store well on your way to having made your brand choice. Once a purchase has been made, companies do what they can to retain your business and get you to evangelize their product. Typical methods are asking you to follow and friend online, adding to you to their email list, asking for your phone number, or getting you to sign up for the store credit card, all of which enables the company to get more information about you while plying you with offers, many of which can be shared with friends and family.

CONSUMER DECISION MARKETING VS. SALES FUNNEL[19]

Need recognition	
Information gathering	Awareness
Evaluation of Alternatives	Consideration
	Preference
Purchase	Purchase
Post purchase behavior	Loyalty/Advocacy

There is an important difference between old sales and marketing and new methods implemented via digital technology as it relates to this process: marketers can insert themselves into multiple "touch points" along the purchase decision timeline. Most importantly, they can engage with consumers at the point of purchase. In the past, you might have seen a commercial, thought, "that's an interesting, cool, functional product," and then didn't think about the product again because you weren't anywhere near a store that sold the product. The best that marketers could do was hope that you would remember their message and buy the product while standing in a store days or even weeks after having seen the ad. Today, marketers are bidding on advertising online while you are shopping. Looking for a vacation in the Bahamas? Ads related to this search will start to follow you around the web. The same is true for theater tickets, clothes, or cars. This is done via online tracking, which will be explained in more detail below, but in simple terms, it works like this. When you go to the Best Buy website to purchase a pair of headphones, a data company like Acxiom or BlueKai will embed code, called a "cookie," on your computer. Ad exchanges—similar to stock exchanges—will then auction off your "cookie" to advertisers wanting to reach headphone buyers, which could be Beats or Taylor Swift's record label. The highest bidder gets to display a headphone ad or an ad for Ms. Swift's last album on your device as you continue to move around the Internet.

Before you even get to the point of purchase, marketers can influence advocacy for products in ways that were never previously possible. We saw this in Chapter 2 when we looked at word-of-mouth (WOM) marketing. Influencers on Twitter and Facebook, BzzAgents, bloggers, and all kinds of people we interact with on social media drive brand preferences. Because of this, it becomes harder and harder to resist the siren call of the marketer because they are subtly singing to you to buy, buy, buy and share, share, share no matter where you are online. These ongoing interactions via social media have changed the sales process into more of a loop than a funnel. Under this new schema, consumers may actually increase their viable options during the consideration stage of the process, which causes them to spend more and more time in consumer decision-making, as well as more time online.

The increasing number of choices is likely to become an issue for marketers because researchers have found that too many choices can overwhelm us to the point where we decide not to buy at all.[20] To attempt to keep that from happening—and to ensure that their brand is the one that stays top of mind—marketers insert themselves into an increasing number of steps along the decision-making process. The need to be seen at more levels of the sales funnel has changed the way advertising is bought and sold. And now, with mobile, advertisers can deliver the entire purchase funnel—from becoming aware of a product to buying it—all in the palm of your hand, and everything is done in a few short minutes.

PROGRAMMATIC MEDIA BUYING

Buying advertising used to be a straightforward process. At its base, an advertiser would select the media vehicles they wanted to use, such as TV, radio, and magazines, and then they would negotiate the terms for placing those commercials or print ads. After the ads ran, the advertiser would assess the effectiveness of the placement based on information provided by companies like Nielsen. To complete the process, they would evaluate the impact on sales numbers and adjust media placements accordingly. Targeting, however, was imprecise, as Nielsen TV ratings are at best an educated guess about who is watching a particular show. And while marketers could place an ad in primetime in order to reach women aged eighteen to forty-nine, for example, they were also getting a lot of other people watching the ad who had no interest in what was being sold. Moreover, most products have a seasonal focus—that is, it would be silly to promote snow blowers in July when no one is thinking about winter—so it would be a rare product category that advertised 24/7, 365 days per year. Finally, as discussed earlier, advertising was purchased based on a CPM model—the number of people viewing the ad (in media terms called impressions) determined its cost.

In its nascent stage, web advertising worked pretty much the same way. Rectangular banner ads on a site appeared the same way a print ad appeared in a magazine, and they were purchased like any other advertising. As time went on, new advertising formats were developed, but the buying process remained essentially the same.

Google was instrumental changing all that. To start, the search giant was a pioneer in native advertising, even before this format had a name. Sergey Brin and Larry Page, the company founders, believed that ads could be as valuable as search results.[21] They produced ads that looked like the results of search queries: a small block of text with a link to the advertiser's landing page.[22] These were a big win for Google. Not only were the ads more effective than the maligned and overlooked banner ads, but Google could also track which visitors were interested in each ad. At this stage in the early 2000s, Google charged advertisers on the old CPM model of selling against impressions, and the ads were sold by sales reps.

The next iteration was the creation of AdWords, which was promoted with the line "Have a credit card and 5 minutes? Get your ad on Google today."[23] Marketers—particularly smaller companies that could not afford traditional advertising—could buy ads on their own for searches distinctly related to their products. Google would sell ads based on the word search, meaning that ads could be for highly specialized businesses. Teaching calligraphy in upstate New York? Great. Selling first editions of Judy Blume? Not a problem. This strategy was based on the "long tail," an economic concept that would be made popular by *Wired*'s Chris Anderson in his book of the same name. Through thousands of small businesses buying little bits of advertising, Google created a successful revenue source, which was something that evaded most other websites in the early dotcom days.[24] Ads ran to the side of the organic search results so as not to create confusion, and each ad was marked as a "sponsored link." The CPM model continued to prevail.

The most significant way in which Google revolutionized ad buying was with AdWords Select, a service created in 2002 to sell ads based on a pay-per-click auction model.[25] Under this system, advertisers only pay if a visitor clicks on the ad. Conversely, if no one clicks, advertisers owe nothing. The percentage of people who click to the advertiser's landing page was dubbed the "click-through rate," or CTR. Placement of the ad is determined at auction with different advertisers bidding against each other to determine the price they're willing to pay if visitors click on their ad. It behooves everyone—the advertiser, the consumer, and Google—to have the ads be pertinent to the search. However, Google did not leave this to chance. According to Steven Levy in *In the Plex*: "There was one feature built in to try to ensure that the most useful ads would appear: advertisers couldn't pay their way to secure the best positions. Instead, the more successful ones—the ones that lured the most people to click on them and go to the advertiser's landing page— would get priority."[26] Thus, if someone on Google is looking for shoes and clicks on an advertiser's link, that advertiser's site had better be the equivalent of Zappos or DSW or they'll either lose the bid or pay a premium for misleading consumers. Sheryl Sandberg, then the vice president of global online sales and operations, said that the "ad quality formula" has been effective because "it made the advertiser do the work to be relevant. You paid less if your ads were more relevant. So you had a reason to work on your keyword, your text, your landing page, and generally improve your campaign."[27] Google optimizes revenue through balancing the maximum bid with the highest ad quality score, and once this is assessed, it can serve up the ad in approximately 0.26 seconds.[28] It also doesn't hurt that more than ten years later, 41 percent of Google visitors could not distinguish between paid search and organic listings, which keeps the CTR high.[29]

Two ideas are important to highlight here. First, auctioning word searches created a major shift in advertising strategy. When buying search terms, marketers are paying for our personal actions, not for content that they think we might be watching. Type "SUV," and Honda or Toyota ads are served to your computer, which may not be a bad thing. More questionable is that when you type "depression," drug ads are sure to follow. This is very different from placing pharmaceutical ads on daytime talk shows because marketers have good evidence that women are watching those programs and are likely prospects for these medications. That sort of content targeting is generic and not attached to a single individual. Admittedly, advertisers claim that they don't care about identifying who we are as individuals so much as they care about our individual buying habits. That's probably true. However, it is very different to search for information about a medical condition and have someone know that you performed that search than it is to watch a commercial in the privacy of your living room—an act that is unknown to advertisers unless they're peering into your window. The extent of this online "spying" is significant when you realize that the vast majority of advertising online is search and that the vast majority of that is Google.

Second, auctioning space via computer has become widely accepted for buying advertising online on all kinds of sites—banner ads, yes, but also other online formats, including native ads. Any advertising on a web page that is bought automatically by computer is now called "programmatic buying." The Internet Advertising Bureau has delineated two types of programmatic buying: direct and RTB (or real time bidding). Direct programmatic is similar to traditional ad buying: advertisers buy guaranteed space on a site without participating in an auction, the only difference being that a computer makes the purchase according to a set of cost and demographic parameters. Alternatively, programmatic RTB is another way of saying online auctions. It works like Google AdWords, but it is intended for display ads instead of search terms, and there are significantly more moving parts. Most of those moving parts require the use of reams and reams of our personal data.

Combining programmatic buying with native advertising has been difficult. That's because creative formats are different for each site. This is purposeful on the part of the publishers. Barry Lowenthal, president of the Media Kitchen, explained it this way: "The news feed ads have their own specs; Facebook has their own specs, Twitter has their own specs, Google has their own specs." Because each site requires different formatting for the ads, each ad has to be individually produced and cannot appear elsewhere unless it's reformatted, which is time consuming and costly. Not surprisingly, advertisers don't like that. They want to produce one piece of creative and have it appear on multiple sites, while still looking like it is native to any site on which it is served. What they want is called "native at scale," and according to Lowenthal, it's starting to happen: "A lot of companies now are working with publishers to create native at scale. So the publishers write the rules, there's a platform that we can upload our ads to, and when the ad is served, it looks like a native in-stream ad. They talk about it as being native, even though it's scalable. Advertisers want scalable native because it looks more like it flows, rather than just a banner ad."[30]

DATA BROKERS, AD EXCHANGES, AND PROGRAMMATIC BUYING

Companies collect, analyze, and package our information and sell it to advertisers and to each other. We used to call these companies direct mail houses. Today they are known as data brokers. We used to call what they did database marketing. In the digital age, it is called customer relationship marketing. It used to be that they just sent you junk mail and catalogs. Today they shadow you around the Internet and send eerily specific advertising that follows you from site to email to cell phone. Importantly, the difference today is that our most sensitive information—lots of it—is bought and sold as a commodity, mostly without our knowledge.

The typical purveyors of information used to be magazine publishers and credit card companies: one knew what you read and where you lived, the other knew what you bought and how much you spent. Brand companies would buy lists of names and addresses from direct marketing firms based on demographics and purchase behavior, and they would use those to send targeted direct mail messages. They might also combine those lists with internal databases they had developed through various methods, including contests, sweepstakes, or loyalty programs, this last being a bonanza of individual purchasing information.

The airline industry was the first to compile information on their most loyal customers when American Airlines launched their frequent flyer program in 1981.[31] Later, with the introduction of UPC codes and in-store scanners, loyalty programs became all the rage and moved well beyond the airline industry. If you have a plastic card on your key ring from CVS or your local supermarket, then you are part of a loyalty program. Every time you give them your card, these companies create dossiers on what you buy, when you buy, and how much you buy. But that's not all. Companies are developing group loyalty programs (like Plenti) that let retailers like Rite Aid, Macy's, AT&T, and Exxon share data on your drugs, your clothes, your contacts, and your driving habits. As noted above, it's not just the brick and mortar retailers. Online companies collect this data as well.

Much of this information is innocuous. After all, who cares if you bought a book on Amazon, a bra at Macy's or researched bicycles at REI? That's not really the issue. What becomes problematic are the topics that are, frankly, no one else's business. They tend to fall into three categories: health, wealth, and sexual preferences and proclivities. Think about it. Our privacy concerns boil down to this: we don't want people to know our medical conditions, how much money we make, and who or how many people we might be sleeping with. But we don't get to decide what information gets collected and what does not. And once accumulated, we have little to no control over how that information is used or who has access to it.

Marketers employ data in a variety of ways. In 2004, for example, Walmart utilized its vast store of buying data to determine that in advance of a major storm, people buy flashlights and bottled water, but they also buy strawberry Pop-Tarts and beer.[32] It seems that people want to prepare for the worst but enjoy themselves while it happens. This is a fairly inoffensive use of data. Not all cases are so harmless. In *The Power of Habit*, Charles Duhigg explained how Target was able to determine that a teenager was pregnant based on a "pregnancy prediction model" that determines impending parental status based on purchases of items such as vitamin supplements and cocoa-butter lotion. Unfortunately, the company spilled the beans to her father by sending coupons for baby items and pregnancy clothing to her home.[33]

Data in and of itself is useless. It is the insights derived from the information that are important. In the case of Walmart, knowing pre-hurricane purchase behaviors enabled the company to stock stores in the path of a storm with lots more pastry and suds, while Target sends out coupons for products they "know" we need with the full understanding that once we are in the store, we will put a number of additional items in our cart. This is important because 92 percent of purchases are still made *offline*.

For ecommerce sites, news sites, or most any site that might serve you an ad, data collection and manipulation works like this: using cookies, a company tracks visitors' movements online and sees who purchases their product and who does not. Then they examine the common attributes of those people who converted (i.e., bought a product). The information derived from the company's own website is called "first-party data." But advertisers do not want to talk only to their own customers. They want to find other people who are like the people who already buy their product. In order to do that, the company does what is known as "lookalike modeling," where they use the information they know about people who buy their product in order to find more like them. This is how Sarah Evans from Great Courses described it: "In a typical first-party data, programmatic campaign—this is what I referred to as lookalike modeling—what we do is we pixel our website . . . so we can catch every single user coming into that site. You basically follow them around the site, figure out how many pages they browsed, figure out if they put something in their cart, and you can track them through to purchase, or conversion. So when we build these lookalike models, what we would theoretically do is take a look at anyone who came into the site and then slice it by only those who converted, and then we'd figure out what all their common attributes are. So maybe out of 70,000 attributes, there were 250 that all of those people had in common. The model is built off of people who are your customers. And the goal would be once you build those models, you facilitate those within the exchanges—hence the lookalike modeling—you wouldn't go out and target those people again, but you would go out into the wild of the exchanges and try to find people who had those 250 attributes of the customers you did get to convert. That's one way to do it."

Another way to find new prospects is to work with big data brokers, companies like BlueKai or Acxiom or Nielsen who have amassed thousands of pieces of information on us that they supply to advertisers. This information is known as "third-party data." Evans explained that this is a more traditional method in that marketers set the behavioral parameters they are interested in and target people who match those behaviors from the data broker—for example, people fifty and over who are in the market for a car and who go on vacations twice a year. Using first-party data and third-party data, marketers work with the advertising exchanges to find people with similar characteristics no matter where they might be online.

More specifically, an ad exchange is a platform where websites that want to sell advertising connect with marketers who want to buy access to potential consumers. As you travel around online, you will inevitably land on a website that is trying to sell advertising inventory through an exchange. As the page loads, if there is ad space available for real-time bidding, information about you and the page you're on are sent to an ad exchange.[34] When that happens, the exchange notifies advertisers of an auction and asks them to bid on the ad space that will be presented to you. Advertisers make a decision about whether to bid for your attention based on "first-party" data, information they have gotten from data brokers, or a combination of the two. If they determine that you are a good fit, they must then determine if they have a campaign running that makes sense to match up with the information attached to the cookie. Of course, there are multiple advertisers bidding at auction for our attention. The exchange selects the winning bid, and that company's ad appears on the website, a process that takes a matter of milliseconds. According to Quantcast, a company that specializes in real-time bidding, "the person loading the page likely has no idea that several advertising companies were virtually fighting to get in front of him or her."[35] That is what is so deceptive and placating in all of this. We think we're seeing a single website, when in truth we're seeing a mashup of a site with multiple entities providing content.

Key components in this mix are the data brokers. Data brokers have taken the old database marketing concept and multiplied it a few dozen times over. While data companies used to collect basic demographic data like name, address, age, gender, number of kids, income, education, and so on, in total, they might have fewer than forty pieces of information on any one person. Today Acxiom, the biggest of these companies, claims to "execute more than 1 trillion global data transactions per week," has "multi-sourced insight into approximately 700 million consumers worldwide [and] demographics, life-stage segmentation, brand affinities, and purchase tendencies for nearly every adult consumer in the U.S."[36] This last translates to 1,500 data points per American.[37] Information comes from our "click stream," but it also comes from sources like the U.S. Post Office (which sells lists of when people move), public voting records, car registration, court filings (of bankruptcies),[38] and those loyalty cards on your key ring, among many others.[39] According to privacy expert Tim Sparapani, "Most retailers are finding out that they have a secondary source of income . . . the data about their customers . . . [which] is probably just about as valuable, maybe even more so, than the actual product or service that they're selling to the individual. So, there's a whole new revenue stream that many companies have found."[40] A major collector of that information from store loyalty cards is Datalogix, owned by computer company Oracle, which claims to have "information on more than $1 trillion in consumer spending 'across 1400+ leading brands,'" according to a report by ProPublica.[41]

But that's just the beginning. Turning offline purchase activity into digital data and connecting that data to what you do online is part of a growing trend called "onboarding."[42] LiveRamp, a company bought by Acxiom in 2014, enables the online data to be linked to offline purchase information. For example, when a store clerk asks for your email address, the retailer might share it with LiveRamp or another onboarding company. Then when you use the email address online to sign into websites the onboarding company does business with, they can link those websites to your devices, and ultimately to your name.[43] Bearing in mind, of course, that the store's request for your email address was framed as a way to offer you discounts and let you know about upcoming sales events, not as a way for the store to secretly amass more information about you.

More covert are the activities of the now combined Verizon/ AOL. Verizon married its cellphone-tracking supercookie with AOL's ad tracking network, which is on 40 percent of websites, to connect online behaviors with offline information. This is done by default— users never opted in and likely don't even know it is happening.[44] And in an effort to appeal to more advertisers, Twitter has created a service called "Partner Audiences" that allows companies to search on the social site for people who buy products in their category—say, dog food. Connecting information from Twitter about purchase behavior (buying pet food) to information from data brokers enables marketers to learn how many people saw the ad and then ultimately bought the pet food brand. This is advertising's Holy Grail—proof positive that running an ad led to a purchase.[45]

Other major big data firms include Corelogic, eBureau, ID Analytics, Intelius, and BlueKai, just to name a few. These companies classify us into behavioral categories, much like psychographics.[46] Because there is so much more information than in the pre-digital era, these segments can be much more granularly defined. Datalogix, for example, has developed 1,800 different audience segments, from car buyers (categorized by maximum spenders, car owners, and likely in the market to buy) to consumer packaged goods (broken down by category, brand, and product) to lifestyles ("Soccer Moms, Green Consumers, Sports Fans").[47] Segments of particular interest to marketers, and readily offered by all the data brokers I looked at, are people going through major life changes, because they are more likely to spend money across a number of different categories. People who purchase a new home, for example, spend more on products and services in six months than an established resident spends in two years, and that might include anything from cleaning products to window blinds to a new refrigerator to services from local merchants like restaurants and gas stations.[48] Having children is another major life change. Not surprising, then, that Target was interested in pregnant women. The goal is to get families to establish a habit of coming to their store for everything, since a one-stop shop is useful to someone with an infant, but also means more money for the retailer. Experian—the same company that provides credit reports—has a separate marketing arm that keeps an up-to-date list of expectant families and those with newborns.[49]

To get the extent of the data these companies acquire on us, we will look at Acxiom, but much of this can also be found on any number of data broker sites. Like Datalogix, Acxiom categorizes us by products we buy, media we use, and industries that are trying to put advertising in front of us. For people into social media, for example, this data broker can find social influencers and those that are socially influenced; they can find heavy users of Facebook, Twitter, LinkedIn, and YouTube, and they can find people who have a propensity to post photos and videos. If an advertiser is one that markets during back-to-school season—now the second largest sales period of the year—they can find just the type of person a marketer might be looking for, as Acxiom provides segments such as "Stylish Students," which might appeal to brands like Express or Diesel, or "Essential Electronics" for companies like Apple, Best Buy, and Samsung. There's even a segment called "The Early Bird" for customers who like to shop early. The company prides itself on its depth of information. In explaining back-to-school shoppers, the website states: "Reach customers likely to shop as early as two months before school starts. Or aim your message at customers that buy their supplies one month ahead, or even the week after classes begin—Acxiom data sets are that specific."[50] Beyond back-to-school, they provide similar breakdowns for eleven other key time periods throughout the year, including the "Big Game" (The Super Bowl), Christmas, and Mother's Day. The last category includes information on "The Getaway Guy," one who is likely to "surprise an overworked wife or a deserving mom with a relaxing cruise or other getaway." Talk about specialization!

You can get a sense of how data brokers and ad exchanges work if you put an extension on your web browser that allows you to see who is tracking you or who wants to feed you advertising. There are two that are particularly useful. Ghostery tracks the data companies and advertising tracking firms that are following you when you go to a website. Disconnect is another extension that does similar analysis. After you install the app and go to any website, a list of the companies tracking you will appear on your computer screen. Companies that will populate on your screen may include DoubleClick (an ad network owned by Google), big data firms like AddThis, and ad exchanges like BrightRoll. On a recent visit to MovieFone.com, Disconnect counted more than 64 advertising requests from companies like Rocket Fuel, BrightRoll, ValueClick, and Datalogix; 10 requests for analytics, all from comScore;

1 social request from AddThis; and 128 content requests, most of which were from DG, a programmatic video provider. In sum, there were more than 200 requests for information about me—okay, my IP address—all from a single web page. In addition to lists, Disconnect will present the information as an infographic by representing the site that you're on as a circle surrounded by spokes, each of which ends with the logo of the company tracking your data. There is something about seeing those bubble-like logos populating the screen that is very disconcerting. More so when you begin to get advertising that does not relate to anything about you. Just the other day I was watching a video, and the pre-roll ad that came up was for bipolar disorder. In the past I might have laughed that off. Now I can only wonder what I might have been doing that would make a marketer at some anonymous company think I need this medication.[51] And while it was later explained to me that this drug ad was likely a demo target (older and female), it did not make me feel any better. In truth, there is no way to know this for certain.

One issue has loomed for marketers until very recently: how to track us once everything moves to mobile. That is because cookies work for computers but not for mobile devices—sort of. Cookies do work on mobile, but they're limited in their functionality, and they vary across applications (apps versus mobile web) and devices. Mobile web browsers accept first-party cookies, but not all will accept third-party cookies.[52] When you are on an app, cookies can be stored (so you can be served all of those really annoying ads), but the cookies are unique to the application, so they can't be shared with other apps or with your mobile web browser.

Companies have been using a workaround to compensate for this. According to Arvind Narayanan, a professor of computer science at Princeton, "Let's say you have a laptop and a smartphone, and you're traveling with them, and you're browsing the web through Wi-Fi . . . The advertiser, or other company, notices that there are two particular devices that always connect to the website from the same network. The chance of this happening coincidentally is similar to the chance of two people having the same travel itinerary, so, after a period of time, if it keeps happening, they can deduce that it's the same person that owns those two different devices. Now they can put your browsing behavior on one device together with your browsing behavior on the other device and use it to build a deeper profile."[53] This is becoming less of an issue as companies such as drawbrig.ge and Tapad are able to track our movements across devices.

Content—particularly video content—is moving increasingly toward mobile, and with that, the ability to integrate data across devices as easily as possible is high on marketers' agenda. I spoke with Kara Goldberg, the PR manager of Virool, one of the major distributors of branded video to multiple devices.[54] Kara explained that the company has three products: active stream (like the pre-roll you see before a YouTube video), social (in games or apps), and their latest tool, the inline video ad unit. When you read an article, either on a website or a mobile device, the inline video ad unit pushes the text down to expose the video, and the audio will play only when you mouse over it.[55] What makes this particularly interesting and effective for advertisers is that it opens up new inventory. Whereas on Facebook, ads appear as another post, this advertising unit is embedded in the content and is therefore harder to avoid. This accounts for the inline units' 2.5 percent clickthrough rate, compared to 0.8 percent with pre-roll, according to Virool. We also spend more time watching these videos (24 seconds versus 5 seconds for pre-roll).

Another company distributing mobile video in native environments is LoopMe. As Carlos Cruz, the company's senior director, explained, feeding video is good, but using data to fine-tune targeting of those videos is the goal. "Data is becoming a larger focus of our industry, and with that comes machine learning. While we still have campaign managers looking at our efforts, AI [artificial intelligence] is now taking the lead on that front. AI can handle multiple data points, like identifying a poor performing publisher, but also recognizing that on a certain day and at a certain time during the week it may be the best performer on the campaign, and deliver inventory accordingly. In addition, it provides sophisticated attention to all advertisers, from the largest to smallest of efforts, all receiving round the clock attention." LoopMe can do this because they gather data at all times, even when they aren't serving up the mobile ads. "Using our data management platform, we can collect up to thirty data points on the viewer when we receive an ad call on mobile or tablet devices, without even serving the ad. This allows us to collect vast amounts of first-party data on the viewers, which can be layered with third-party (BlueKai, Neustar), or second-party advertiser data, to create a custom target and better reach our target viewer."[56]

All of this goes to show that as big as Big Data is now, it will only continue to grow as we provide ever-increasing amounts of data, not only on our phones and our tablets but through our FitBits and our Apple Watches and whatever else becomes part of the Internet of Things. We can be sure that ads will find us on these devices as well.

THE PROBLEM OF BIG DATA

What is incredible to grasp is that no one has been able to determine how many of these data companies there are. In part that is because they all do a number of different things, so it's difficult to categorize them. Yes, they amass data, but they also do data analytics.[57] Some companies just analyze the data. Some use the data to sell advertising (ad networks and ad exchanges). Other companies, like Google, gobble up data and keep it for their own purposes. It is confusing, and as with other aspects of black ops advertising, it is designed to be that way. The best guesses, however, are that thousands of companies hold millions of pieces of information.

But while the companies collect data, they don't always get it right. And the more data they collect, the more opportunities they have to get it wrong. Acxiom allows you to see some of the data they have on you through aboutthedata.com.[58] For the most part, my information was incorrect, and this isn't an isolated case. Recently, I tried to log into my health provider's website but had forgotten my password. They asked if I would like to answer a couple of questions so that they could identify me. I said sure. The question that came up was: "At which of the following addresses did you live with Estee Einstein?" Estee Einstein is my ex-husband's ex-wife, and I can assure you that I never lived with her.

What was disconcerting was that the company made inferences about me. In this case, it was creepy, but not ultimately detrimental. However, data mining is increasingly used to infer behavior and preferences that can be used against consumers. Far worse is that we have no control over this because decisions are being made not based on what we post, but what our friends post—about us, yes, but also what they post about themselves, which then reflects on us.[59] The U.S. Army, for example, uses Facebook for recruitment purposes because they can infer that if a number of your friends are in the military, you are more likely to enlist. Mac users are considered more discerning and will spend more money for computers, so Orbitz showed Mac users more expensive hotel options.[60] More broadly, companies use "dynamic pricing," meaning that they offer different prices based on where you live and how you shop.[61] The *Wall Street Journal* found that major companies like Staples, Office Depot, and Home Depot "were consistently adjusting prices and displaying different product offers based on a range of characteristics that could be discovered about the user" based on information derived from browsing history and geolocation.[62] Similarly, banks determine whether you're a good credit risk based on whether you associate with people who pay their bills on time.[63] Shockingly, in August 2015, Facebook announced that they were granted a patent on technology that discriminates against borrowers based on their social network. The company described how it would work in the patent application:

> When an individual applies for a loan, the lender examines the credit ratings of members of the individual's social network who are connected to the individual through authorized nodes. If the average credit rating of these members is at least a minimum credit score, the lender continues to process the loan application. Otherwise, the loan application is rejected.[64]

This is the digital version of redlining, when banks drafted maps of U.S. communities in the 1930s and cut off from credit those that were unworthy of mortgage lending—typically because of race. Facebook is not alone in this. Racial inferences are also made about services necessary for different Internet users. In a study by Harvard professor Latanya Sweeney, research determined that names that sound black, like "Trevon Jones," will generate ads suggesting that the person has an arrest record 25 percent more often than a white-sounding name.

In his book *Black Box Society*, Maryland law professor Frank Pasqual terms these misuses of information "runaway data." Other scholars have dubbed it "big data hubris," which is the "implicit assumption that big data are a substitute for, rather than a supplement to, traditional data collection and analysis."[65] An example here is the oft-cited Google Flu, whereby the search engine claimed that they would be able to track an influenza outbreak faster than the CDC under the assumption that people will search for remedies for their flu symptoms. On the face, this seemed like a good idea. Turned out, not so much: people are not good at diagnosing themselves and typed in "flu" whether they had it or not. Subsequent research found that Google Flu was wrong 100 out of 108 weeks.[66]

The latest trend is for companies to put on a friendly face when explaining why you got the ad you did. Facebook has a video that does this, as do a number of publishing sites like Cosmopolitan, which redirect you to the web page for the Digital Advertising Alliance (http://www.aboutads.info/).[67] This site's rhetoric frames Big Data-driven advertising as serving us "better ads" in the same way that content marketing is framed as "informative and entertaining." That is all fine and well, but we should also consider why all of this information is being collected. Google, for example, compiles thousands of pieces of data about us, and most of it is unnecessary. Craig Heimbuch of Barefoot Proximity/BBDO explained that while Google has all of this information on us, there are really only six things that he is interested in knowing: "how did they find it [the website/content], how long did they stay, if they left where did they go, if they stayed what did they do, what did they click on next, and volume."[68] So why are companies collecting so much more information? In part, it allows marketers to justify their jobs. In the digital space, marketing can be tracked and quantified. Marketers talk endlessly about return on investment (ROI). In the past, the ROI was all about sales. Today, it's all about the relationships they've made with consumers, and particularly with Millennials.

No matter what data brokers or marketers claim, however, consumers are not happy about Big Data. Here are some stats:

- 82 percent of global consumers believe that companies collect too much information on consumers. (Adobe, June 2013)
- 86 percent of U.S. Internet users have attempted to remove or mask their online activities, despite only 37 percent believing it possible to be completely anonymous online. (Pew Research Center, September 2013)
- 93 percent of email users believe that users should be able to opt

out if they don't want the content of their emails to be scanned in order to target ads. (GfK & Microsoft, November 2013)[69]

Even more recently, research by Joseph Turow of the University of Pennsylvania and his associates found that we do not want to pay with our data, even if it allows us access to platforms like Facebook and Google for free or gives us discounts on purchases.[70] What we are paying now, in terms of the value of our data and attention, is far more than what we paid in an analog world.

In the United States, not much has been done to protect consumers from marketers and their manipulation of our data. FTC Commissioner Julie Brill has pushed for more oversight, but to little avail, even given the new FTC guidelines.[71] Senator Jay Rockefeller, chair of the Senate Commerce Committee, proposed legislation to increase transparency and spent more than a year investigating the industry, only to be stonewalled by Acxiom, Epsilon, and Experian.[72] But this is not the case everywhere, and particularly not in Western European countries. According to Julia Angwin, "Those countries require all data collectors to provide individuals with access to their data, the ability to correct errors in that data, and, in some cases, the right to delete the data."[73] These are the so-called "right to be forgotten laws," whereby if you ask a corporation to delete unflattering material, they must comply. Not surprisingly, Google has appealed the case and from all appearances intends to fight this vociferously.[74]

6
THE (DIS)EMPOWERED CONSUMER

In March 2015, Starbucks initiated a campaign to generate conversation about race relations in America. As part of that effort, baristas were instructed to write #racetogether on coffee cups and to instigate race-related conversations with customers while preparing cappuccinos and blueberry scones. The negative reaction was palpable. Tweets included "I don't have time to explain 400 years of oppression to you & still make my train," and "Y'all realize there are no coloured hands in the press photos, right? @Starbucks #RaceTogether" and "Would #Starbucks lower their prices in order to offset the emotional cost of discussing #RaceTogether with a clueless Barista?" In fact, the comments reached such vitriol that a Starbucks executive had to suspend his Twitter account. Within days, the campaign was eliminated.

A different Twitter strategy—in which celebrities or brands invite consumers to ask any question they want—has also proven to be less than successful. In one November 2014 example, talk show host Mehmet Oz ("Dr. Oz") asked people to tweet their "biggest question for me" with the hashtag #OzsInbox. In June of the same year, Oz had been called in front of the United States Senate to respond to consumer protection concerns as it related to health claims he made on his show, particularly recommendations for weight loss. The subsequent

#OzsInbox campaign was likely intended as a means to bolster the doctor's reputation in light of these very public quackery allegations, as well as to provide an inexpensive means of generating show ideas through viewer input. Questions about serious health concerns began to fill "Dr. Oz's Inbox," but there were also a flurry of tweets like: "Can you go an entire show without saying the words 'miracle,' 'toxin,' and 'belly fat'?" and "I accidentally dropped my sonic crystals in the dirt. Are they dishwasher safe?" as well as some from physicians asking, "Why have you not been censured or fired from @ColumbiaSurgery for conduct unbecoming a physician, scientist, and gentlemen?" and "How do I get my patients to stop believing your bull?"[1] Oz is not alone. McDonald's had similar results when they asked people to share their #McDstories (people shared stories of fingernails in their food, getting food poisoning, and preferring to eat feces), Bill Cosby's meme generator did not produce the positive spin the actor/accused rapist was looking for, and #MyNYPD generated pictures of police brutality rather than the hoped for smiling faces of community members hugging New York City cops.[2]

Events like these lead consumers—that is, us—to believe that we have some level of control over corporate and municipal interests. Companies create a flatfooted or insensitive social media campaign, we post to social media *en masse* to take them to task, and the campaign gets shut down or taken over. Conclusion: consumers have power. But do we?

Let's say an airline leaves you stranded on a tarmac for five hours. In the past, the best you could do was to write a letter to the CEO or make a phone call to customer service and hope that someone would respond to your complaint. These individual complaints were simple for the company to ignore. It was done in isolation (no one else knew you were dissatisfied except perhaps a few close friends), and companies rarely responded unless a critical mass of consumers made the same complaint. One might organize a letter writing campaign or a product boycott, but such efforts take time and considerable coordination. Social media changed this; feedback is instantaneous and has the potential to become widespread, given a large enough number of followers or friends who willingly pass the message along to others. But so what?

Negative consumer conversations rarely have a long-term effect on brands. A month after the Starbucks campaign, the only tweets still listed under the #RaceTogether hashtag stated that the campaign continued, with a link to a CNN puff piece claiming that Starbucks was a better company for having gotten involved in race relations. The only negative comment was: "You think you're going against the #racetogeher [sic] campaign? Posting your dislike about it on social media helps spread the word about it." The campaign had no negative effect on sales, and the company overall has sustained increased revenue and profit.[3] As for Mehmet Oz, he is still on staff at a prestigious hospital, and his show started its seventh season in fall 2015.

Given our inability to affect significant change, such as getting Bill Cosby arrested or removing Dr. Oz from the airwaves, why do we keep on posting and tweeting? The answer is simple. For a brief time, we could use social media to make a difference. But not anymore, not in the consumer marketplace.[4] Unfortunately, that reality doesn't seem to have caught up with us yet.

FROM BRAND HIJACK TO BRAND HIJACK 2.0

From around 2000 and through the early 2010s, rapidly developing technology allowed companies to include consumer generated content (CGC) in their web presences. With that, consumers were able to influence companies in a way they never had before.[5] We were able to give immediate feedback to marketers—first through blogs and then through an array of social media—and much of that feedback was not positive. Greenpeace hijacked Nestle's Facebook page in opposition to the company deforesting Indonesia for palm oil.[6] Mommy bloggers were able to get Motrin to pull an online ad suggesting that baby slings lead to neck and back pain, which the bloggers viewed as bashing "baby wearing." Domino's Pizza employees made a disparaging—and rather disgusting—video highlighting bad conditions at their store and posted it on YouTube.[7]

There were early promotions using CGC, but like today's Twitter campaigns, these did not always work as the company intended. Take, for example, a General Motors Chevy Tahoe campaign that ran in 2006. The company invited people to build their own ad and provided online tools and beautiful footage of their SUVs. Environmentalists took GM up on the offer and used the technology to create commercials that condemned not only Tahoes but also SUVs generally for being utterly unsustainable.

In light of these events and others like them, and since there seemed to be no effective way to prevent us from commenting negatively on brands—or at least no effective way had been developed yet—marketing consultants recommended that companies begin to actively integrate consumers into the process of creating brand messages.[8] These consultants widely talked and wrote about the "empowered consumer" and how "the consumer is in control" when it came to brand creation. Engaging consumers in the marketing process came to be known broadly as participatory marketing. It was also called "co-creation," "vigilante marketing," "open source" branding, and "creative consumers,"[9] among others.[10] None of these gained wide usage either in academia or in corporate America.

The term that did catch on was "brand hijack," a phrase coined by Alex Wipperfurth in his 2005 book of the same name. The author delineates two ways in which consumers affect the meaning of brands:

"Serendipitous hijack [is] the act of consumers seizing control of a brand's ideology, use, and persona. It is most often practiced by brand fanatics within subcultures, and is largely unanticipated by—and independent of—the brand's marketing department."[11] The author includes Napster, Doc Martens boots, and Pabst Blue Ribbon beer among the brands whose meanings have been defined by the market rather than by marketers. What is important to note here is that while the brand's message was taken over, there was nothing negative about this takeover, and in all three cases the brands were revitalized. Alternatively, Wipperfurth describes a "co-created hijack [as] the act of inviting subcultures to co-create a brand's ideology, use, and persona, and pave the road for adoption by the mainstream,"[12] which is the sort of participatory marketing that consultants were recommending at the time. In the first case, consumers overtake the brand message; in the second, the brand invites in a small group to do the same—*both with positive outcomes.*

Given this, "brand hijack" is a misnomer, and more so today than a decade ago. First, it doesn't matter whether consumers manipulate brand communications on their own or we are asked to participate: the process as defined is more like a pep rally than a hostage taking. Second, the term gives the illusion that consumers have control, when this is simply no longer the case, at least not in the vast majority of marketing interactions and not as it relates to fundamental tenets of a brand. Finally, the term is too limited. Participatory marketing can occur in a variety of ways. Overtaking a brand is certainly one of them, though this very rarely happens. More often, interactions are stage managed to ensure utterly positive results.

Marketers have become adept at manipulating consumer communications, particularly by limiting the framework within which we can talk back. We saw this in Chapter 2 when looking at Consumer Generated Advertising (CGA), specifically the annual Doritos Super

Bowl campaign. Unlike with the Chevy Tahoe, these CGC commercials are screened—some might say censored—so as to curtail negative consumer commentary. Understanding how to harness the message has made asking consumers to create commercials a popular strategy with a growing number of companies, including Nike, Unilever, and Google, among others.[13] A twist on this idea is to ask consumers to create the product itself. Frito-Lay ran a contest to come up with a new potato chip favor, and the winner got to share in the profits of the product.[14] Media companies now conceive films and other video content assuming that users will appropriate it. With Universal's animated film *Despicable Me*, the Minions characters were developed simplistically, the company made the creative assets available to online users, and thus a large number of site visitors used those assets to make their own content, which ultimately helped to sell the films and ancillary products.[15]

A better definition for brand hijacking—though a more appropriate word might be "borrowing"—would be *the hostile takeover of a brand message by an individual or community unrelated to the brand*. Note here that it is a takeover of the *brand message* and not a wholesale takeover of the brand itself. Such hijackings do still occur, but when they do, they tend not to have the same impact that they used to. The usurped communiques tend to be short term and of limited consequence for the brand.

Coca-Cola's obesity campaign provides an example of how this manifests in the current media environment. On January 15, 2013, Coca Cola launched an anti-obesity project. The cornerstone of this effort was a two-minute commercial which aired on cable TV and online and in which the company extolled the litany of initiatives they were implementing in order to help Americans lose weight while retaining Coke products as part of their diet.[16] The short film begins with nostalgic footage of a typical 1950s American soda fountain. It then shows people smiling, eating salads, and recycling plastic bottles. The video shows a plethora of Coke products with large, bright red arrows moving in a downward direction to represent the reduction in calories of many of the brand's products. This is followed by scenes of overweight children exercising, a montage of culturally diverse and smiling people, and a final call to action telling viewers to go to coke. com/comingtogether. The voiceover of the commercial says, in part:

> For over 125 years we've been bringing people together. Today we'd like people to come together on something that concerns all of us: obesity. The long-term health of our families and the country's [sic] at stake . . . Across our portfolio of more than 650 beverages, we now offer over 180 low and no calorie choices . . . [and] we've created smaller, portion-controlled sizes for our most popular drinks.

Two days later, a video called "The Honest Coca-Cola Obesity Commercial" appeared on YouTube. Using the same footage as the original, producers changed the voiceover. The text begins in the same way as the original, but is altered to highlight the hypocrisy of a company that produces a sugar-laden beverage claiming to care about the country's health:

> These diet beverages still pose serious health risks even though we've reduced the calories per serving. These beverages can still cause kidney problems, obesity, metabolic syndrome, cell damage, and rotting teeth, which leaves 470 beverages which have extremely high unhealthy levels of calories. Consuming large amounts of rapidly digested sugar and high fructose corn syrup . . . can lead to inflammation and insulin resistance, both of which may increase your risk of stroke, heart disease, diabetes, obesity, and cancer . . . All calories are not the same, and the calories in Coca-Cola

products have no nutritional value . . . If you drink Coke, you'll get fatter and fatter. The solution is simple, and it's right in front of your eyes. Don't drink Coke. It's killing you and your family. Coca-Cola: We're partially responsible for America's obesity problem.

Coca-Cola's response: quietly remove all traces of its anti-obesity efforts. The website no longer exists, and even links to healthier living initiatives are dead ends. Other than the "honest" ad still living on YouTube, it is as if the campaign never happened. Moreover, Coca-Cola sales went up: in addition to "disappearing" the offending campaign, they overwhelmed the system with the new, positive message (your name on a soda can), à la the Mormons.

This softer form of brand hijack represents a shift from criticizing a corporation's brand based on how the corporation runs its business—i.e., using palm oil or producing environmentally irresponsible vehicles—to primarily criticizing the corporation's messages. Coca-Cola was attacked for trying to "own" anti-obesity, and Starbucks for thinking it should have a say in race relations. Both were ridiculous concepts, and people rightly criticized the corporations. But neither was an example of the old brand hijack, characterized by sustained effort and long-term impact. In neither the Coca-Cola nor Starbucks case was a brand fundamentally changed, or sales affected. Current brand hijacks have become a watered-down version of their predecessors, and by and large they have been replaced by brand evangelism.

NOT CONSUMER EMPOWERMENT, BRAND EVANGELISM

While the marketing landscape has changed, the discourse around consumer empowerment continues unabated. Admittedly, some clear-thinking marketers and consultants saw as early as 2011 that consumers controlled nothing.[17] Others, however, continue to perpetuate the myth of consumer empowerment. Bob Jeffrey, CEO of advertising agency J. Walter Thompson, has said: "It is about the power of consumers to choose their own destiny, define their world, their media, their interactions with the world, and their ability to control communications. They are now the critic and the creative, marketer and advertiser, creator and consumer, all rolled into one."[18] Lego claims "we own the logo, but our consumers own the brand."[19] And articles in *Advertising Age* still make ridiculous claims like "If you want to talk to this group of consumers [Millennials], you cannot control them. If you want to stay in touch with them, let them express themselves,"[20] and "The consumer is in control! Remember that rallying cry from the first decade of the century? The advertising industry goes through so many fads so rapidly, you'd be forgiven for forgetting. As it turns out, consumers are still in control—perhaps even more so."[21] We also see this rhetoric in commentary about consumer/bloggers and their ability to set trends, such as off-the-shoulder styles and helping to revitalize Birkenstocks. However, while these bloggers might help set trends, the vast majority of them are living on a shoestring while they lick the boots of the Bethennys and Beyonces.[22]

Whether blogger or social media maven, consumers do not control brands now any more than they did prior to interactive media. Do brands respond to us more on Twitter? Yes. Are marketers listening in on our conversations about their products? Yes. But they are doing that so they can manage the conversation, not to let us do the talking. The reason a company will respond within 24 hours or less is not simply to provide service, but also to manage the communication.[23] True, we may affect individual campaigns or some small part of the brand messaging, as we did with Starbucks and race relations, but the underlying system is left untouched. Rather, as we saw in earlier chapters, we are being used to spread marketing messages. Our ability to continually communicate about brands has been framed by the industry as consumer empowerment; it is not. It is brand evangelism—also known as word of mouth marketing, which we now all know is integral to the new sharing paradigm.[24]

Brand evangelism is the *positive promotion and selling of a product or service by an individual or community unrelated to the brand*. This is the most extreme, most passionate form of sharing. Consumers may forward a video produced by a company or retweet a picture or write a review, but they are also investing significant time and energy to produce content for a product or brand. These are the "super fans" who become brand Influencers, although unlike some of the Influencers discussed earlier, they do not get paid. Their goal in creating content and sharing it endlessly is to spread the good word, much in the same way that a religious evangelist would spread the "good news." We are becoming brand evangelists either through our own passion for the brand or, more typically, because the brand has assisted us in evangelizing it.

We looked at two examples of organic brand evangelism in Chapter 2 when we talked about word of mouth marketing, specifically in relationship to consumer generated content. There we discussed Nutella—a brand with passionate followers who created the World Nutella Day—and Chipotle consumers, who created and maintain the www.chipotlefan.com website.

Entertainment properties—including movies, TV shows, and sports teams—also elicit committed brand evangelists. Star Trek fans (known as Trekkies) and Star Wars fans are excellent examples. The lovers of Harry Potter are incredibly passionate: while J. K. Rowling wrote the books, fans have created a wealth of content around the English wizard that has nothing to do with the original texts. "Potter Pals" (a series of videos created with puppets representing characters from Harry Potter), college Quidditch leagues (real world competitions based on the game in the books), and *James Potter* (a sequel to the series written by a fan) are just a few illustrations of this.

These are some of the rare true examples of unadulterated brand evangelism. But just as wholesale brand hijacks are outliers, the same is true for brand evangelism. What passes for evangelism is, in truth, word of mouth that a marketer is manipulating in order to frame us as passionate advocates for the brand and as empowered consumers.

Beyond paying Influencers to tell us about products and services (black ops evangelizing?), marketers facilitate brand evangelism through what are known as brand communities.[25] A brand community is defined as "a specialized, non-geographically bound community, based on a structured set of social relations among admirers of a brand."[26] In other words, people create rituals and practices around a consumer brand that aid in enforcing and sustaining connections among the members of the community. What makes these communities so effective are the relationships generated among the participants. Deciding not to use a brand is easy. Deciding to walk away from a group of people that you have become friendly with and committed significant time to is more difficult. This is why marketers (and Mark Zuckerberg) are gung-ho on creating communities. These communities typically exist online, though members may also meet in the real world. Brand community interactions may be instigated by a passionate group of fans (Nutella), but more typically are enabled by brand marketers, such as when Jeep holds its Jeep Jamboree weekends to bring families together in order to teach them how to drive off road. Apple and Harley Davison's brand communities have such obsessive followers that they have been called brand cults.[27]

Brand communities with engaged followers exist across product categories. Particularly passionate are car lovers. Tesla owners are crazy about the brand,[28] and BMW lovers have their driving experience.[29] Mobile apps also generate considerable consumer affinity. People love to share apps that make their lives better, easier, or more efficient. This is what propelled the meteoric rise of Uber. Finding a car quickly, knowing how long it would take to show up, and not having to deal with cash or credit at the end of the ride makes for a more pleasant traveling experience. HBO Go has serious fans, as does Netflix and for younger users, Snapchat. In each of these cases, though, a marketer helped seal the deal: in the case of the car companies by holding events and facilitating brand communities, in the case of the app companies by using early adopters to influence sharing.[30]

One company that stuck out as generating considerable enthusiasm is lululemon, a manufacturer of yoga apparel for women. For some—such as the bloggers who maintain sites like lululemon addict (http://www.luluaddict.com/) and lulu mum (http://www. lululemonblogger.com/), which started in 2008 and 2009 respectively, and both of which remain active—the company inspires true brand evangelism. But what lululemon did and does to foster consumer connections isn't as hands off as it first appears. Lululemon has been committed to consumer engagement, and its employees are adept at utilizing social media. They maintained a website forum called "the White Board," where they ran polls and where company employees gently responded to customer complaints.[31] Here is the empowerment message from the site: "Here at lululemon athletica we are all about collaboration, ideation and creativity . . . Your insights and ideas shape our future, and this online community allows us to engage in two-way conversations in order to co-create."[32] But the White Board was more sounding board than influencer—sort of like when you talk to someone at an 800-number and they read back to you from a script—and today it lies dormant. Beyond that site, the company has "fitness ambassadors," local yoga or CrossFit teachers who wear the company's clothes while they work and endorse the brand to their students—an up-close and personal version of black ops marketing. As for social media, the company is active on YouTube, Facebook, and Twitter, all of which it uses to promote its products, but which it also uses to provide inspiration about running, meditating, and yoga. A recent Facebook post said: "Most of the time we spend looking outside of ourselves for answers. Meditation allows us to access the wisdom that is already there. Practicing silence helps us to listen to our inner voice. Give it a try." Then there is a link that sends you to the company's podcast series on SoundCloud, which displays a large lululemon logo and asks you to create an account.[33] This is manipulation through spirituality, repackaged to sell high-end yoga wear. There is simply no situation under which spiritual manipulation is acceptable, and yet lululemon uses the tactic because it creates, well, evangelists.[34] It is sad to say that they are not alone. SoulCycle, a company that runs very high-end exercise spinning classes, uses a similar strategy. They have a "mantra" on their wall, and candles burn during workout sessions. Perhaps not surprisingly, the brand is routinely referred to as a cult.[35]

Socially conscious brands tap into our passions rather than our spiritual belief systems to help drive evangelism. The clothing brand Patagonia comes to mind. Patagonia has long been known for its commitment to outdoor living and the environment. As a company with a longstanding vision to do no harm, protect the environment, and not perpetuate overconsumption (they placed a full-page ad in the *New York Times* saying "Don't Buy This Jacket" on Black Friday), Patagonia demonstrates again and again its commitment to its values. So much so that the company has even said that they are not looking to grow—an idea that is anathema to capitalism and marketing. Connecting social responsibility to the bottom line has created a brand that evokes commitment and passion on the part of its consumers. Socially responsible brands like this hold significant appeal for Millennials, which is why more companies look to embed these values into their brands. In addition to Patagonia, we could include TOMS shoes, Warby Parker eyewear, and Interface carpet. Unlike lululemon, these companies demonstrate a commitment to the values they espouse,[36] and through these practices come closest to the ideal of brand co-creation that was envisioned in the early days of participatory marketing.

Most examples in this book fall in the area of company-facilitated brand evangelism. Are Red Bull users big fans of the product? Clearly. If you think that's because the drink tastes good—you probably haven't tried it. Mega-fans exist because the company is skilled at creating stories and events that their consumer wants to be connected with—music, extreme sports, technology—and share. In fact, Red Bull is now considered a media company almost more than it is an energy drink producer.

Finally, let's not forget Starbucks. The brand has been incredibly successful in building a following of loyal customers. Some of that loyalty is related to their products, which people genuinely like. But coffee alone did not make people pushers of this caffeine purveyor. A series of marketing tools also led to Starbucks's reputation. For example, like lululemon, Starbucks has a site where people can offer ideas (http://mystarbucksidea.force.com/) and visitors are asked to "Share. Vote. Discuss. See."—all key terms of co-creation. Starbucks was also early to develop a mobile app that is both useful and that keeps consumers connected to the brand. Customers can order ahead with the app to avoid in-store lines, as well as pay for their coffee and even digitally tip the barista. And like Frito-Lay, the company asks for consumer input when picking new products, such as the newest flavor for their Frappuccino.[37] All the goodwill generated by these marketing activities makes the #racetogether debacle a blip on the map.

• • •

Staying conscious of the role we have been given within this stealth framework is key to understanding the power relationships that marketers have prescribed. While the marketers' come-on is to say that they want a "relationship" (co-creation), the makeup of that interaction is more like one of boss to employee. We perform the labor of sharing, and we do it for free to boot. When we do speak up with complaints, they're either quickly squelched by a conscientious listener from the company, who placates us, or we complain about something trivial, like a misguided marketing campaign.

Rather than the consumer empowerment of the early 2000s, which involved some vague level of brand hijacking, what exists today is a more tightly controlled communication environment. The goal has been to move consumers away from brand hijack toward brand evangelism, and by and large, that movement has been successfully executed. And while marketers talk about co-creation, it is hard to say that that is what occurs in the real world because corporations set the guidelines within which the conversation about their brand takes place. We saw that with the Super Bowl ads and with the T Mobile Facebook app, and there are many more examples. Everyone can submit videos to GoPro, but not every video is posted. Everyone can submit a new Lays flavor, but Frito-Lay decides the winner (while simultaneously generating thousands of flavor suggestions voted on by millions of people without having to pay for research and development or the accompanying free publicity). Socially conscious brands come close to co-creation, but those companies are a limited few. Evangelism equals sharing, and just like religious institutions, marketers want to keep a very tight rein on the message that gets dispersed.

According to the marketing firm Edelman, 66 percent of consumers feel that interactions with corporations are tilted in favor of the brands, and 70 percent "feel that brands are motivated by a self-centered desire to increase profits rather than by a sincere commitment to their customers."[38] But still we do their bidding. The problem is not that we're unaware that corporations control the message; it's that when we're online, we don't behave as if we know it. Corporations grabbed back the megaphone, and they are using it to loudly proclaim our empowerment, even though nothing could be farther from the truth.

If you want real consumer empowerment, there's one simple thing you can do: stop sharing content.

7
ADVERTISING OURSELVES TO DEATH

Click a button and we can read the *New York Times* or watch our favorite TV show or stream the latest movie. Submit a query to Google and a world of knowledge appears on the screen, albeit algorithmically delimited. Newspaper or magazine, TV or movie, fact, tidbit, or commentary, no matter how big or small, how significant or trivial: it's all available at our fingertips, and it's all absolutely free.

This is the perception we have been lulled into believing. It is time to wake up. There is no free lunch, free movie, news report, or factoid. We are paying and paying dearly.

We pay with our time and our attention—a scarce and valuable resource in the twenty-first century—and the coin of the realm in today's "attention economy."[1] We pay by being forced to engage with what has become an unending stream of advertising blurred to be indistinguishable from legitimate news stories, leading to the utter skewing of our sense of reality. We pay by providing our personal data to marketers, who then use that data to sell us an increasing array of products "specifically targeted to us" by manipulating and whipsawing our emotions. We pay by turning our relationships into monetizable opportunities, making personal interactions into market transactions, and remaining in a constant state of buying or selling, albeit one that's been prettied up to look like sharing and making "friends." Exaggeration? I don't think so. Not if dating apps like Tinder exist that allow us to dismiss people with the swipe of a thumb, or apps like Peeple are created with the sole purpose to rate anyone, anytime, without their say, as if they were a plate of food or a room to rent from Airbnb. No matter where we turn in this digitally "enhanced" world, our agency—our personal ability to act freely and independently—is being quashed. We can't choose the type of content we want to watch or read; we can't represent who we are; we are emotionally manipulated in the name of corporate profit. This is what marketers call consumer empowerment. I heartily disagree.

Until now, we could be excused for passively interacting with whatever content appears on our mobile device or laptop. Few beyond those working in the industry knew or understood the level of stealth activity associated with digital technologies, and many of them don't even comprehend it. I sympathize: I'm not a Luddite, but I'm not a tech person either; it all seems too complex and confusing and ultimately overwhelming.

In truth, it was designed that way. You see, we've been duped—and by some really smart people. Jeff Hammerbacher, Facebook's first "research scientist" and a Harvard-trained mathematician, is widely quoted as saying, "The best minds of my generation are thinking about how to make people click ads . . . and it sucks."[2] It's the reason he left the company. But tricking us into clicking on ads certainly doesn't happen only on Facebook, and manipulation doesn't happen only at the level of content. The user interface keeps our eyes locked and our hands glued to screens big and small. In 1996, B. J. Fogg—another smart guy, this time from Stanford University—coined the term "Captology," based on an acronym for Computers As Persuasive Technologies. His work, which has been embraced by numerous companies, uses a combination of tools to increase our interaction with a screen. These are: positive or negative motivation (pleasure or pain), ability (simplify tasks), and triggers (say, a noise cue). So every time a push notification comes through our phone, we leap from whatever we are doing to pick it up, typically in anticipation of a pleasurable reward like a text from a loved one.[3] Of course, it is more likely to be a come-on from a corporation. But once we've been triggered to pick up the phone, we're hooked, and so we end up clicking and clicking, creating endless data and interacting with untold ads every day—and most of the time, we're painfully unaware that that is what we are doing. It is utterly Pavlovian. Combine that addictive technology with ambiguous information, and we have content confusion writ large.

As bad as all this is, it's about to get worse. The media industry as we know it is imploding.

ADVERTISING AND AGENCY

There has long been a tacit agreement media companies had with their audiences: if we sit through the commercials, the networks will provide us with high quality news and entertainment. Barring that, we buy a monthly subscription to programming like HBO or Showtime in order to avoid having to deal with commercials.

While many of us complained about this structure, in truth, it wasn't that bad.[4] Commercials may be irrelevant to you or inane in their execution, but some are incredibly entertaining, such as Apple's "1984," Budweiser's "Whassup," Nike's Michael Jordan ads, and more recently, VW's "Darth Vader" and Old Spice's "The Man Your Man Could Smell Like." It doesn't get much better than Under Armour's Misty Copeland ad. Smart, captivating, strategically aligned advertising is typically so good that you want to watch it. And if you don't, you can always get up and grab a beer or go to the bathroom or walk the dog.

In this scenario, no company knew in any detail who you were or what you watched or what you bought. You might see some advertising that didn't relate directly to you, but so what? More importantly, you knew it was a commercial, and *it was your choice whether or not to watch it*.

At the beginning of the Internet, the high social ideal was that it would somehow exist outside this revenue model. In the boom days before the Internet bubble and even after, company business plans were drawn up without a hint of how the organization was going to generate income. Facebook is a great example here in that they didn't try to make money for almost six years, yet they still had millions of dollars of investment capital. It was a cyberspace gold rush, but no one knew what they were mining.

Making money ultimately came down to two things: sell stuff (ecommerce) or sell time and space (advertising). Subscription models like Netflix or Hulu didn't take off until later, when broadband became widely available (and ultimately, they qualify as ecommerce too). When the dust finally settled, the Internet turned out to be no different than the legacy media that preceded it. The Internet—and with it, every mobile device we carry, no matter where we go, no matter what we do—is nothing more than a purveyor of sales messages. Your phone is an advertising medium.

So the advertising model you hated on television now exists online, only it's worse. While you might not have liked commercials breaking up your favorite TV show, ads now follow you around the Internet instead, moving from your computer to your iPad to your cell phone. Along the way, myriad companies are collecting more and more data about you without your even knowing it, though you may suspect it is happening and don't like it.[5] And the advertising is no longer obvious, so you're never quite sure if you're getting news or some sort of biased claptrap. With TV, you were anonymous and you knew when you were watching a commercial. Not anymore. Today that cute animal video might be an ad for a mobile phone company, and that article about cocaine use turns out to be an ad for Netflix.[6] Of course, commercials have long been manipulative and designed to pull at our heartstrings, but we knew we were being manipulated. Today, our emotional world is up for grabs so that we will do the labor of sharing commercial messages with our friends.

While we grumble about commercials, the truth is that advertising was and still is the economic support for all the music and entertainment and news we have come to want and need. It isn't free and it never was, no matter how much it feels like it is. But we'll get to the point (and we're getting close to it) when media outlets can't sell enough advertising to support the content they need to create.[7] That's not just an issue for traditional media. Ad blockers, browser extensions that prevent ads from being loaded onto your screen, may become so pervasive as to threaten the existence of online outlets. Ad blockers have been around for a while but only recently achieved wide acceptance, in no small part due to their ability to improve download times because the browser doesn't have to spend resources on delivering ads. Around the globe, 41 percent of Internet users block ads, and that number is growing.[8] This latest, greatest means of ad avoidance seems great for us, but it may destroy the advertising-based revenue model as more and more money moves to digital.

Once there isn't enough advertising income to support media companies, their only alternative is to charge us for every manner of content. It's already started with HBO Now, CBS All Access, Netflix, Hulu, and so on and so on and so on. It's also why Google and Apple and Amazon have all gotten into TV, and why Amazon is preventing its competitors from selling TV products on their site. Most telling is the sales pitch for Apple TV, which reads in part: "TV is a major part of our lives . . . Yet somehow, the overall experience of TV has continued to stagnate. Until now. It all starts by recognizing that apps are the future of television. HBO NOW, WatchESPN, Netflix, Hulu, iTunes—apps are quickly becoming how we watch today . . . This is where television is headed." TV equals apps, and apps equal money coming out of your pocket. Soon, very soon, that $150-a-month cable bill is going to start looking pretty sweet in comparison to all the individual subscriptions we'll have to buy because we didn't want to know we were looking at advertising.

Advertising Age calculated what that possible ad-free media universe might look like. A subscription to the *New York Times* would increase from $195 a year to $334 a year; television would cost about $1,800 a year ($1,200 without premium channels like HBO) for at most a dozen TV channels (rather than the 500-channel universe you are used to because those networks could no longer afford to exist); and Facebook would cost $12 a year. (They also noted that the fee for BuzzFeed would be zero, because no one would pay for that content, and "A World without Advertising Is a World without BuzzFeed.")[9] The ad-free media universe posits a reversion to the times of early newspapers, when the only people who could afford access to information were the wealthy. It is a world for the one percenters.

Given this doomsday scenario, I am all for watching TV with commercials—knowing full well they are commercials—and paying for advertising-free online content. I'd pay to use Google; it's a valuable service. If at some later time I decide that its algorithms are too out of whack, I might change my mind. But let us all decide for ourselves. And at the risk of sounding like a libertarian, let the market decide. Given the choice, $12 a year for Facebook is a pittance in comparison to the price we pay in personal data, skewed reality, and dehumanized personal relationships.[10]

TOO BIG TO FAIL

The boys of Silicon Valley were smart enough to bleed the media system. They weren't smart enough to create a better revenue model than the advertising one that preceded it. (Ecommerce rates only as a minor innovation.) Google and Facebook both claimed—no, bragged vociferously—that they would not be purveyors of advertising. That would be funny if it wasn't so sad and dangerous and deceptive. Their "cleverness" may yet come back to bite them, and we could end up paying the bill. But for now, the "four horsemen of tech"—Google, Facebook, Amazon, and Apple—just keep on with their deceptive and monopolistic practices.

Google has become the biggest advertising platform, and with that status has come bullying tactics. In April 2015, for instance, the company changed its search algorithm for mobile because, as we know, mobile is the future. Any advertiser that hadn't made their site mobile friendly enough for Google found themselves losing the advertising bid. "So what?" you might say. After all, that only affects the companies. Not so. Google was giving higher search result rankings to sites "with large text, easy-to-click links, or those with responsive design," the last meaning a site whose webpage URL was consistent across devices. Sites from eBay to Nintendo to the Daily Mail got lost in the search rankings.[11] When one company controls that much gatekeeper power, they have untold ability not only to affect other companies' bottom line, but also our ability to access information.

Facebook, too, is immersed in advertising and commerce, including selling news. In October 2015, they finally launched their long-awaited Instant Articles, news stories from leading publications like the *New York Times*, the *Washington Post, National Geographic*, and the *Atlantic,* among others. Dozens more are slated to join, with the real possibility that "very soon, every digital publisher, journalistic or non, that wants to be a serious online player will host a large portion of their content on Facebook's servers."[12] While the service is touted for its faster downloads, the real reason news organizations have signed on is so that they can get a piece of Facebook's advertising revenue. Some publishers will outsource their advertising sales to Facebook, but others—mostly the larger entities—will sell their own advertising, some of which will be of the native variety.[13]

The most obvious and ubiquitous way that Facebook displays its commitment to all things commercial is the "Like" button. After announcing that the company would respond to users' requests for a "Dislike" button, Zuckerberg came back with a series of emotional options, without a "Dislike" button among them.[14] Few industry followers were surprised; "Dislike" is anti-advertising. What Facebook did come up with was a series of emoticons, which helps Facebook and advertisers more than it helps you. While the "Like" button says that you accept being associated with a brand (Susie Smiths likes XYZ Company), emoticons move feelings (and we know how important those are) from verbiage to structured data.[15] It is deceptive, systematized emotional tracking from the company that brought you emotional contagion experiments. They are also the company that enables other companies to evaluate your social connections to determine your ability to get a loan, to target you for military service, and to assess your job qualifications. How long do you think it will be before you hit the sad emoticon one too many times and an antidepressant medication ends up in your news feed?

The manipulative and monopolistic practices of Google and Facebook are reflected on the ecommerce side at Amazon. This online shopping site is now a behemoth and the leading search option when it comes to shopping, with 44 percent of people starting on the site when they purchase online.[16] With size comes power, which the company uses to bully other companies. Notable here are the almost year-long price-setting fight with publisher Hachette and the announcement that Amazon had banned the sale of streaming devices from its key competitors, Apple and Google.[17] As Amazon moves into more and more businesses, there is every reason to believe that these practices will continue. And we know that they are going into lots of different businesses: they spend billions of dollars annually in research and development to come up with things like delivery drones and electronics like the Kindle and Fire TV, and most recently they have taken on retailers in a handful of cities like New York, San Francisco, and San Antonio by offering one-hour delivery through Amazon Prime Now, which threatens not big competitors but little mom-and-pop stores.[18] Lastly, Amazon has become notorious for its reportedly abysmal labor practices, which affect employees from temporary warehouse help to white collar workers.[19] But all we see is the convenience, the box with the smile on our doorstep. What we don't see are the overworked people and the monopolistic practices that deny us access to products. Nor are we privy to how they track our data, from what we buy right down to how much we read and what we highlight on our Kindle.[20]

Providing the foundation for and fueling the perpetuation of triggers and clicks is, of course, Apple. They make the technology, sure, but they also distribute content (via iTunes and Apple TV) and collect purchase data through Apple Pay, which is tying in with an untold number of brick-and-mortar retail outlets. We can only begin to guess how they will combine what we watch to what we buy to who we text in new and more hidden ways. What concerns me more at this point is that they are on the cutting edge of supporting ad blocking. This is great for them, because they primarily generate revenue from products rather than advertising. But for us, again, it has costs. As I have discussed throughout the book, there have always been ways to avoid advertising. What Apple is doing (per B. J. Fogg's methodology) is to make the task simpler by allowing developers to create ad blocking tools for its new iOS 9 operating system. Now that Apple has gotten into the fight, the expectation is that ad blockers will gain still broader acceptance. The immediate issue for us: ad blockers don't detect content marketing. So, either we will not know we are engaging with ads because we will have assumed that ad blockers caught the advertising, or the advertising will become even more black ops in order to avoid being detected by ad blockers. In the longer term, they may be the avoidance tool that sinks the entire advertising-based media system.

In thinking about these companies, I couldn't help but remember when I began teaching media, and we used to show students an illustration of an octopus with tentacles wrapped around the logos of the major media companies like Disney and Viacom and Newscorp. Now, that octopus looks downright quaint in comparison to the subversive digital-techno behemoths. Those legacy media were regulated in a way that today's media giants simply are not. And while Disney might be vertically integrated—producing TV shows and games based on films, which in turn get syndicated onto the Disney Channel—today's media companies are also increasingly horizontally integrated so that their tentacles reach into more and more industries. Google makes cars and maps; Apple has Apple Pay; Amazon creates drones, and all of them sell data, with Facebook being the most encompassing because of its ability to interconnect people, whether they are on the site or not.[21] Instead of the banks, it will be Facebook and Google and Amazon and Apple who have become too big to fail, and it won't be one industry but several that will take the fall.

We are not there yet. In the meantime, there is other fallout from digital technologies and advertising we need to address.

CONTENT CONSEQUENCES

Throughout the book, we've discussed ways in which content is deceptive. Native advertising hides commercial messages in existing content.

Content marketing turns product placement on its head, forcing legitimate information to find a home within corporately sponsored material. And while marketers claim their expertise (which is true), they also claim journalistic objectivity (which is not). Finally, content has to be engaging to keep our attention and motivate us to share, so content creators will gear more content to be entertaining, making serious news increasingly harder to find. Dependence on big data is only making it worse.

Big data is concerned with behavior, not context. What this means is that digital advertisers don't care what we watch (context), they simply care what we do (behavior). Since advertisers care primarily about reaching us as far down the sales funnel as possible, then the content the advertising appears in is superfluous. It is utterly disconnected from the ad buy.

Let me explain. Traditional media models were all about aggregating eyeballs for advertisers. Marketers made educated guesses about who was watching what TV programming. Today, companies are chasing individuals, or individual IP addresses, and they have a very good idea of who each individual is. Based on this, advertising is sent instantly to wherever you are on the web. You could be reading the news, watching cat videos, or taking a pop quiz. In this environment, the content simply doesn't matter.

If the content doesn't matter, there is no incentive to produce anything of substance or something that might take time or money, say like investigative reporting. I often tell students that the TV networks would show a test pattern if they thought people would watch it. We won't do that for TV. On the Internet, though, we come pretty close. There are numerous examples of wasted resources throughout this book, but the one that tops the list is a website called www.blahairlines .com. It is a stripped down, downscale version of a typical airline website. Its most outstanding feature is an alert on the bottom of the page that says, "breaking news on a video you should not watch!!!!" Ultimately, you will be taken to a five-hour-and-45-minute video of a bunch of dummies in seats for a supposed flight from Newark to San Francisco. The video is not static; there is audio of babies crying, a flight attendant gives the usual announcements, and periodically someone off screen manipulates a dummy's arm as if to move hair out of her face. I'm not sure which boggles the mind more: that Virgin Airlines spent the time and money and energy to produce this, or that more than 850,000 people viewed it.[22] Another example of disjointed content is the "No" website (http://noooooooooooooooo.com) consisting of a single page with a picture of Darth Vader and a button you can push that says "Noooooo." This site—a single page really—has received more than 27 million views, has 673,000 Facebook "Likes," and has been tweeted more than 75,000 times, thus qualifying as suitable for advertising placement. If the content isn't inane or ridiculous, it veers toward stunts like Marc Ecko pretending to tag Air Force One or a story of a naked man crawling out of a Buckingham Palace window, which was covered by NBC News only for the network to be embarrassed to learn that it was a stunt for a show called *The Royals* that appears on one of its own networks.[23] That's right: a media company's marketing team created fake news that was picked up by its real news division.

Underlying all of this are the economic consequences of moving revenue out of traditional media and into digital marketing, including lost jobs, lower pay, and evergreen content. Many of the people writing content marketing today are former journalists who can no longer find a position because newspapers are dead or dying. These writers, who can very skillfully make an ad look like news, have no choice because marketers are becoming the only ones with enough money to pay a decent wage. Even given that, many of these skilled writers are working as freelancers rather than full-time salaried employees. Maintaining freelancers is one way for a company to keep costs in check. The other common practice is to use evergreen content—content that is not tied to a particular point in time, meaning that it can be used over and over again. Remember, the goal is to distribute content that people will read. Online, you can constantly be getting new people in front of content, which you can't do with a newspaper that has subscribers or loyal folks that pick up the paper at the newsstand every day. The problem for writers, then, is that once there is a stockpile of content that can be continually re-purposed, there is less need for writers. Don't forget, too, the increasing amount of written content that is produced for free (read: Huffington Post) and videos produced as user-generated content. In the latter case, it won't just be writers out of jobs, but all the creative people in agencies, including art directors, copywriters, producers, casting directors, and the dozens of more junior people who report to them. And if this continues to play out, many personnel at television networks will be out of work, too.

Newspapers and broadcasters "comfort the afflicted and afflict the comfortable," confronting us with issues we must face. They investigate corrupt politicians, report on the local school board meetings, and discover the source of tainted food when the government doesn't spend the money to do so. If it were not for newspapers and local broadcasters, we would likely never have known about Watergate (*Washington Post*) or the AIDS epidemic (*San Francisco Chronicle*) or the financial improprieties of RNC chairman Michael Steele (WBAL). Who's going to do those stories online? The Drudge Report? BuzzFeed?

PERSONAL CONSEQUENCES

"You're just an old-time marketer."

That's what one of the people I interviewed said to me. In fact, he said it as if I was scum he'd found on the bottom of his shoe. Truth is, he's right. I am an old-time marketer, and because of that, I didn't—and still don't—see what all the fuss is about when it comes to using digital technologies as a marketing tool. Digital isn't magical; it's advertising. And our cellphones and mobile devices aren't mechanisms of wonder; they are an advertising distribution system. Sure, the gizmos and gadgets of our mobile devices are fun, and for marketers, it's nice to see sales numbers grow and to use big big data to generate pretty, colorful graphs. But an ad medium is an ad medium is an ad medium. I really couldn't get all that excited about it.

What bothered me, though, was how excited the people I interviewed seemed about things like A/B testing (putting two pictures up online to see which one will generate more sales) and tracking people around the Internet in pursuit of data—all without people knowing they are participating in ongoing, unpaid market research.

Being able to look at this from the outside, what I could see that most people I interviewed could not (or would not admit to seeing) were the serious consequences of all this stealth activity. People who work in advertising say things like "more information means better targeting so that ads are more relevant for consumers" or "market testing is just about making the online product better" or "content marketing is less disruptive and more entertaining." They also say that consumers aren't stupid, that consumers can see that the work they produce is advertising. Not so. In presenting parts of this book over the last year, the audible gasps that come up in the room are evidence that people don't know, and that includes classrooms full of Millennial college students—the ones who are supposed to be so hip to this information. Content confusion is real. The skewing of reality is real.

The social media feeding this subversive content has its own negative hidden agenda. We already know that sharing is about buying and selling. We also know that our relationships have become market transactions. But that's not all. Just as women feel inferior after reading magazines, the same is true online—only we find ourselves competing with friends, rather than some unattainable model. Statistics are that one-third of Facebook users feel envious of others and worse about themselves after leaving the site.[24] That is because "confessionalism, exhibitionism, prideful consumerism, and, above all, a relentless positivity . . . are the values and practices of today's social media."[25] We feel compelled to consistently project a positive image, even if that image has no basis in reality. Take the examples of Kiersten Rickenbach Cerveny, a stunning, successful Long Island doctor found dead of a drug overdose in the vestibule of a New York City apartment building, and Madison Holleran, the Ivy League track star who leapt to her death from a nine-story parking garage.[26] Both were beautiful and smart and successful by any measure; both led double lives, with the online life projecting an all-too-perfect world that no one could ever possibly live up to, not in a million years. These are extreme, for sure, but the pressures to fit in are not. But we can understand why this happens. The rules of advertising—everything has to look good, everything has to be perfect, everything is not real—have spilled over onto sites that were originally meant for community but that are now all about commerce. The online space becomes the storefront for our own personal brands, which in turn sells the clothes we wear and the stores we shop and the bars we frequent. We become walking, talking advertisements. In thinking about this, it suddenly struck me why the pitch for the new iPhone was primarily all about the camera—the better the camera, the better able we are to make products look good.

Our world is further skewed by the manipulation of data. Data collected about us can be inadequate or flat-out wrong. It limits who we are because it is derived from what we did, not who we might become. It is the difference between Amazon offering suggestions for books and going to the library to see what's on the shelf. Algorithms that generate this data are a "black box," and they are not neutral.[27] It's possible that companies might make good use of the personal data we're providing, but there's no way for us to know everything that's involved in the process of collecting it and using it: I've outlined much of that process in this book, but even that can only begin to skim the surface. The sad reality is that we don't know—and from my research, I've found that even marketers don't fully understand—what happens with all the information we provide by living our lives increasingly online.

Finally, because we are increasingly tethered to technology, we live increasingly mediated lives rather than engaging with the world. The marimba ringtone makes every head turn. We step on an elevator and pull out our cell phones instead of talking to one another. If there is a phone on a table, personal conversations or conversations of depth are less likely to come up.[28] In her latest book, MIT professor Sherry Turkle outlines how Millennials have determined an appropriate etiquette for when you can pull out a cell phone when among a group of people. She notes as well that boredom for this generation has become a fate worse than death.[29] They are not alone. Ask a friend, "How are you?" and the response is likely to be, "Busy." We should ask ourselves why that has become a badge of honor, why we have become too busy to engage with each other. Some of that is economic, but technology has culpability here, too.[30] We are more willing to engage with advertising—because that's what we are doing if we're online—than with the living, breathing person standing next to us. It is madness.

WHERE'S THE GOOD?

It's not in my nature to be a pessimist. In thinking about these issues, though, I'm not sure that I have what could qualify as a neatly packaged solution. The best I can do is to provide some insights and suggestions.

First: I like really good, smart advertising. The GE moon landing piece with Thrillist fits that bill. Intel's inside films are gorgeously executed. Whole Foods has a blog called Whole Story that is beautiful and contains informative content. As long as these ads are clearly marked, as far as I'm concerned, it's all good.

Having read this book, my hope is that you can more easily spot the advertisements on your own, but you should not have to do all the work. The FTC has held meetings with members of the advertising industry and given them veiled threats, but to little avail.[31] That lack of action, along with the sense I got from speaking with someone at the agency, makes me believe that the organization doesn't have teeth—even with their new guidelines. An alternative route should be found. As the FTC guidelines suggest, advertising needs to be clearly marked using a consistent language: when it says "Sponsored Content," we should know that it means ADVERTISING. This should not merely be guidelines but full-fleshed regulation with consequences attached. Implementing this should not be hard to put into place. As for tracking: government regulations already prohibit the Marine Corps websites from using cookies.[32] How about we apply that regulation to all online advertising, while providing enough flexibility in the language to cover whatever new technology comes along when cookies soon become obsolete?

Second: there are a lot of really good uses for data collection, and I don't want to throw the baby out with the bath water. But accumulating data on how to better target us for ads doesn't make the Top 10. Believing that big data allows correlation (connections between events happening concurrently) to trump causation (one event causing another) also doesn't make the cut.[33] Nor does misleading people on dating sites, a skeevy tool that I would rank up with the conversion tactics of religious cults. Instead, smart, life-affirming data analysis and positive uses for technology are happening outside the realm of advertising and marketing, and we should look to them for inspiration. One example is the work of Crisis Text Line (CTL), the first twenty-four-hour hotline via text. Because it is text based and data driven, the organization has been able to develop an understanding of what issues teens are facing (cutting, depression, eating disorders) and when crises are most likely to occur (Sunday is the day of the week when they get the most texts about suicide, for example) and uses that to better serve those in need.[34] In another example, ProPublica has a website called "Dollars for Docs" that allows people to search for payments made by pharmaceutical companies to doctors and hospitals in order to suss out underlying biases.[35] As for technology itself, cellphones enable personal freedom for young Saudis by providing a space for debates on Twitter, flirting on Snapchat, and business opportunities on Instagram which would be verboten in the real world.[36] Even the much maligned drone can be used for good, as they have been in the service of transporting medical supplies around the world. This is what the best minds of this generation should be working on, not getting us to click on another ridiculous, time-wasting ad.

Third: individual actions to repel technology are good, but they won't turn the tide. More and more of my friends have begun to take Facebook vacations. This turns out to be quite common. In 2013, Pew Research found that 61 percent of Americans have at "one time or another in the past . . . voluntarily taken a break from using Facebook for a period of several weeks or more."[37] People use the term "digital detox," and we would do well to adopt this strategy. There's also something called conscious computing, some of which is ridiculous because it involves wearing technology to remind you to stop using technology. But some advice is useful, such as only looking at your email at defined times during the day.[38] These types of individual changes in the digital space are fine, but it's like recycling and the environment: every little bit helps, but only collective action, not individual choices, will affect the system and the techno-behemoths.[39] Standard Oil was the innovator of its day, but the Supreme Court saw fit to order its breakup in 1911. We should do no less with Google and Amazon and Apple and Facebook.[40] We might also add Uber and Airbnb to that list. Additional regulations should address issues such as the "right to be forgotten," where search engines are required to delete information that is no longer relevant or is misrepresentative. This policy is the law in Europe.[41] Many have argued that there are free speech issues at play. That's ridiculous. The press in the United States is protected by the First Amendment, but it can still be taken to task for libel. This is no different. Silicon Valley clings to some long forgotten notion that the digital space is open source and free. It is not, and it needs to be regulated like the mature business that it is.

I'm not particularly optimistic when it comes to data and our privacy. That cat's already out of the bag.[42] However, there are things you can do to reduce your online presence or to help be more aware of how and when you are being tracked. I use a number of ad blockers, but I use them for detection rather than for blocking purposes. Seeing 6,697 requests for information about me when I went on Salon.com made me disconcerted enough to think about whether that's a site that I will visit again any time soon. Ghostery and Disconnect are easy to add to your browser, and both help you to see who's tracking you. Ad Detector lets you know when a news article is really an advertisement, which is terrifically useful for spotting content marketing. Tor, TrackMeNot, and Ad Blocker or Ad Blocker Plus were all recommended during my research as tools to get control over the tracking and advertising that we cannot see. Be aware, however, that an increasing number of sites will not allow access to their content if you don't agree to see the ads. In truth, that's not so bad. At least you know what you are looking at.

• • •

If we continue on the current trajectory, confusion, manipulation, and obfuscation will only get worse. Independent media voices will be overtaken by marketers, who will be the only ones left who can afford to pay for content, leaving us with a warped perception of reality. Sites we think of as places of entertainment and personal interaction will have been transformed into shopping malls.

Eliminating digital technologies is unrealistic. Eliminating the corporations that have a chokehold on the system is not. Until that happens, we can become more aware, and through awareness, we can increase our agency. Some of that will come through downsizing our digital life and enabling ad detectors that help us to better understand the content we are engaging with. Some will come from remembering this one thing: your mobile device is a purveyor of advertising—no more, no less—and it exists to keep us in a constant state of buying and selling.

We need to stop thinking about digital technology as something scary and hidden and complex. It's not complex. It's incredibly simple. Every time you go online, you are giving a piece of yourself away. Every time you go online, you are not interacting with a single site, but with a plethora of marketers all trying to sell you something. Every time you go online, you are exposing yourself to content that has no basis in reality.

Real empowerment comes from refusing to be a consumer—of content or of anything else. Maybe instead of pulling out your phone when you step on an elevator, you could start a conversation with the person standing next to you, or maybe you could just be bored.

If we don't do that, we just might advertise ourselves to death. Now you know.

ACKNOWLEDGEMENTS

I thought writing books would get easier. It doesn't. Rather, I have found it is like raising a child: it takes a village.

Fortunately, many people were graciously willing to give of their time and energy to help me put these ideas on paper and for that I am truly grateful. First, I must acknowledge John Oakes at OR Books who valued this work from its nascent stages, and whose enthusiasm for it almost surpasses my own. Thanks as well to others at the press, including Jeanne Thornton and Justin Humphries, who have made this book a reality, and to Jen Overstreet for designing a truly awesome cover. To my scholarly colleagues across a wealth of disciplines who provided information, support, and encouragement: Katie Lofton, Brooke Duffy, Michael Serazio, Lynn Schofield Clark, Michele Rosenthal, Amy Herzog, Susan MacMillan, Melissa Aronczyk, Matthew Quint, and my newfound colleagues Mark Hannah and Chris Hoofnagle. Most of all, to my colleagues and friends—inside the academy and out—who read various drafts or segments of this work and provided thoughtful insights and pushed me to hone my ideas, particulary Matt McAllister, Richard Kedzior, Steven Schreibman, and Barry Lowenthal. Thank you, thank you, thank you.

In addition, I owe a huge debt of gratitude to the many people who helped me better understand the complexities of the current digital marketing environment, including Marykate Byrnes, Carlos Cruz,

Jiayi Ying, Julia Gometz, Jeff Chester, Jeremiah Boehner, Matt Cooper, Paul Josephson, Todd Pruzan, Julie Brill, Mary Engle, Kara Goldberg, Shafqat Islam, John McCarus, Jonathan Allen, the folks at SocialBakers, Jeff Pundyk, Courtney Colwell, Wes Yee, Peter Berman, Scott Ableman, Sarah Evans, Suzanne Hermalyn, Sarah Albert, Collin McCarthy, Craig Heimbuch, and Kevin Stetter. If I missed anyone from this list, please know that it is unintentional and my apologies. I'll pay for cocktails if you come to New York.

Finally, this book would not have had the audience it deserves without the tenacity and generosity of Douglas Rushkoff. Your belief in me has been a blessing. You have seen in me what I had not been able to see in myself and held the mirror up. You are the very embodiment of "mensch." I only hope that one day I will be able to pay back the favor.

Personally, I could not have made it through this process without friends and my "new family." To Karyn Slutsky, Roni Caryn Rabin, and Vashti Bernard, thanks always for your love and support. To David Langer, you push me to be my best and to question, justify, and support my thinking as any good attorney should. I hate that and love it. It is a godsend to have such a smart and caring partner. I'm sorry I made you afraid of the Internet. And, to my daughter, Cayla: even though you didn't get the dedication page this time, this book—like all the others—is all about you.

ENDNOTES

INTRODUCTION

1   S. Adam Brasel & James Gips, "Red Bull 'Gives You Wings' for better or worse: A double-edged impact of brand exposure on consumer performance," in "Nonconscious Processes in Consumer Psychology," special issue, *Journal of Consumer Psychology*, 21 (2011): 57–64.

2   Not every extreme athlete is so lucky. A number of Red Bull athletes have died creating marketing content for the company. See *Red Bull and The Dangers of Red Bull's Extreme Athletic Event Marketing (Full Documentary)*. Accessed September 1, 2015 from https://www.youtube.com/watch?v=6uAC8vQ36Sg.

3   "Top Ad Campaigns of the 21st Century," *Advertising Age*, 2015. Accessed March 1, 2015 from http://adage.com/lp/top15/#stratos.

4   Darren Heitner, "Red Bull Stratos Worth Tens of Millions of Dollars in Global Exposure of the Red Bull Brand," *Forbes*, 2012, http://www.forbes.com/sites/darrenheitner/2012/10/15/red-bull-stratos-worth-tens-of-millions-of-dollars-in-global-exposure-for-the-red-bull-brand/ (accessed January 2, 2015); *Red Bull and The Dangers of Red Bull's Extreme Athletic Event Marketing*.

5   "Top Ad Campaigns of the 21st Century."

6   Kelly D. Martin and N. Craig Smith, "Commercializing Social Interaction: The Ethics of Stealth Marketing," INSEAD Business School Research Paper No. 2008/19/ISIC (February 2008), http://ssrn.com/abstract=1111976; Rob Walker, *Buying In: What We Buy and Who We Are* (New York: Random House, 2010).

7   Melanie Deziel, "Women Inmates: Why the Male Model Doesn't Work," *New York Times*, http://paidpost.nytimes.com/netflix/women-inmates-separate-but-not-equal.htm (accessed January 14, 2015).

8   Maia Szalavitz, "This is Your Brain on Facebook," August 31, 2013, http://healthland.time.com/2013/08/31/this-is-your-brain-on-facebook/ (accessed October 16, 2015).

9   James Meikle, "Twitter is harder to resist than cigarettes and alcohol, study finds," *The Guardian*, February 3, 2012, http://www.theguardian.com/technology/2012/feb/03/twitter-resist-cigarettes-alcohol-study (accessed October 16, 2015).

10   http://www.ragan.com/Main/Articles/48687.aspx. One study claimed that spending ten minutes on Twitter raises oxytocin levels, which is the hormone that reduces anxiety and creates feelings of security. However, it was a limited study and therefore questionable in terms of its findings.

11   "Average daily media use in the United States from 2010 to 2014 (in minutes)," Statista, 2015, http://www.statista.com/statistics/270781/average-daily-media-use-in-the-us/ (accessed June 15, 2015).

12   Douglas Rushkoff, *Program or Be Programmed: Ten Commands for a Digital Age* (New York: OR Books, 2010).

13   Not just anyone can do this. Evan's father owns a video production company, and you can see the high production values in the content.

14   Daniel Roberts, "Yelp's fake review problem," *Fortune*, September 26, 2013, http://fortune.com/2013/09/26/yelps-fake-review-problem/ (accessed March 2, 2015); David Streitfeld, "Give Yourself 5 Stars? Online, It Might Cost You," *New York Times*, http://www.nytimes.com/2013/09/23/technology/give-yourself-4-stars-online-it-might-cost-you.html (accessed October 15, 2015). Additional information about the industry of sponsored mentions online can be found in the following chapter.

15   According to the Boston Consulting Group, "37 percent of younger Millennials said that they feel as if they are 'missing something' if they are not on Facebook or Twitter every day." Christine Barton, Lara Koslow, and Christine Beauchamp, "How Millennials Are Changing the Face of Marketing Forever," *BCG Perspectives*, 2014, https://www.bcgperspectives.com/content/articles/marketing_center_consumer_customer_insight_how_millennials_changing_marketing_forever/?chapter=3 (accessed March 25, 2015); "Roughly half of Millennials say they like to be one of the first to buy new/trendy products," *Marketing to Millennials U.S. Report*, February 2015, Mintel Group Ltd.

16   Roo Ciambriello, "Groupon Posted this Product on Facebook, Then Replied to Everyone Who Made a Sex Joke," *Adweek*, March 27, 2015, http://www.adweek.com/adfreak/groupon-posted-product-facebook-then-replied-everyone-who-made-sex-joke-163737 (accessed April 12, 2015).

17   https://twitter.com/yoginigangsta/status/448587759641694208.

18   Tim Ash, "Smart Remarketing: Psychological Tricks to Bring Back Abandoned Visitors," December 5, 2014, http://marketingland.com/smarter-remarketing-psychological-tricks-abandoned-cart-visitors-108950 (accessed October 15, 2015).

19   Gregory S. McNeal, "Facebook Manipulated User News Feeds to Create Emotional Responses," *Forbes*, June 28, 2014, http://www.forbes.com/sites/gregorymcneal/2014/06/28/facebook-manipulated-user-news-feeds-to-create-emotional-contagion/ (accessed February 17, 2015).

20   For information regarding legal notices and their ramifications, see Cullen Hoback, *Terms and Conditions May Apply* (2013, documentary), and Jacob Silverman, *Terms of Service: Social Media and the Price of Constant Connection* (New York: HarperCollins, 2015).

21 Some companies, such as *Consumer Reports*, use a subscription-only model so as not to be influenced by marketers. These, however, are limited in number.

22 "Reinvention of MTV Will Drive Advertising Growth," Trefis, 2014, http://www.trefis.com/stock/via/articles/244083/reinvention-of-mtv-will-drive-the-networks-advertising-growth/2014-06-23 (accessed February 5, 2015).

23 Anthony Crupi, "Your Favorite Show is Going to Be Canceled . . . And It's All Your Fault," *Advertising Age*, April 3, 2015, http://adage.com/article/special-report-tv-upfront/ad-skipping-modern-viewing-killing-favorite-tv/297897/ (accessed April 4, 2015).

24 "Media, Tech and Big Data" (Center for Communications event, 2015, April 13).

25 Jack Neff, "Brutal TV upfront ahead as buyers, sellers toughen bargaining positions," *Advertising Age*, April 20, 2015, 4.

26 "National ADS, Wired-Cable & Over-The-Air Penetration Trends." Television Bureau of Advertising, 2015, http://www.tvb.org/research/media_comparisons/4729/72512. The NCTA is the cable and telecommunications association tasked with presenting these facts (accessed June 13, 2015). Of late, their website has become opaque and confusing, as if to obscure the industry's decline (see www.NCTA.com).

27 Jack Loechner, "Netflix To Grow Fourfold From 2010 to 2020," *Media Post*, March 5, 2015, http://www.mediapost.com/publications/article/244737/netflix-to-grow-fourfold-from-2010-to-2020.html (accessed March 30, 2015).

28 Alexandra Sifferlin, "Americans Are Watching More Streaming Video and Less Live TV," *Time*, March 11, 2015, http://time.com/3740865/more-americans-streaming-television/ (accessed March 30, 2015).

29 Jack O'Dwyer, "2014, the year in review," *O'Dwyers*. January 2015, 12. Other media spending declined. Print saw an 11 percent decline in advertising revenue and radio dropped more than 3 percent. Ninety-nine magazines folded in 2014 versus fifty-six in 2013. Newspaper revenues are at $20 billion, down from $47 billion in 2007.

30 Alison McCarthy, "US Ad Spending: Q4 2014 Complete Forecast," *eMarketer*, December 19, 2014; Bill Cromwell, "Alas, 2014 wasn't good for advertising," *Media Life*, February 27, 2015, http://www.medialifemagazine.com/alas-2014-wasnt-good-for-advertising/ (accessed March 3, 2015).

31 Sean Corcoran, "Defining Earned, Owned and Paid Media," *Forrester Research*, December 16, 2009, http://blogs.forrester.com/interactive_marketing/2009/12/defining-earned-owned-and-paid-media.html (accessed March 10, 2015).

32 For an in-depth analysis of guerilla marketing tactics, see Michael Serazio, *Your Ad Here: The Cool Sell of Guerrilla Marketing*, (New York: New York University Press, 2013).

33 Megan Garber, "Welcome to the Grumpy Cat Industrial Complex," *The Atlantic*, December 8, 2014, http://www.theatlantic.com/technology/archive/2014/12/Welcome-to-the-Grumpy-Cat-Industrial-Complex/383532/ (accessed March 30, 2015).

CHAPTER 1

1   Jessica Pressler, "Bullsh*t. The art of the sell, a half-century after Mad Men," *New York Magazine*, May 4–17, 2015, 41.

2   Farhad Manjoo, "Ad Blockers and the Nuisance at the Heart of the Modern Web," *New York Times*, August 20, 2015, http://www.nytimes.com/2015/08/20/technology/personaltech/ad-blockers-and-the-nuisance-at-the-heart-of-the-modern-web.html (accessed August 21, 2015).

3   George Stenitzer, "As More Say 'No' to Ads, It's Time to Immunize Content Marketing," April 10, 2015, http://contentmarketinginstitute.com/2015/04/no-ads-content-marketing/ (accessed April 10, 2015).

4   Steve Rose, "As seen on TV: why product placement is bigger than ever," *The Guardian*, June 24, 2014, http://www.theguardian.com/tv-and-radio/2014/jun/24/breaking-bad-tv-product-placement (accessed January 3, 2015); Researchers found that privacy concerns and ad irritation lead to advertising avoidance, though "perceived personalization" decreases ad avoidance. Tae Hyun Baek & Mariko Morimoto, "Stay Away From Me," *Journal Of Advertising*, 41(1), 2012: 59–76.

5   "Advertising: It's Everywhere," *Media Smarts*, http://mediasmarts.ca/marketing-consumerism/advertising-its-everywhere (accessed February 2, 2015).

6   For an overview and history of the insertion of products into content, see: Cristel Antonia Russell, *Advertainment: Fusing Advertising and Entertainment* (Yaffee Center for Persuasive Communication, University of Michigan, 2007), http://www.bus.umich.edu/facultyresearch/researchcenters/centers/yaffe/downloads/advertainment_teaching_materials.pdf (accessed February 3, 2015); Joe Turow, *Niche Envy: Marketing Discrimination in the Digital Age* (Cambridge, MA: MIT Press, 2008); and Kathleen J. Turner, "Insinuating the product into the message: An historical context for product placement," *Journal of Promotion Management* 10.1–2 (2004): 9–14.

7   Jean-Marc Lehu, *Branded entertainment: Product placement & brand strategy in the entertainment business* (London: Kogan Page, 2008).

8   "2014 ARRIS Research Reveals Consumers Are Finding New Ways to Get Entertainment on Their Terms," PR Newswire, May 28, 2014, http://ir.arrisi.com/mobile.view?c=87823&v=203&d=1&id=1935112 (accessed February 3, 2015).

9   To help combat the use of DVRs, broadcast and cable networks are offering more of their content on video on demand (VOD) through cable systems. In this format, people cannot fast forward through the commercials.

10 "PQ Media: Double-Digit Surge in Product Placement Spend in 2014 Fuels Higher Global Branded Entertainment Growth As Media Integrations & Consumer Events Combo for $73.3B," PQ Media, March 13, 2015, http://www.prweb.com/releases/2015/02/prweb12487911.htm (accessed September 12, 2015).

11 Matthew Fleischer, "'House of Cards,' or more like house of product placement?" *Los Angeles Times*, May 3, 2013, http://articles.latimes.com/2013/may/03/entertainment/la-et-st-house-of-cards-netflix-product-placement-20130503 (accessed February 5, 2015).

12 Vildan Jusufović Karışık, "20 Years of Research on Product Placement in Movie, Television and Video Game Media," *Journal Of Economic & Social Studies (JECOSS)*, 4(2), 2014: 253–283.

13 Greg Sterling, "Nielsen: More Time On Internet Through Smartphones Than PCs," February 11, 2014, http://marketingland.com/nielsen-time-accessing-Internet-smartphones-pcs-73683 (accessed February 3, 2015).

14 ARRIS.

15 Lehu, 63; Robert B. Zajonc, "Attitudinal effects of mere exposure." *Journal of Personality and Social Psychology* 9.2p2 (1968): 1.

16 "Movies May Carry a Hidden Pitch," 2014, http://www.thefreelibrary.com/Movies+May+Carry+a+Hidden+Pitch.-a058037919 (accessed September 8, 2015).

17 "Bang & Olufsen Luxury Headphones," KPFR, http://kfpr.tv/product-seeding (accessed June 15, 2015).

18 It was recently announced that theAudience was being sold because movie studios refused to pay to help talent promote their online followings. I suspect the new funding source is likely to be advertisers. Brooks Barnes, "TheAudience, a Social Media Company, Is Sold to Al Ahli Holding Group," *New York Times*, September 15, 2015, http://www.nytimes.com/2015/09/16/business/media/theaudience-a-social-media-company-is-sold-to-al-ahli-holding-group.html (accessed September 17, 2015).

19 Douglas Rushkoff, "Generation Like," *PBS Frontline*, 2015, http://www.pbs.org/wgbh/pages/frontline/media/generation-like/transcript-57/ (accessed March 15, 2015).

20 "It's Child's Play: Advergaming and the Online Marketing of Food to Children," Kaiser Family Foundation, 2013, https://kaiserfamilyfoundation.files.wordpress.com/2013/01/7536.pdf (accessed February 5, 2015); Anna Almendrala, "'Advergames' that Market Food to Children Push Mostly Junk, Study Says," *Huffington Post*, October 9, 2013, http://www.huffingtonpost.com/2013/10/09/advergames-food-children-junk_n_4071978.html (accessed February 5, 2015). For a comprehensive look at advertising practices that specifically target children, see "Advertising to Children and Teens: Current Practices," Common Sense Media, January 28, 2014, https://www.commonsensemedia.org/research/advertising-to-children-and-teens-current-practices (accessed February 5, 2015).

21 Sara M. Grimes, "From advergames to branded worlds: The commercialization of digital gaming," in *Routledge Companion to Advertising and Promotional Culture*, ed. Matthew P. McAllister & Emily West (New York, NY: Routledge, 2013).

22 Graeme Wood, "Anthropologie Inc," *The Atlantic*, 2013, http://www.theatlantic.com/magazine/archive/2013/03/anthropology-inc/309218/ (accessed March 20, 2013); "The Adidas Method," *The Economist*, August 24,2013, http://www.economist.com/news/business/21584002-german-firms-unusual-approach-designing-its-products-adidas-method (accessed February 10, 2015).

23   Online, this is known as netnography and is increasingly being used by researchers. It is, however, beyond the scope of this work. See Robert Kozinets, *Netnography: Doing Ethnographic Research Online* (Thousand Oaks, CA: Sage Publications, 2010).

24   For more on history of branding see Marcel Danesi, *Brands* (London: Routledge, 2006); Douglas B. Holt, *How Brands Become Icons: The Principles of Cultural Branding* (Cambridge, MA: Harvard Business School Press, 2004); Celia Lury, *Brands: The Logos of Global Economy* (London: Routledge, 2004); Jonathan Schroeder and Miriam Slazer-Mörling, ed., *Brand Culture* (London: Routledge, 2006); James Twitchell, *Branded Nation: The Marketing of Megachurch, College Inc., and Museumworld** (New York: Simon & Schuster, 2005); Albrecht Rothacher, ed., *Corporate Cultures and Global Brands* (Hackensack, NJ: World Scientific Publishing, 2004); Gareth Williams, *Branded? Products and Their Personalities* (London: V & A, 2000); Randolph J. Trappey III and Arch G. Woodside, *Brand Choice: Revealing Customers' Unconscious-Automatic and Strategic Thinking Processes* (New York: Palgrave Macmillan, 2005), Robert Goldman and Stephen Papson, *Nike Culture: The Sign of the Swoosh* (Thousand Oaks, CA: Sage Publications, 1988).

25   Louise Story, "Anywhere the Eye Can See, It's Likely to See an Ad," *New York Times*, January 15, 2007.

26   David Court, Dave Elzinga, Susan Mulder, and Ole Jørgen Vetvik, "The Consumer Decision Journey," June 2009, http://www.mckinsey.com/insights/marketing_sales/the_consumer_decision_journey (accessed March 10, 2015).

27   "Changing Channels: Americans View 17 Channels Despite Record Number to Choose From," Nielsen, 2014, http://www.nielsen.com/us/en/insights/news/2014/changing-channels-americans-view-just-17-channels-despite-record-number-to-choose-from.html (accessed Febuary 12, 2015).

28   Psychographics have been falling out of favor, but to date are still in use. See Nielsen's Prizm: http://www.claritas.com/MyBestSegments/Default.jsp?ID=70&pageName=Learn%2BMore&menuOption=learnmore and VALS, the originator of psychographic segmentation: http://www.strategicbusinessinsights.com/vals/ustypes.shtml.

29   Christine Barton, Lara Koslow, and Christine Beauchamp, "How Millennials Are Changing the Face of Marketing Forever," BCG Perspectives, January 15, 2014, https://www.bcgperspectives.com/content/articles/marketing_center_consumer_customer_insight_how_millennials_changing_marketing_forever/ (accessed March 25, 2015).

30   "Millennials Outnumber Baby Boomers and Are Far More Diverse, Census Bureau Reports," US Census Data, June 25, 2015, https://www.census.gov/newsroom/press-releases/2015/cb15-113.html (accessed September 13, 2015).

31   "Post-Demographic Consumerism," Trendwatching, November 2014, http://trendwatching.com/trends/post-demographic-consumerism/ accessed January 3, 2015.

32   For an in-depth analysis of guerilla marketing tactics, see Michael Serazio, *Your Ad Here: The Cool Sell of Guerrilla Marketing* (New York: New York University Press, 2013).

33   "Millennials in Adulthood: Detached from Institutions, Networked with Friends," Pew Research Center, March 7, 2014, http://www.pewsocialtrends.org/files/2014/03/2014-03-07_generations-report-version-for-web.pdf (accessed September 13, 2015).

34   Mary Burns, "The Millennial Generation at Work" (lecture, Kellogg Alumni Career & Professional Development, September 26, 2013).

35   There is an ongoing academic debate about whether digital technologies are improving social relations or making us more atomized and disconnected. Those believing in the positive aspects of this include Lee Rainie and Barry Wellman, *Networked: The New Social Operating System* (Cambridge, MA: MIT Press, 2012); danah boyd, *It's Complicated: The Social Lives of Networked Teens* (New Haven: Yale University Press, 2014); and Henry Jenkins, Sam Ford, and Joshua Green, *Spreadable Media: Creating Value and Meaning in a Networked Culture* (New York: New York University Press, 2013). Less sanguine about this are Clay Sharky, *Here Comes Everybody: The Power of Organizing Without Organizations* (New York: Penguin Press, 2008); Astra Taylor, *The People's Platform: Taking Back Power and Culture in the Digital Age* (New York: Metropolitan Books, 2014); Robert McChesney, *Digital Disconnect: How Capitalism Is Turning the Internet Against Democracy* (New York: The New Press 2013); and Siva Vaidhyanathan, *The Googlization of Everything (And Why We Should Worry)* (Berkeley, CA: University of California Press, 2011).

36   https://www.whitehouse.gov/sites/default/files/docs/millennials_report.pdf.

37   Ali Driesman (presentation, Ypulse Conference, June 17, 2013).

38   MarketingCharts Staff, "Millennials Mostly Talk About Brands Offline. Which Media Drive Their W-O-M Impressions?" September 16, 2014, http://www.marketingcharts.com/traditional/millennials-mostly-talk-about-brands-offline-which-media-drive-their-w-o-m-impressions-46011/ (accessed March 25, 2015).

39   "How Millennials Are Changing the Face of Marketing Forever."

40   Berj Kazanjian and Sandra Lopez (presentation, Ypulse Conference, June 17, 2013).

41   Micah Solomon, "2015 is the Year of the Millennial Customer: 5 Key Traits These 80 Million Consumers Share," *Forbes*, December 24, 2014, http://www.forbes.com/sites/micahsolomon/2014/12/29/5-traits-that-define-the-80-million-millennial-customers-coming-your-way/ (accessed March 11, 2015); Jeff Fromm, Celeste Lindell, and Lainie Decker, "American Millennials: Deciphering the Enigma Generation," 2011, https://www.barkleyus.com/AmericanMillennials.pdf (accessed March 11, 2015).

42   https://www.youtube.com/watch?v=NyG3eXF89Ow.

43   Jeff Fromm, "The Secret to Bud Light's Millennial Marketing Success," Forbes, October 7, 2014, http:// www.forbes.com/sites/jefffromm/2014/10/07/the-secret-to-bud-lights-millennial-marketing-success (accessed March 11, 2015). Doritos had a similar event where they drove Millennials to Las Vegas for a spur of the moment weekend.

44   Budweiser has also gotten into trouble with this campaign, notably when they promoted overdrinking among college-aged women during a time of national attention about rape on college campus.

45   See ad here: https://www.youtube.com/watch?v=R9J9FobsXEQ.

46   See pictures here: http://www.shareacoke.com/#gallery.

47   Mike Esterl, "'Share a Coke' Credited With a Pop in Sales," *Wall Street Journal*, September 25, 2014, http://www.wsj.com/articles/share-a-coke-credited-with-a-pop-in-sales-1411661519 (accessed September 8, 2015).

48   To view the video, go to: https://www.youtube.com/watch?v=XpaOjMXyJGk.

49   James Cooper, "10 Trends Shaping the Future of Branded Content," *Adweek*, March 20, 2015, http://www.adweek.com/news/advertising-branding/10-trends-shaping-future-branded-content-163591 (accessed March 22, 2015).

CHAPTER 2

1   In communications literature, this is the work of Elihu Katz and Paul Lazarsfeld, who advanced the "two-step flow" model of communication. Elihu Katz and Paul Felix Lazarsfeld, *Personal Influence: The Part Played by People in the Flow of Mass Communications* (Piscataway, NJ: Transaction Publishers, 1970). See also Jacqueline Johnson Brown and Peter H. Reingen, "Social Ties and Word-of-Mouth Referral Behavior," *Journal of Consumer Research* 14 (December 1987): 350–362.

2   Serazio, 97. This book provides an extensive history of word of mouth marketing and other guerrilla tactics. For more on the history of PR, see Stewart Ewen, *Captains of Consciousness: Advertising and the Social Roots of the Consumer Culture, 25th Anniversary Edition* (New York: Basic Books, 2001); and *PR! A Social History of Spin* (New York: Basic Books, 1996).

3   The average number of Facebook friends for those between thirty and forty-nine years of age is two hundred; for those under 30, the average is three hundred. See Aaron Smith, "6 New Facts about Facebook," Pew Research Center, February 3, 2014, http://www.pewresearch.org/fact-tank/2014/02/03/6-new-facts-about-facebook/ (accessed March 15, 2015).

4   "9 Big Reasons for Serious WOMM," Lithium (n.d.), http://www.lithium.com/pdfs/infographic/lithium_nine_big_reasons_for_serious_WOMM.pdf (accessed March 16, 2015).

5   Jacques Bughin, Jonathan Doogan, and Ole Jørgen Vetvik, "A New Way to Measure Word-of-mouth Marketing," April 2010, http://www.mckinsey.com/insights/marketing_sales/a_new_way_to_measure_word-of-mouth_ marketing (accessed March 15, 2015).

6   "Why People Share Online," New York Times Consumer Insight Group, November 26, 2012, http://www.slideshare.net/Somatica/why-people-share-online (accessed March 15, 2015).

7   Mikal E. Belicove, "Measuring Offline Vs. Online Word-of-Mouth Marketing," Keller Fay Group, 2012, http://www.kellerfay.com/measuring-offline-vs-online-word-of-mouth-marketing-2/ (accessed September 15, 2015).

8   Techopedia, s.v. "Word-of-Mouth Marketing (WOMM)." http://www.techopedia.com/definition/26413/word-of-mouth-marketing-womm (accessed April 20, 2015).

9   "Under the Influence: Consumer Trust in Advertising," Nielsen, 2013, http://www.nielsen.com/us/en/insights/news/2013/under-the-influence-consumer-trust-in-advertising.html (accessed April 20, 2015). Lithium puts that statistic at 92 percent.

10 Andrew M. Kaikati, and Jack G. Kaikati, "Stealth Marketing: How to reach consumers surreptitiously," *California Management Review* 46 (4) (2004): 6–21.

11 Colin Campbell, Justin Cohen, and Junzhao Ma, "Advertisements Just Aren't Advertisements Anymore: A New Typology for Evolving Forms of Online Advertising," *Journal of Advertising Research* 54 (1) (2014):7–10. Although this article was written in 2014, the terminology is already outdated. For example, the authors had native advertising under unpaid, which is no longer the case. Also, they do not use the term content marketing, which is now the industry standard. I have revised the chart for simplicity and clarity.

12 After I wrote this, information came out that Coke had been sponsoring scientists to downplay the importance of calorie counting on diet while emphasizing exercise. New York Times Editorial Board, "Coke Tries to Sugarcoat the Truth on Calories," *New York Times*, August 14, 2015, http://www.nytimes.com/2015/08/14/opinion/coke-tries-to-sugarcoat-the-truth-on-calories.html (accessed August 15, 2015).

13 "Medaling In Media: P&G Proud Sponsor of Mom," Advertising Education Foundation (n.d.), http://www.aef.com/pdf/jay_chiat/2013/p&g_olympic_proudsponsor.pdf (accessed April 20, 2015).

14 Campbell et al. make a distinction between social video and viral video in their version of this chart, suggesting that the success of social video is based on "consumer engagement" while viral video success is based on "pass along." From the audience's perspective, that distinction is meaningless.

15 For information on the origins of the Ice Bucket Challenge, see Alexandra Sifferlin, "Here's How the ALS Ice Bucket Challenge Actually Started," *Time*, August 18, 2014, http://time.com/3136507/als-ice-bucket-challenge-started/ (accessed April 23, 2015).

16 Melissa Coker, "How We Made A Viral Video Of Strangers Kissing And Increased Sales By Nearly 14,000%," *Business Insider*, March 24, 2014, http://www.businessinsider.com/wren-first-kiss-viral-success-2014-3 (accessed January 27, 2016).

17 Suzanne Vranica, "Best and Worst Ads: Marketers Pitched in New Places in 2014; But Array of Venues Increased Clutter Facing Consumers," *Wall Street Journal*, December 19, 2014.

18 "Mobile Ad Spend to Top $100 Billion Worldwide in 2016, 51% of Digital Market," April 2, 2015, http://www.emarketer.com/Article/Mobile-Ad-Spend-Top-100-Billion-Worldwide-2016-51-of-Digital-Market/1012299 (accessed October 17, 2015).

19 Zuberance, "Brand Advocate Data & Insights," January 2011, www.gleanster.com (accessed September 17, 2015).

20 Definitional confusion exists among these terms as well. A major consumer behavior textbook I reviewed (Frank Kardes, Maria Cronley and Thomas Cline, *Consumer Behavior, second edition* [South-Western College Pub, 2014]), for example, states that buzz marketing, viral marketing, stealth, and grassroots marketing are interchangeable terms. While that may be true in practice, there are important distinctions among them. See "Word of Mouth 101: Types," 2008, https://digitalvibes.wordpress.com/tag/womma/ (accessed September 17, 2015).

21 "Word of Mouth 101: Types."

22 Liat Kornowski, "Celebrity Sponsored Tweets: What The Stars Get Paid for Advertising in 140 Characters," The Huffington Post, May 5, 2013, http://www.huffingtonpost.com/2013/05/30/celebrity-sponsored-tweets_n_3360562.html (accessed April 21, 2015).

23 Angela Doland, "Chinese Social Media Marketing Explained, Through One Super-Viral Selfie," *Advertising Age*, June 15, 2015, http://adage.com/article/digital/chinese-social-media-marketing-explained-super-viral-selfie/298969/ (accessed September 17, 2015).

24 Shareen Pathak, "These Vine Celebs Made $10,000 in Six Seconds on Their Mobile Phones," *Advertising Age*, August 26, 2013, http://adage.com/article/digital/vine-users-team-brands-talent-agency/243773/ (accessed April 25, 2015); Kurt Wagner, "Stealth Marketing: How Brands Infiltrate Vine With Product Placement," July 22, 2014, http://mashable.com/2014/07/22/sneaky-vine-ads/#Lrxx6cfbbGqt (accessed October 13, 2015).

25 Per the FTC, "Required disclosures must be clear and conspicuous." Federal Trade Commission Guidelines, ".com Disclosures: How to Make Effective Disclosures in Digital Advertising," 2013, https://www.ftc.gov/tips-advice/business-center/guidance/com-disclosures-how-make-effective-disclosures-digital (accessed April 21, 2015).

26 See http://www.amazon.com/gp/vine/help.

27 See video here: https://www.youtube.com/watch?list=PLrA2uPvinhdVgv2NxLEH-XFWmkyOiMvPy&v=ahs_hPeHNBQ.

28 They can be viewed here: https://www.youtube.com/watch?v=kn2iOwlMNhk&index=2&list=PLrA2uPvinhdVgv2NxLEH-XFWmkyOiMvPy.

29 Lizzie Widdicombe, "Perfect Pitching," *The New Yorker*, September 21, 2015, http://www.newyorker.com/magazine/2015/09/21/perfect-pitching (accessed October 17, 2015).

30 Grateful to David Kamerer of Loyola for this work. See "Plug Away: Disclosure of material connections in social media channels," http://www.slideshare.net/dkresearch. See also Paul Moura, "Harmless Tweets or Deceptive Speech? The Problem of Stealth Marketing in New Media, the Dual Regulatory Roles of the FTC, and the market for Social Capital," *Whittier Law Review* 33, no. 3 (2012): 613–650.

31 Christine Hauseraug, "F.D.A. Warns Company Over Kardashian Instagram Marketing," *New York Times*, August 12, 2015, http://www.nytimes.com/2015/08/13/health/fda-warns-company-over-kardashian-instagram-marketing.html?_r=1 (accessed August 24, 2015).

32 "'The Green Party offered to pay me for positive tweets,'" El Daily Post, June 9, 2015, http://www.eldailypost.com/news/2015/06/the-green-party-offered-to-pay-me-for-positive-tweets/ (accessed June 11, 2015).

33 Neither company is part of the advertising conglomerate Dentsu.

34 "The paper finds that teenagers like being buzz agents, they view this role as a job, they usually conceal the fact that they are buzz agents, and they generally see no ethical dilemma in not revealing their status." Roshan D. Ahuja, Tara Anne Michels, Mary Mazzei Walker, and Mike Weissbuch, "Teen perceptions of disclosure in buzz marketing," Journal of Consumer Marketing 24, no. 3 (2007): 151–159.

35 Melanie Wells, "Kid Nabbing," February 2, 2004, quoted in "P&G's Tremor: Reinventing Marketing by Word of Mouth," http://ibscdc.org/Free%20 Cases/P&G%E2%80%99s%20Tremor%20%E2%80%93%20Reinventing%20 Marketing%20by%20pl.htm (accessed April 30, 2015).

36 Ibid.

37 Interview with the author, Paulette Yarosz, vice president of creative services at Vocalpoint, May 1, 2015.

38 Jack Neff, "P&G's Buzz-Building Networks Thrive in Age of Social Media: How BzzAgent, Tremor Stay Top of Mind Despite Rise of Twitter, Facebook," Advertising Age, October 10, 2010, http://adage.com/article/digital/p-g-s-buzz-building-networks-thrive-age-social-media/230280/.

39 Jason Del Ray, "Facebook Starts Turning Messenger into a Shopping Platform," Re/Code, March 25, 2015, http://recode.net/2015/03/25/facebook-starts-turning-messenger-into-a-shopping-platform/ (accessed June 30, 2015).

40 Victoria Taylor, "Lupita Nyong'o's Clarins lip balm from the Oscars sells out, becomes a social media sensation," Daily News, March 4, 2014, http://www.nydailynews.com/life-style/oscars-2014-lupita-nyong-lip-balm-viral-article-1.1710752 (accessed April 30, 2015).

41 Pierre Berthon, Leyland Pitt, and Colin Campbell, "Ad Lib: When Customers Create the Ad," California Management Review 50, no. 4 (2008): 6–30.

42 Campbell et al.

43 Bernard Cova and Stefano Pace, "Brand community of convenience products: new forms of customer empowerment—the case 'my Nutella The Community'," European Journal of Marketing 40 (9/10) (2006): 1087–1105.

44 Alan Cassinelli, "10 Great Examples of User Generated Content Campaigns," Postano, April 21, 2014, http://www.postano.com/blog/10-great-examples-of-user-generated-content-campaigns (accessed April 30, 2015).

45 Brooke Erin Duffy, "Empowerment through Endorsement? Polysemic Meaning in Dove's User-Generated Advertising," Communication, Culture & Critique 3 (2010): 26–43. Duffy notes that "much of the discourse on user-generated content (UGC) situates it within a framework of either exploitation or empowerment," which reflects utopian/dystopian arguments about the Internet generally. For the consumer empowerment argument, see Henry Jenkins, Convergence Culture: Where Old and New Media Collide (New York: New York University

Press, 2006); and Henry Jenkins, Sam Ford, and Joshua Green, *Spreadable media: Creating value and meaning in a networked culture* (New York: New York University Press, 2013). For exploitation critiques, see Tiziana Terranova, "Free Labor: Producing Culture for the Digital Economy," *Social Text* 63, no. 18 (2000): 33–58. On appropriating consumer labor in helping to sell branded products, see Adam Arvidsson, "Brands: A Critical Perspective," *Journal of Consumer Culture* 5, no. 2 (2005): 235–58.

46   Gemma Crave, "Writing for Social Media" (slide presentation for social@Ogilvy, 2013), http://www.slideshare.net/Gemsie/why-people-share-copywriting-for-social-nov-2013 (accessed April 30, 2015).

47   Rosanna E. Guadagno, Daniel M. Rempala, Shannon Murphy, and Bradley M. Okdie, "What makes a video go viral? An analysis of emotional contagion and Internet memes," *Comput. Hum. Behav.* 29, no. 6 (2013): 2312–2319, http://dx.doi.org/10.1016/j.chb.2013.04.016.

48   For an academic analysis of how we represent ourselves online and in particular why we share, see Russell W. Belk, "Extended Self in a Digital World," *Journal of Consumer Research*, October 2013, http://www.msi.org/uploads/files/ATreview13-Belk.pdf (accessed October 27, 2015).

49   David R. Brake, *Sharing Our Lives Online: Risks and Exposure in Social Media* (Palgrave, 2014), 131.

50   "6 New Facts About Facebook."

51   Jessica L. Lakin, Valerie E. Jefferis, Clara Michelle Cheng, and Tanya L. Chartrand, "The Chameleon Effect as Social Glue: Evidence for the Evolutionary Significance of Nonconscious Mimicry," *Journal of Nonverbal Behavior* 27, no. 3 (2003): 145–162.

52   Sheldon Stryker and Richard T. Serpe, "Commitment, Identity Salience, and Role Behavior: A Theory and Research Example," in *Personality, Roles, and Social Behavior*, William Ickes and Eric S. Knowles, ed. (New York: SpringerVerlag, 1982), 199–218.

53   Fred Turner, *From Counterculture to Cyberculture: Stewart Brand, the Whole Earth Network, and the Rise of Digital Utopianism* (Chicago: University of Chicago Press, 2006). See also Astra Taylor, *The People's Platform: Taking Back Power and Culture in The Digital Age* (New York: Metropolitan Books, 2014); and Jacob Silverman, *Terms of Service: Social Media and the Price of Constant Connection* (New York: HarperCollins, 2015).

54   Andrea Shea, "Facebook Envy: How The Social Network Affects Our Self-Esteem," WBUR, 2013, http://www.wbur.org/2013/02/20/facebook-perfection (accessed April 25, 2015).

55   Kurt Opsahl, "Facebook's Eroding Privacy Policy: A Timeline," Electronic Frontier Foundation, April 28, 2010, https://www.eff.org/deeplinks/2010/04/facebook-timeline (accessed April 25, 2015).

56   "Facebook Principles," https://www.facebook.com/principles.php.

57   *New York Times*, April 24, 2015, page B7.

58 Vindu Goel, "Facebook's Growth Slows Slightly, but Mobile Shift Intensifies," *New York Times*, April 22, 2015, http://www.nytimes.com/2015/04/23/technology/facebook-ql-earnings.html (accessed April 24, 2015).

59 Nicholas John, "Sharing and Web 2.0: The emergence of a keyword," *New Media and Society* 15, no. 2 (2013): 167–182.

60 "Keeping count of sharing across the web," Facebook, 2009, http://blog.facebook.com/blog.php?topic_id=167544352390.

CHAPTER 3

1 See a pdf of the ad here: http://poynter.org/extra/AtlanticScientology.pdf.

2 For an in-depth scholarly analysis of native advertising, see Matt Carlson, "When news sites go native: Redefining the advertising–editorial divide in response to native advertising," *Journalism* 16, no. 7 (2015): 849–865.

3 Julie Moos, "The Atlantic publishes then pulls sponsored content from Church of Scientology," *Poynter*, January 15, 2013, http://www.poynter.org/news/mediawire/200593/the-atlantic-pulls-sponsored-content-from-church-of-scientology/ (accessed May 3, 2015).

4 This link provides a snapshot of the original page, which includes reader comments: http://freze.it/talscientology.

5 Statement from the Atlantic, https://www.magnetmail.net/actions/email_web_version.cfm?recipient_id=699462885&message_id=2459857&user_id=NJG_Atlan&group_id=0&jobid=12656579.

6 Access this ad here: http://paidpost.nytimes.com/shell/cities-energized.html.

7 Dating apps are popular for this kind of promotion because they reach the coveted Millennial demographic. Tinder is predominantly (83 percent) made up of sixteen to thirty-four year olds, and they have promoted everything from Budweiser to pizza to movies since April 2015. Twentieth Century Fox promoted the movie *Spy*, for example, by putting up pictures of the movie's star, Melissa McCarthy. People could swipe right for a chance to get tickets to free advance screenings. The promotion garnered 17 million social impressions. Similarly, Match.com promoted Mariah Carey's album, while Madonna launched her album *Rebel Heart* on Grindr. See Shepherd Laughlin, "Cupid Goes Native," JWT Intelligence, June 15, 2015, https://www.jwtintelligence.com/2015/06/cupid-goes-native/ (accessed September 11, 2015).

8 Steven Perlberg, "CNN Unveils New Studio to Produce Content for Advertisers," *Wall Street Journal*, June 8, 2015, http://blogs.wsj.com/cmo/2015/06/08/cnn-courageous-branded-content-studio/ (accessed June 10, 2015).

9 CNN Commercial Case Studies, http://commercial.cnn.com/case-studies (accessed October 18, 2015).

10 Perlberg.

11 *The rise of native advertising in the news media* (Al Jazeera, April 12, 2015), flash video, http://www.aljazeera.com/programmes/listeningpost/2015/04/native-advertising-trust-sale-150411130613310.html (accessed June 10, 2015).

12   Erik Wemple, "The Atlantic's Scientology problem, start to finish," *Washington Post*, January 15, 2013, http://www.washingtonpost.com/blogs/erik-wemple/wp/2013/01/15/the-atlantics-scientology-problem-start-to-finish/ (accessed June 10, 2015); Josh Sternberg, "The Atlantic Tries Native Ads," *Digiday*, September 25, 2012, http://digiday.com/publishers/the-atlantic-tries-native-ads/ (accessed June 10, 2015).

13   "How Native Ad Campaigns Are Shaping Up: Definitions of native advertising still vary," eMarketer, July 22, 2013, http://www.emarketer.com/Article/How-Native-Ad-Campaigns-Shaping-Up/1010064 (accessed June 10, 2015).

14   "Going Native," *Creative Review* 34, no. 12 (2014): 44–48.

15   "Blurred Lines," *NZ Marketing*, http://stoppress.co.nz/features/blurred-lines (accessed May 10, 2015).

16   Tobi Elkin, "Native Advertising Update: Marketers See Healthy Spending Growth in 2015," *eMarketer*, November 20, 2014.

17   Mark Hoelzel, "Spending on native advertising is soaring as marketers and digital media publishers realize the benefits," *Business Insider*, May 20, 2015, http://www.businessinsider.com/spending-on-native-ads-will-soar-as-publishers-and-advertisers-take-notice-2014-11 (accessed May 21, 2015).

18   Ian Batten, "The Rise of Native Advertising: Usage, Stats & Examples," SearchStar, February 2, 2014, http://www.search-star.co.uk/blog/the-rise-of-native-advertising-usage-stats-examples/ (accessed May 21, 2015).

19   Giselle Abramovich, "15 Mind-Blowing Stats About Native Advertising," *CMO* (n.d.), http://www.cmo.com/articles/2013/10/21/15_Stats_Native_Advertising.html (accessed September 11, 2015).

20   Jack Loechner, "Where's The State of Native Advertising?" November 19, 2013, http://www.mediapost.com/publications/article/213640/wheres-the-state-of-native-advertising .html?print (accessed May 11, 2015).

21   See ad at: https://www.youtube.com/watch?v=djo6i3J7CoO.

22   Stephanie Georgopulos, "We've Disguised this Newcastle Ad as an Article to Get You to Click It," Studio@Gawker, January 28, 2014, http://studioatgawker.kinja.com/weve-disguised-this-newcastle-ad-as-an-article-to-get-1508339241 (accessed May 11, 2015). For additional examples of native advertising, see http://blog.hubspot.com/marketing/native-advertising-examples; http://www.wordstream.com/blog/ws/2014/07/07/native-advertising-examples.

23   Grant McCracken, "TV Got Better," Wired (n.d.), http://www.wired.com/partners/netflix/ (accessed October 19, 2015).

24   See full descriptions of IAB formats at http://www.iab.net/nativeadvertising.

25   To see advertising case studies for these sites, see http://www.voxmedia.com/vox-advertising (Vox), http://media.salon.com/2014/05/MediaKit5.7.14.pdf (Salon), and http://innovate.slate.com/#/showcase and http://innovate.slate.com/#/custom (Slate).

26   Kunal Gupta, "So we all know what native ads are, right? Maybe not," *Venture Beat*, January 23, 2014, http://venturebeat.com/2014/01/23/so-we-all-know-what-native-ads-are-right-maybe-not/ (accessed May 15, 2015).

27   "*Forbes* BrandVoice," from http://www.brandvoice.com/ (accessed September 12, 2015).

28   Michael Sebastian, "Media Companies Take Pains to Avoid Scarlet 'A' for 'Ad,'" *Advertising Age*, June 15, 2015, 8.

29   Martin Beck, "How Twitter's Changing Promoted Tweets to Look More Like Regular Ones," Marketingland, April 29, 2015, http://marketingland.com/new-twitter-makes-promoted-tweets-less-obvious-127072 (accessed April 30, 2015). The company claims that the revised promotional cue is intended to make the "Promoted Tweets" blend in more easily with the rest of the Twitter feed. Its motivation for this may involve Twitter's sinking revenues and plummeting stock price, which fell 25 percent after first quarter 2015 sales numbers were announced. While the site had reached 302 million monthly active users, a change in the advertising formats Twitter offered led to reduced spending. Twitter offers direct-response ads, which advertisers only pay for if consumers engage with the marketer in some way: for example, by installing an app or clicking to a website. Those ads have not been proven to drive results. See Jack Marshall and Yoree Koh, "The problem with twitter ads," *Wall Street Journal*, April 30, 2015, http://www.wsj.com/articles/the-problem-with-twitter-adsthe-problem-with-twitter-ads-1430438275 (accessed September 12, 2015). We can only assume that Twitter is attempting to improve its clickthrough rate by further disguising promoted content.

30   Dan Shewan, "Native Advertising Examples: 5 of the Best (and Worst)," The Wordstream Blog, July 7, 2014, http://www.wordstream.com/blog/ws/2014/07/07/native-advertising-examples (accessed May 10, 2015).

31   Federal Trade Commission, "Native Advertising: A Guide for Businesses," 2015, https://www.ftc.gov/tips-advice/business-center/guidance/native-advertising-guide-businesses (accessed January 29, 2016).

32   Jeremy Barr, "The IAB Is 'Concerned' About The FTC's New Native Advertising Rules, but Publishers Play It Cool," *Advertising Age*, December 29, 2015, http://adage.com/article/media/iab-concerned-ftc-s-native-advertising-rules/301948/ (accessed January 29, 2016).

33   Martin Goefron, "BuzzFeed's Editorial Fumble Doesn't Have to Be a Buzzkill for Native Advertising," *Advertising Age*, May 7, 2015, http://adage.com/article/digitalnext/buzzfeed-s-editorial-fumble-a-buzzkill/298386/ (accessed September 17, 2015).

34   Anastasia Dyakovskaya, "BuzzFeed CEO Jonah Peretti: Creating a Media Empire with a 'Marriage Between Data and Creativity,'" Newscred, 2014, http://blog.newscred.com/buzzfeed-ceo-jonah-peretti-creating-a-media-empire-with-a-marriage-between-data-and-creativity/ (accessed September 17, 2015).

35   http://blog.newscred.com/buzzfeed-ceo-jonah-peretti-creating-a-media-empire-with-a-marriage-between-data-and-creativity/.

36   Stephanie N. Berberick, and Matthew P. McAllister, "You got Piper: Online quizzes as viral, consumption-based identities," (presentation at the International Communication Association, San Juan, Puerto Rico, May 2015).

37   David Carr, "Significant and Silly at BuzzFeed," *New York Times*, February 5, 2012, http://www.nytimes.com/2012/02/06/business/media/at-buzzfeed-the-significant-and-the-silly.html (accessed May 20, 2015).

38   Jacob Silverman, *Terms of Service: Social Media and the Price of Constant Connection* (New York: HarperCollins, 2015).

39   Alyson Shontell, "Inside Buzzfeed: The Story of How Jonah Peretti Built the Web's Most Beloved New Media Brand," *Business Insider*, December 11, 2012, http://www.businessinsider.com/buzzfeed-jonah-peretti-interview-2012-12?page=2 (accessed May 10, 2015).

40   Andy Goldberg, "Buzzfeed's website: Is it the enemy or the future?" *Business Recorder*, 2013, October 6, 2013, http://www.brecorder.com/pages/article/1238552/2013-10-06/buzzfeeds-website:-is-it-the-enemy-or-the-future.html (accessed September 12, 2015).

41   Jennifer Yeh, "Bright Lights, Bright-Line: Toward Separation and Reformation of the Transformative Use Analysis," *Cardozo Arts & Ent LJ* 32 (2014): 995–1027.

42   Peretti said in an interview on Bloomberg that 76 of the top 100 brands have advertised with BuzzFeed, and a perusal of their website suggests that this is the case. The company charges a modest $8 to $10 CPM according to *Ad Age*, but it generates additional revenue from advertisers by creating their advertising for them—an option that is only available "once they reach a certain spending threshold." See Michael Sebastian, "Reality Check: Sizing Up VC-Backed Publishers' Prospects," *Advertising Age*, February 10, 2015, http://adage.com/article/media/private-equity-plowing-money-buzzfeed-vox/297034/ (accessed September 17, 2015).

43   Michelle Castillo, "For Brands, These Are the Do's and Don'ts of Working With BuzzFeed," *Adweek*, October 7, 2014, http://www.adweek.com/news/technology/hey-brands-here-are-dos-and-donts-working-buzzfeed-160617 (accessed May 15, 2015).

44   "New Kids on the Block," CIMA, 2014, http://myjobs.cimaglobal.com/article/new-kid-on-the-block/ (accessed January 27, 2016).

45   Michelle Castillo, "After Removing Article Critical of Dove, BuzzFeed Says It Wants to Avoid Publishing 'Hot Takes,'" *Adweek*, April 10, 2015, http://www.adweek.com/news/press/after-removing-article-critical-dove-buzzfeed-says-it-wants-avoid-publishing-hot-takes-164001 (accessed May 10, 2015); Benjamin Mullin, "BuzzFeed yanks post critical of Dove ad," *Poynter*, April 10, 2015, http://www.poynter.org/news/mediawire/334591/buzzfeed-yanks-post-critical-of-dove-ad/ (accessed May 10, 2015).

46   Mark Duffy, "Top 10 Best Ever WTF OMG Reasons Buzzfeed Fired Me, LOL!" *Gawker*, November 25, 2013, http://gawker.com/top-10-best-ever-wtf-omg-reasons-buzzfeed-fired-me-lol-1471409834 (accessed May 10, 2015). For additional BuzzFeed missteps, see Goefron (2015) and Krishnadev Calamur, "BuzzFeed Deleted Stories After Complaints from Advertisers," NPR, April 20, 2015, http://www.npr.org/sections/thetwo-way/2015/04/20/401005384/buzzfeed-deleted-stories-after-complaints-from-advertisers (accessed September 17, 2015).

47   CIMA.

48   Ryan Kim, "BuzzFeed's Peretti: Design engaging ads made for sharing," *GigaOm*, April 17, 2012, https://gigaom.com/2012/04/17/buzzfeeds-peretti-design-engaging-ads-made-for-sharing/ (accessed May 10, 2015).

49   Mike Shield, "Thrillist Takes Native Advertising to the Moon with GE-Produced Sneaker," *Wall Street Journal*, August 11, 2014, http://blogs.wsj.com/cmo/2014/08/11/thrillist-takes-native-advertising-to-the-moon-with-ge-produced-sneaker/ (accessed September 12, 2015).

50   Personal interview with the author, April 29, 2015. See also Michael Sebastian, "Reality Check: Sizing Up VC-Backed Publishers' Prospects," *Advertising Age*, February 10, 2015, http://adage.com/article/media/private-equity-plowing-money-buzzfeed-vox/297034/ (Accessed September 17, 2015).

51   "The Post launches new native ad feature: BrandConnect Perspective," press release, *Washington Post*, November 19, 2014, http://www.washingtonpost.com/pr/wp/2014/11/19/the-post-launches-new-native-ad-feature-brandconnect-perspective/ (accessed March 10, 2015).

52   About WP Brand Connect: http://www.washingtonpost.com/sf/brand-connect/.

53   Lucia Moses, "The Washington Post's Native Ads Get Editorial Treatment," *Adweek*, March 3, 2014, http://www.adweek.com/news/press/washington-posts-native-ads-get-editorial-treatment-156048 (accessed May 10, 2015).

54   See GE's content hub as an example: http://online.wsj.com/ad/bizruption.html.

55   Available at http://paidpost.nytimes.com/netflix/women-inmates-separate-but-not-equal.html#.VRltlPnF-So.

56   Lucia Moses, "Inside T Brand Studio, The New York Times' native ad unit," Digiday, December 2, 2014, http://digiday.com/publishers/new-york-times-native-ad-unit/, (accessed May 20, 2015).

57   Joe Pompeo, "Times to Staff Up Content Studio," Politico, January 16, 2015, http://www.capitalnewyork.com/article/media/2015/01/8560278/emtimesem-staff-content-studio (accessed May 20, 2015).

58   New York Times Idea Lab website is here: http://www.nytimes.com/ads/idealab/#projects/PaidPost. This site is broken up into Advertising Innovations, which is the native advertising described in the text, and Newsroom Innovations. This latter included a quiz about the Westminster Dog Show, for example. There is no explanation for the purpose of the Newsroom Innovations, and the last example is from February 2015, which leads me to believe that it has been folded into the Advertising Innovation area.

59   *The rise of native advertising in the news media.*

60   "Research from The New York Times T Brand Studio and Chartbeat Shows That Branded Content Can Generate Significant Audience Engagement," *New York Times* press release, March 10, 2015, http://investors.nytco.com/press/press-releases/press-release-details/2015/Research-from-The-New-York-Times-T-Brand-Studio-and-Chartbeat-Shows-That-Branded-Content-Can-Generate-Significant-Audience-Engagement/default.aspx (accessed June 10, 2015).

61   Tessa Wegert, "Why The New York Times' Sponsored Content Is Going Toe-to-Toe with Its Editorial," Contently, March 27, 2015, http://contently.com/strategist/2015/03/27/why-the-new-york-times-sponsored-content-is-going-toe-to-toe-with-its-editorial/ (accessed June 12, 2015).

62   Dominic Ponsford, "*The Guardian* signs seven-figure deal to build on 'shared values' and provide branded content for Unilever," PressGazette, February 13, 2014, http://www.pressgazette.co.uk/guardian-signs-seven-figure-deal-build-shared-values-provide-branded-content-unilever (accessed September 12, 2015). One of the main initiatives under this agreement is an area on *The Guardian* site called the Unilever Partner Zone. The page looks like almost any page on the site, with the newspaper's masthead running along the top. It is covered with pictures over headlines, again making it look like editorial content. The U.S. page has no indication that it is sponsored content until you click a link to an "article" page. For example, if you click on the headline "Low flow showers and more water saving tips," it will take you to a story about saving water and in the left column it states "Live Better—Unilever Partner Zone." Accessed January 27, 2016 from http://www.theguardian.com/live-better-unilever/low-flow-showers-and-more-water-saving-tips.

63   Peter Oborne's resignation letter: https://opendemocracy.net/ourkingdom/peter-oborne/why-i-have-resigned-from-telegraph.

64   Michael Sebastian, "New York Times Tones Down Labeling on Its Sponsored Posts," *Advertising Age*, August 5, 2014, http://adage.com/article/media/york-times-shrinks-labeling-natives-ads/294473/ (accessed June 15, 2015).

65   Tessa Wegert, "Why The New York Times' Sponsored Content Is Going Toe-to-Toe With Its Editorial."

66   Jeanine Poggi, "What NBCU's Investments in BuzzFeed, Vox Could Mean for Advertising," *Advertising Age*, August 18, 2015, http://adage.com/article/media/nbcu-s-investments-buzzfeed-vox-advertising/300005/7j (accessed October 20, 2015).

67   Lizzie Widdicombe, "The Bad-Boy Brand," *The New Yorker*, April 8, 2013, http://www.newyorker.com/magazine/2013/04/08/the-bad-boy-brand (accessed June 25, 2015).

68   Vice advertising case studies: http://company.vice.com/en_us/casestudies, see also FastCompany's "Brilliant Minds" campaign for Virgin Atlantic: http://www.fastcompany.com/section/brilliant-minds.

69   As we saw with Net-a-Porter, fashion is a major segment in content marketing. See also Hilary Milnes, "The Asos approach to native content: authenticity," Digiday, August 5, 2015, http://digiday.com/brands/asos-commerce-content/ (accessed August 24, 2015).

70   Jordan Crook, "Refinery29 Raises $50 Million in Series D," Techcrunch, April 27, 2015, http://techcrunch.com/2015/04/27/refinery29-raises-50-million-in-series-d/ (accessed June 20, 2015).

71   Ann Gynn, "Content Marketing Experts Reveal Which Brands Are Pushing the Envelope," Content Marketing Institute, July 17, 2015, http://contentmarketinginstitute.com/2015/07/experts-brands-pushing-envelope/

72   About Refinery29: http://www.corporate.r29.com/about/.

73   Steven Perlberg, "Conde Nast Unveils Branded Content Shop Powered By Editors," CMO Today, January 26, 2015, http://blogs.wsj.com/cmo/2015/01/26/23-stories-conde-nast-branded-content/ (accessed June 20, 2015). Hearst Publications also has an in-house advertising agency, which is called iCrossing. They claim to be independent from the parent company. It remains to be seen if this is true, as this agency is quite new.

74   Kylie Jane Wakefield, "What Content Marketers Can Learn from Journalists," NewsCred blog (n.d.), http://blog.newscred.com/article/what-content-marketers-can-learn-from-journalists/1cd109f4d6629ab3663c495072176d09 (accessed September 12, 2015).

75   Josh Sternberg, "The Atlantic Tries Native Ads," Digiday, September 25, 2012, http://digiday.com/publishers/the-atlantic-tries-native-ads/ (accessed June 10, 2015).

76   Josh Sternberg, "Publishers Must Think Like Agencies," Digiday, January 13, 2013, http://digiday.com/publishers/why-publishers-need-to-think-like-agencies/ (accessed June 14, 2015).

77   *Time CEO Ripp: We're Not Just a Magazine Company* (Bloomberg), flash video, http://www.bloomberg.com/news/videos/b/d3786419-2d0b-4e73-afb1-b31d53149926.

78   Gabriel Sherman, "The Matter of Time: What should a magazine company be now? The most storied one in America has to come up with an answer fast," *New York Magazine*, August 24, 2014, http://nymag.com/news/features/time-inc-magazines-2014-8/ (accessed September 15, 2015).

79   Association of National Advertisers, "ANA Study Reveals Marketers Are Increasing Spend on Native Advertising but Disclosure, Ethics and Measurement Are Key Issues," press release, January 29, 2015, https://www.ana.net/content/show/id/33530 (accessed June 14, 2015).

80   "Going Native."

81   Demian Farnworth, "12 Examples of Native Ads (And Why They Work)," Copyblogger (n.d.), http://www.copyblogger.com/examples-of-native-ads/ (accessed June 14, 2015).

82   Joshua Benton, "Like it or not, native advertising is squarely inside the big news tent," Nieman Foundation, September 15, 2014, http://www.niemanlab.org/2014/09/like-it-or-not-native-advertising-is-squarely-inside-the-big-news-tent/ (accessed June 24, 2015).

83   Chris Jay Hoofnagle, Eduard Meleshinsky, "Native Advertising and Endorsement: Schema, Source-Based Misleadingness, and Omission of Material Facts," *Technology Science*, December 15, 2015, http://techscience.org/a/2015121503.

84   Amar C. Bakshi, "Why and How to Regulate Native Advertising in Online News Publications," *University of Baltimore Journal of Media Law & Ethics* 4 (2014): 4.

85   Bartosz W. Wojkynski & Nathaniel J. Evans, "Going Native: Effects of Disclosure Position and Language on the Recognition and Evaluation of Online Native Advertising," *Journal of Advertising* (2015), http://www.tandfonline.com/doi/full/10.1080/00913367.2015.1115380 (accessed January 29, 2016).

86   Anne Pilon, "Native Advertising Survey: Very Few Know of Native Advertising Concept," AYTM (Ask Your Target Market), May 22, 2013, http://aytm.com/blog/daily-survey-results/native-advertising-survey/ (accessed June 24, 2015).

87   Giselle Abramovich, "15 Mind-Blowing Stats About Native Advertising," *CMO* (n.d.), http://www.cmo.com/articles/2013/10/21/15_Stats_Native_Advertising.html (accessed September 11, 2015); "Consumers Feel Duped by Sponsored Video Ads, Facebook Sponsored Stories." Marketing Charts, November 7, 2012, http://www.marketingcharts.com/television/consumers-feel-duped-by-sponsored-video-ads-facebook-sponsored-stories-24601/ (accessed February 10, 2015).

CHAPTER 4

1   Interview with author, Matt Cooper, CEO of Visually.

2   OK Go came to fame with a video consisting of them dancing on treadmills. They have produced a number of music videos with sponsors including Samsung, Google, State Farm, and Chevrolet.

3   The Content Marketing Institute limits this term to content that only appears on the marketer's website. My analysis suggests that this is too limited, because it would not include things like the music video, which is most decidedly content marketing, even if it doesn't appear on Honda's website.

4   Interview with the author, June 1, 2015.

5   Chris Welch, "Comcast reportedly taking on YouTube and Facebook with rival video platform," The Verge, August 14, 2015, http://www.theverge.com/2015/8/14/9154397/comcast-watchable-video-platform (accessed August 15, 2015).

6   A vast majority of content marketing today is business-to-business. American Express Open Forum (https://www.americanexpress.com/us/small-business/openforum/explore/?linknav=us-openforum-global-header-home) is a good example. The site provides information for small businesses in a magazine-like format. Producing a website based on the expertise of a company executive—demonstrating "thought leadership"—is the backbone of many of these marketing strategies. Companies can blog or create podcasts, and most offer white papers expounding on the latest trends and executive insights, which visitors can download once they provide their email address and company information. The latest trend is to turn aspects of these sites into infographics and use that to entice people to visit the website.

7   For YouTube's case study of GoPro, see https://www.thinkwithgoogle.com/case-studies/gopro-youtube-case-study.html.

8   GoPro and Red Bull have a partnership wherein Red Bull uses GoPro cameras to produce their stunts while GoPro gets access to Red Bull's extreme sports talent.

9   Billie Goldman and Josh Brandau, "The Next Wave of Digital Marketing" (slide presentation, iMedia conference, Austin, Texas, October 20–23, 2013), http://www.slideshare.net/imediaconnection/2013-10breakthroughintelpereira-odell (accessed June 30, 2015).

10   Paul Zak, "How Stories Change the Brain," Greater Good in Action, December 17, 2013, http://greatergood.berkeley.edu/article/item/how_stories_change_brain (accessed July 1, 2015).

11   Paul Zak, "Why Your Brain Loves Good Storytelling," *Harvard Business Review*, October 28, 2014, https://hbr.org/2014/10/why-your-brain-loves-good-storytelling/ (accessed July 1, 2015).

12   Natalya Minkovsky, "'Will It Blend?' Company Embarks on New Influencer Marketing Program," Content Marketing Institute, June 28, 2015, http://tiny.cc/los7zx (accessed July 1, 2015).

13   Microsoft Stories: https://news.microsoft.com/stories/index.html.

14   http://viralvideochart.unrulymedia.com/facebook?id=10152404556832413 (accessed April 20, 2105). This information is now only available via subscription.

15   This is not to be confused with The Creators Project, a division of VICE Media and sponsored by Intel.

16   Michael Meyer, "The Wolf at the Door," *Columbia Journalism Review* (November/December 2014): 24–29.

17   J. Max Robins, "GE Burnishes Content Marketing Legacy With Nat Geo Series," MediaPost, April 17, 2015, http://www.mediapost.com/publications/article/247962/ge-burnishes-content-marketing-legacy-with-nat-geo.html (accessed October 13, 2015).

18   Marty Biancuzzo, "Why GoPro is Set for a Strong Wall Street Debut," *Wall Street Daily*, May 21, 2014, http://www.wallstreetdaily.com/2014/05/21/gopro-ipo/ (accessed July 8, 2015).

19   Christopher Ratcliff, "A look inside GoPro's dazzling YouTube strategy," Econsultancy, February 20, 2014, https://econsultancy.com/blog/64370-a-look-inside-gopro-s-dazzling-youtube-strategy/ (accessed July 8, 2015). While I was working on this chapter, a reporter contacted me to comment on GoPro's anticipated foray into full-length documentaries in order to help differentiate them from Red Bull. I was not able to do so and have yet to see the article come out. If I'd had the opportunity to comment, I would have said it was the obvious next step, but not necessarily something that would differentiate GoPro from other brand companies, who—as we have seen—are producing documentaries.

20   Goldman, Billie and Josh Brandau (2013, October 20–23), "The Next Wave of Digital Marketing," slides presented at iMedia Conference in Austin, Texas. Accessed June 30, 2015 from http://www.slideshare.net/imediaconnection/2013-10breakthroughintelpereira-odell.

21   Jessica Pressler, "The World is Not Enough," *New York Magazine*, August 10–23, 2015, 50–58, http://nymag.com/thecut/2015/08/net-a-porter-bigger-better-future.html.

22   Tessa Wegert, "The New Red Bulls: Why Every Big Brand Is Launching a Media Company," Contently, June 22, 2015, http://contently.com/strategist/2015/06/22/the-new-red-bulls-why-every-big-brand-is-launching-a-media-company/ (accessed July 3, 2015).

23 AFP, "Indian officials order Coca-Cola plant to close for using too much water," *The Guardian*, June 18, 2014, http://www.theguardian.com/environment/2014/jun/18/indian-officals-coca-cola-plant-water-mehdiganj (accessed October 1, 2015).

24 Chiung Hwang Chen, "Marketing Religion Online: The LDS Church's SEO Efforts," *Journal of Media and Religion* 10, no. 4 (2011): 185–205.

25 Justin Briggs, "Breaking Down the Mormon Strategy," Distilled, 2010, https://www.distilled.net/blog/seo/breaking-down-the-mormon-seo-strategy/ (accessed October 21, 2015).

26 For other examples of corporate entities producing online magazines, see IQ from Intel, Virgin Media Presents, *Food & Family* from Kraft, and The Adrenalist from Degree deodorant.

27 Michael Meyer, "The Wolf at the Door."

28 Dumb Ways to Die: https://www.youtube.com/watch?v=IJNR2EpSOjw.

29 Mike O'Brien, "YouTube Video Series Shows Branded Content's Success," ClickZ, March 16, 2015, http://www.clickz.com/clickz/news/2399914/youtube-video-series-shows-branded-contents-success (accessed July 14 2015).

30 Nathalie Tadena, "Google Makes Push for YouTube Branded Content With New Video Series," CMO Today, March 16, 2015, http://blogs.wsj.com/cmo/2015/03/16/google-makes-push-for-youtube-branded-content-with-new-video-series/ (accessed July 14, 2015). See also Think With Google: https://www.thinkwithgoogle.com/.

31 Kelsey Duchesne, "Creating a Stir: Why Oreo is Succeeding at Content Marketing," inSegment, 2015, http://blog.insegment.com/creating-stir-oreo-succeeding-content-marketing/ (accessed September 12, 2015).

32 MTV used a similar technique with "I want my MTV." It was previously the tagline for an oatmeal product, "I want my Maypo," and would have been known to people being introduced to the music channel.

33 As of July 2015, the ad has been shared almost a million times and has more than 19.5 million YouTube views as of September 17, 2015. See Tara Mulloy, "The Most Shared Video Ads of 2015(So Far)," Unruly, 2015, July 28, 2015, https://unruly.co/blog/article/2015/07/28/the-most-shared-video-ads-of-2015-so-far/ (accessed September 17, 2015).

34 Mara Einstein, *Brands of Faith: Marketing Religion in a Commercial Age* (London: Routledge, 2007).

35 Christine Birkner, "Lifestyle Brands Make It Personal," American Marketing Association, February, 28, 2011, https://lifestylebrandsblog.files.wordpress.com/2012/04/marketing-news_lifestyle-brands1.pdf (accessed July 20, 2015).

36 Jill Cress (presentation at Newscred Insights conference, 2015), http://library.fora.tv/2015/05/14/Setting_a_Creative_Standard_in_a_Regulated_Environment (accessed September 17, 2015).

37 Tim Nudd, "Droga5's Gisele Campaign for Under Armour Scores the Cyber Grand Prix at Cannes," *Adweek*, June 24, 2015, http://www.adweek.com/news/advertising-branding/droga5s-gisele-campaign-under-armour-scores-cyber-grand-prix-cannes-165541 (accessed July 3, 2015).

38   "Marketers Continue to Rate Email the Most Effective Digital Marketing Tactic." Marketing Charts, September 23, 2014, http://www.marketingcharts.com/online/marketers-continue-to-rate-email-the-most-effective-digital-marketing-tactic-46295/ (accessed July 10, 2015).

39   Joe Pulizzi and Ann Handley, "B2C Content Marketing: 2015 Benchmarks, Budgets and Trends—North America," Content Marketing Institute (n.d.), http://contentmarketinginstitute.com/wp-content/uploads/2014/10/2015_B2C_Research.pdf (accessed August 1, 2015).

40   Personal interview with the author, May 18, 2015.

41   See *Generation Like.*

42   David Griner, "Oreo Surprises 26 Million Facebook Fans with Gay Pride Post," *Adweek*, June 25, 2012, http://www.adweek.com/adfreak/oreo-surprises-26-million-facebook-fans-gay-pride-post-141440 (accessed January 23, 2015).

43   Tessa Wegert, "The New Red Bulls: Why Every Big Brand Is Launching a Media Company."

44   Wills Robinson, "Dog Owners Describe Horror of Watching their Pets Suffer Violent Seizures," *Daily Mail*, March 10, 2015, http://www.dailymail.co.uk/news/article-2985819/Dog-owners-horrific-effects-claim-Purina-Beneful-beloved-pets-including-violent-seizures-kidney-failure-cases-death.html (accessed July 14, 2015).

CHAPTER 5

1   See Christian Rudder, *Dataclysm: Who We Are When We Think No One is Looking* (New York: Crown, 2014); Kevin Poulsen, "How a Math Genius Hacked OkCupid to Find True Love," *Wired*, 2014, http://www.wired.com/2014/01/how-to-hack-okcupid/all/ (accessed July 14, 2015).

2   Christian Rudder in his book *Dataclysm* notes: "Outside researchers rarely get to work with private messages like this—it's the most sensitive content users generate and even anonymized and aggregated, message data is rarely allowed out of the holiest of holies in the database. But my unique position at OkCupid gives us special access." (65)

3   Charlie Warzel, "OkCupid Data Scientist: 'I'm Not Playing God,'" BuzzFeed, July 28, 2014, http://www.buzzfeed.com/charliewarzel/ok-cupid-data-scientist-im-not-playing-god (accessed July 14, 2015).

4   Douglas MacMillan and Elizabeth Dwoskin, "Smile! Marketing Firms Are Mining Your Selfies," *The Wall Street Journal*, October 9, 2014, http://www.wsj.com/articles/smile-marketing-firms-are-mining-your-selfies-1412882222 (accessed February 1, 2015). Advertisers will post multiple versions of an advertisement and compare the effectiveness of one piece of creative over the other. They also analyze their social information versus the competition. Companies to see in relationship to this are Curalate, BuzzSumo, Social Bakers, and Mantii.

5   Google Search Statistics can be seen at http://www.Internetlivestats.com/google-search-statistics/. The base website provides real-time Internet statistics: http://www.Internetlivestats.com/.

6   Erin Griffith, "Youtube CEO: 'Video views on Facebook are different,'" *Fortune*, July 13, 2015, http://fortune.com/2015/07/13/youtube-ceo-facebook-video/ (accessed August 29, 2015).

7   "The Top 20 Valuable Facebook Statistics," Zephoria, May 2015, https://zephoria.com/top-15-valuable-facebook-statistics/ (accessed September 17, 2015).

8   Luke Brynley-Jones, "8 Useful Social Media Statistics," Our Social Times, December 22,2014, http://oursocialtimes.com/8-useful-social-media-statistics-for-2015/ (accessed September 13, 2015).

9   Jeff Bullas, "33 Social Media Facts and Statistics You Should Know in 2015," personal blog, 2015, http://www.jeffbullas.com/2015/04/08/33-social-media-facts-and-statistics-you-should-know-in-2015/ (accessed September 17, 2015).

10   "Internet Users by Country," Internet Live Stats, 2014, http://www.Internetlivestats.com/Internet-users-by-country/(accessed August 30, 2015).

11   Andrew Perrin and Maeve Duggan, "Americans' Internet Access: 2000–2015," Pew Research Center, June 26, 2015, http://www.pewInternet.org/2015/06/26/americans-Internet-access-2000-2015/ (accessed August 29, 2015).

12   For critiques on big data, surveillance, and data and advertising, see: Joseph Turow, *Daily You: How the New Advertising Industry Is Defining Your Identity and Your Worth* (New Haven: Yale University Press, 2012); Julia Angwin, *Dragnet Nation: A Quest for Privacy, Security, and Freedom in a World of Relentless Surveillance* (New York: Times Books, Henry Holt and Company, 2014); Adam Tanner, *What Stays in Vegas: The World of Personal Data—Lifeblood Of Big Business—And The End Of Privacy As We Know It* (New York: PublicAffairs, 2014); Jacob Silverman, *Terms of Service: Social Media and the Price of Constant Connection* (New York: HarperCollins, 2015); Robert Scheer and Sara Beladi, *They Know Everything About You: How Data-Collecting Corporations and Snooping Government Agencies Are Destroying Democracy* (New York: Nation Books, 2015); Siva Vaidhyanathan, *The Googlization of Everything (and Why We Should Worry)* (Berkeley, CA: University of California Press, 2011); Frank Pasquale, *The Black Box Society: The Secret Algorithms That Control Money and Information* (Cambridge, MA: Harvard University Press, 2015).

13   Michael Barbaro and Tom Zeller, Jr., "A Face Is Exposed for AOL Searcher No. 4417749," *New York Times*, August 9, 2006, http://www.nytimes.com/2006/08/09/technology/09aol.html?pagewanted=all&_r=0 (accessed September 13, 2015).

14   Arvind Narayanan and Vitaly Shmatikov, "Robust De-anonymization of Large Sparse Datasets," *Proceedings of the 2008 IEEE Symposium on Security and Privacy* (2008): 111–125.

15   Julia Angwin, 169.

16   Michal Kosinski, David Stillwell, and Thore Graepel, "Private traits and attributes are predictable from digital records of human behavior," Proceedings of the National Academy of Sciences of the United States, April 9, 2013, http://www.pnas.org/content/110/15/5802.full (accessed September 13, 2015).

17   For more on big data from a pro-business perspective, see Viktor Mayer-Schonberger and Kenneth Cukier, *Big Data: A Revolution That Will Transform How We Live, Work, and Think* (Boston: Houghton Mifflin Harcourt, 2013); "Big Data," Teradata (n.d.), http://www.teradata.com/business-needs/Big-Data-Analytics/#tabbable=0&tab1=0&tab2=0&tab3=0&tab4=0 (accessed September 13, 2015); Executive Office of the President, "Big Data: Seizing Opportunities, Preserving Values," May 1, 2014, https://www.whitehouse.gov/sites/default/files/docs/big_data_privacy_report_may_1_2014.pdf (accessed August 30, 2015). For examples of large data sets, see http://aws.amazon.com/public-data-sets/.

18   For some consumers, social media complicates and reconfigures this process. They consider products based on websites, blogs, or email, and they evaluate the brand by watching YouTube or reading reviews. They buy the product, follow brand experts on Twitter, and "Like" it on Facebook. They may even tell friends when they visit a store via Foursquare. This process becomes a continuing loop, with the evaluation stage eliminated after the first purchase. Some consulting groups, such as McKinsey, have suggested that the sales equivalent is less of a funnel and more of a feedback loop, with consumers adding choices throughout the process. There is validity to this theory, but practitioners still overwhelmingly use the funnel metaphor, which is why I include it here.

19   There are many different versions of the sales funnel. The key points in the funnel, however, are always awareness, consideration, purchase, and loyalty.

20   Barry Schwartz, *Paradox of Choice: Why More is Less* (New York: Ecco Books, 2004); Sheena S. Iyengar and Mark R. Lepper, "When choice is demotivating: Can one desire too much of a good thing?" *Journal of Personality and Social Psychology* 79, no. 6 (2000): 995.

21   Steven Levy, *In the Plex: How Google Thinks, Works, and Shapes Our Lives* (New York: Simon & Schuster, 2011), 78.

22   When first developed, the ads would have a shaded box around them to denote that visitors were looking at advertising. Today, ads have a small box that says "AD" below the link for the site, much like Twitter's arrow used to look.

23   Scott Karp, "Google AdWords: A Brief History of Online Advertising Innovation," Publishing 2.0, May 27, 2008, http://publishing2.com/2008/05/27/google-adwords-a-brief-history-of-online-advertising-innovation/ (accessed August 29, 2015).

24   Google maintained a separate sales team to sell to premium advertisers.

25   They came to this idea via competitor Bill Gross and his GoTo search engine, which showed paid advertising among the organic search results. When presenting this concept at a TED talk in 1998, Gross was hissed at for unethical behavior. Google did not integrate ads with organic, but it did quickly adopt pay-per-click and auction buying, turning AdWords into AdWords Select.

26   Steven Levy, 85–6.

27   Ibid., 92.

28   Christopher Ratcliff, "What is Google AdWords and how does it work?" October 30, 2014, https://econsultancy.com/blog/65682-what-is-google-adwords-and-how-does-it-work (accessed August 18, 2015).

29   Graham Charlton, "40% of consumers are unaware that Google Adwords are adverts," February 28, 2013, https://econsultancy.com/blog/62249-40-of-consumers-are-unaware-that-google-adwords-are-adverts (accessed August 18, 2015). Companies can also optimize their ability to be at the top of the Google search through Search Engine Optimization strategies. This is, however, tangential to the current discussion.

30   Personal interview with the author. Combining first party data with third party data is done via data management platforms (DMPs). To see interrelations among advertising technology firms, see http://adage.com/lp/bigdata2014/#DataManagementPlatforms.

31   Adam Tanner, 24.

32   Constance L. Hays, "What Wal-Mart Knows About Customers' Habits," *New York Times*, November 14, 2004, http://www.nytimes.com/2004/11/14/business/yourmoney/14wal.html (accessed August 20, 2015).

33   Charles Duhigg, "How Companies Learn Your Secrets," *New York Times Magazine*, February 16, 2012, http://www.nytimes.com/2012/02/19/magazine/shopping-habits.html (accessed September 13, 2015); Charles Duhigg, *The Power of Habit: Why We Do What We Do In Life And Business* (New York: Random House, 2012), 193.

34   Christopher Ratcliff, "A super accessible beginner's guide to programmatic buying and RTB," August 19, 2015, https://econsultancy.com/blog/65677-a-super-accessible-beginner-s-guide-to-programmatic-buying-and-rtb/ (accessed September 2, 2015).

35   "The Real World of Real-time Advertising" Quantcast, 2014, https://www.quantcast.com/wp-content/uploads/2014/10/Quantcast-Advertise-Real-World-of-Real-Time-Advertising-White-Paper-2014.pdf (accessed September 13, 2015).

36   Katy Bachman, "Confessions of a Data Broker," *Adweek*, March 25, 2014, http://www.adweek.com/news/technology/confessions-data-broker-156437 (accessed August 18, 2015).

37   Bachman, Katy (2014, March 25), "Confessions of a Data Broker," *Adweek*. Accessed August 18, 2015 from http://www.adweek.com/news/technology/confessions-data-broker-156437.

38   See http://www.pklistmarketing.com/index.htm.

39   Scheer and Beladi, 59.

40   "The Data Brokers: Selling Your Personal Information," *60 Minutes*, http://www.cbsnews.com/news/data-brokers-selling-personal-information-60-minutes/ (accessed September 30, 2014).

41   Lois Beckett, "Everything We Know About What Data Brokers Know About You," ProPublica, June 13, 2014, https://www.propublica.org/article/everything-we-know-about-what-data-brokers-know-about-you (accessed September 5, 2015).

42   "What is Data On-Boarding," *Advertising Age*, June 24, 2014, http://adage.com/article/glossary-data-defined/data-boarding/293651/.

43   Simon Hill, "How much do online advertisers really know about you? We asked an expert," Digital Trends, June 27, 2015, http://www.digitaltrends.com/computing/how-do-advertisers-track-you-online-we-found-out/ (accessed August 30, 2015).

44   Julia Angwin and Jeff Larson, "Verizon's Zombie Cookie Gets New Life," ProPublica, October 6, 2015, https://www.propublica.org/article/verizons-zombie-cookie-gets-new-life (accessed October 13, 2015).

45   Michael Bollinger, "A Lot for CPG Brands To Like In Twitter," MediaPost, May 13, 2015, http://www.mediapost.com/publications/article/249884/a-lot-for-cpg-brands-to-like-in-twitter.html (accessed October 13, 2015).

46   See Nielsen for examples of psychographic segmentations: https://www.claritas.com/MyBestSegments/Default.jsp?ID=30&menuOption=segmentexplorer&pageName=Segment%2BExplorer#. Acxiom's categories are here: https://isapps.acxiom.com/personicx/personicx.aspx.

47   "Over 1,800 segments at your fingertips," Datalogix (n.d.), http://www.datalogix.com/audiences/online/syndicated-segments/.

48   "Life-event triggers." Experian Marketing Services (n.d.), http://www.experian.com/marketing-services/life-event-marketing.html (accessed September 13, 2015).

49   Ibid.

50   "Data Packages," Acxiom (n.d.), http://www.acxiom.com/data-packages/.

51   To check out your own information about your profile, see analytics.twitter.com and https://blog.twitter.com/2012/your-twitter-archive (Twitter) and https://support.google.com/accounts/answer/3024190?hl=en (Google).

52   "Understanding Mobile Cookies," IAB (n.d.), http://www.iab.net/media/file/IABDigitalSimplified MobileCookies.pdf (accessed September 3, 2015).

53   Simon Hill, "How do online advertisers really know about you? We asked an expert."

54   Personal interview with the author.

55   For more information on inline advertising: https://www.virool.com/inline.

56   Email with the author, September 15, 2015.

57   Chuck Hemann and Ken Burbary, *Digital Marketing Analytics: Making Sense of Consumer Data in a Digital World* (Indianapolis, Indiana: Que Printing, 2013).

58   You can see some of the data that Acxiom has about you personally if you register on their site, called About the Data (https://aboutthedata.com/). You can also edit the information, should you choose to do so. When I first went to the site in early 2015, the company thought that I was still married after having been divorced for ten years. By mid-2015, the company had changed this information to "inferred single"—still no proof that I was divorced, but getting

closer. The only other information they showed that they had on me was that I owned two credit cards (wrong) and that I had made one purchase on one of these and four purchases on the other (also wrong). They had purchase data—mostly related to books and magazines—and information about offline as well as online purchases, which too seemed incorrect. The site also listed a number of interests, which seemed more connected to the magazines that I read than they did to my true interests. (BlueKai has a similar site which you can access at: http://www.bluekai.com/registry/).

59   Adam Tanner, 101.

60   Dana Mattioli, "On Orbitz, Mac Users Steered to Pricier Hotels," *Wall Street Journal*, August 23, 2012, http://www.wsj.com/articles/SB10001424052702304458604 577488822667325882 (accessed September 5, 2015).

61   Thorin Klosowski, "How Web Sites Vary Prices Based on Your Information (and What You Can Do About It)," Lifehacker, January 7, 2013, http://lifehacker. com/5973689/how-web-sites-vary-prices-based-on-your-information-and-what-you-can-do-about-it (accessed September 5, 2015).

62   Jennifer Valentino-Devries, Jeremy Singer-Vine, and Ashkan Soltani, "Websites Vary Prices, Deals Based on Users' Information," *Wall Street Journal*, December 24, 2012, http://www.wsj.com/article_email/SB10001424127887323777204578189391813881534-lMyQjAxMTAyMDIwMzEyNDMyWj.html (accessed September 5, 2015).

63   Eli Pariser, *The Filter Bubble: What the Internet is Hiding from You* (New York: The Penguin Press, 2011).

64   Mark Sullivan, "Facebook patents technology to help lenders discriminate against borrowers based on social connections," *Venture Beat*, August 4, 2015, http:// venturebeat.com/2015/08/04/facebook-patents-technology-to-help-lenders-discriminate-against-borrowers-based-on-social-connections/ (accessed August 5, 2015).

65   Steven Salzberg, "Why Google Flu is a Failure," *Forbes*, March 23, 2014, http:// www.forbes.com/sites/stevensalzberg/2014/03/23/why-google-flu-is-a-failure/ (accessed September 7, 2015).

66   David Lazer, Ryan Kennedy, Gary King, and Alessandro Vespignani, "The Parable of Google Flu: Traps in Big Data Analysis," *Science* 343, no. 6176 (March 14, 2014): 1203–1205.

67   About Facebook ads: https://www.facebook.com/help/585318558251813; about Cosmopolitan ads: http://www.cosmopolitan.com/about/oba-policy.

68   Personal interview with the author, May 18, 2015.

69   "7 Consumer Trends to Run with in 2014" Trendwatching, January 2014, http:// trendwatching.com/trends/7trends2014/#no-data (accessed March 7, 2015).

70   Joseph Turow, Michael Hennessy, and Nora Draper, "The Tradeoff Fallacy: How Marketers Are Misrepresenting American Consumers and Opening Them Up to Exploitation," Annenberg School for Communication, University of Pennsylvania, 2015, https://www.asc.upenn.edu/sites/default/ files/TradeoffFallacy_1.pdf (accessed October 1, 2015).

71   Federal Trade Commission, "Data Brokers: A Call for Transparency and Accountability," May 2014, https://www.ftc.gov/system/files/documents/reports/data-brokers-call-transparency-accountability-report-federal-trade-commission-may-2014/140527databrokerreport.pdf (accessed July 27, 2015).

72   "The Data Brokers," *60 Minutes*.

73   Julia Angwin, *Dragnet Nation*, 86.

74   Sam Schechner, "Google Appeals French Order to Apply 'Right to Be Forgotten' Globally," *Wall Street Journal*, July 30, 2015, http://www.wsj.com/articles/google-appeals-french-order-to-apply-right-to-be-forgotten-globally-1438273521 (accessed July 31, 2015).

CHAPTER 6

1   Julia Belluz, "Here's what happened when Dr. Oz asked Twitter for health questions," *Vox*, November 12, 2014, http://www.vox.com/2014/11/12/7203269/dr-oz-health-twitter (accessed September 1, 2015); Ann Oldenburg, "Dr. Oz asks Twitter for questions, gets hate," *USA Today*, November 13, 2014, http://www.usatoday.com/story/life/people/2014/11/13/dr-oz-ssks-for-twitter-questions-gets-hate/18958203/ (accessed September 1, 2015).

2   Hannah Roberts, "#McFail! McDonalds' Twitter promotion backfires as users hijack #McDstories hashtag to share fast food horror stories," *Daily Mail*, January 24, 2012, http://www.dailymail.co.uk/news/article-2090862/McDstories-McDonalds-Twitter-promotion-backfires-users-share-fast-food-horror-stories.html (accessed September 20, 2015); Brian Koerber, "Bill Cosby's meme generator hijacked by reminders of rape allegations," Mashable, November 10, 2014, http://mashable.com/2014/11/10/bill-cosbys-meme-generator/ (accessed September 20, 2015); Abby Phillip, "Well, the #MYNYPD hashtag sure backfired," *Washington Post*, April 22, 2014, https://www.washingtonpost.com/news/post-nation/wp/2014/04/22/well-the-mynypd-hashtag-sure-backfired-quickly/ (accessed September 29, 2015).

3   Julie Jargon, "Starbucks Profit Jumps, as Revenue Surges 18%," Wall Street Journal, July 23, 2015, http://www.wsj.com/articles/starbucks-profit-jumps-as-revenue-surges-18-1437684114 (accessed July 24, 2015).

4   Political situations are an exception: Arab Spring, activist takeovers of hashtags such as "Ask Bobby" (a Twitter Q&A with Louisiana Government Bobby Jindal), and LGBT groups appropriating McDonald's #CheerstoSochi hashtag to highlight the mistreatment of gays and lesbians in Russia. See Scott Eric Kaufman, "Who thought that an #AskBobby Jindal Twitter dialogue would be a good idea?" Salon, June 30, 2015, http://www.salon.com/2015/06/30/who_thought_that_an_askbobby_jindal_twitter_dialogue_would_be_a_good_idea/ (accessed October 24, 2015); Tony Merevick, "LGBT Activists Launch 'Cheers To Sochi' Parody Site After 'Hijacking' McDonald's Hashtag," BuzzFeed, 2014, http://www.buzzfeed.com/tonymerevick/lgbt-activists-launch-cheers-to-sochi-parody (accessed October 24, 2015).

5   John A. Deighton and Leora Kornfeld, "Digital Interactivity: Unanticipated Consequences for Markets, Marketing, and Consumers," *Harvard Business School Working Paper*, 08–017 (2008); Lauren I. Labrecque, Jonas vor dem Esche, Charla Mathwick, Thomas P. Novak, and Charles F. Hofacker, "Consumer power: Evolution in the digital age," *Journal of Interactive Marketing* 27, no. 4 (2013): 257–269.

6   Elliott Fox, "Nestle hit by Facebook 'anti-social' media surge," *The Guardian*, March 19, 2010, http://www.theguardian.com/sustainable-business/nestle-facebook (accessed October 24, 2015).

7   Stephanie Clifford, "Video Prank at Domino's Taints Brand," *New York Times*, 2009, http://www.nytimes.com/2009/04/16/business/media/16dominos.html (accessed from October 24, 2015).

8   Craig J. Thompson, Aric Rindfleisch, and Zeynep Arsel Zeynep, "Emotional Branding and the Strategic Value of the Doppelgänger Brand Image," *Journal of marketing, 70*(1) (2006): 50–64; David Edelman and Brian Salsberg, "Beyond paid media: Marketing's new vocabulary," McKinsey & Company, 2010, http://www.mckinsey.com/insights/marketing_sales/beyond_paid_media_marketings_new_vocabulary (accessed October 24, 2015).

9   C. K. Prahalad and Venkat Ramaswamy, *The Future of Competition: Co-Creating Unique Value with Customers* (Boston, MA: Harvard Business School Press, 2004); Nat Ives, "Unauthorized campaigns used by unauthorized creators to show their creativity become a trend," *New York Times*, December 23, 2010; Albert M. Muniz, Jr., and Hope Jensen Schau, "Vigilante marketing and consumer-created communications," *Journal of Advertising* 36, no. 3 (2007): 187–202; Susan Fournier and Jill Avery, "The uninvited brand," *Business Horizons* 54, no. 3 (2011): 193–207; Bob Garfield, "Listenomics," *Advertising Age*, October 10, 2005, http://adage.com/article?article_id=104909 (accessed from February 1, 2014); Pierre Berthon, Leyland Pitt, Ian McCarthy, and Steven Kates, "When customers get clever: Managerial approaches to dealing with creative consumers," *Business Horizons* 50, no. 1 (2006): 39–47; Robert V. Kozinets, Andrea Hemetsberger, and Hope Jensen Schau, "The wisdom of consumer crowds: Collective innovation in the age of networked marketing," *Journal of Macromarketing* 28, no. 4 (2008): 339–354; Susan Fournier and Claudio Alvarez, "Brands as relationship partners: Warmth, competence, and in-between," *Journal of Consumer Psychology* 22, no. 2 (2012): 177–185.

10   Communication scholars have also written about this phenomenon, using terms like "appropriation," see Sarah Banet-Weiser and Charlotte Lapsansky, "RED is the New Black: Brand Culture, Consumer Citizenship and Political Possibility," *International Journal if Communication* 2, no. 21 (2008): 1248–1268; "prosumption," see Ashlee Humphreys and Kent Grayson, "The Intersecting Roles of Consumer and Producer: A Critical Perspective on Co-production, Co-creation and Prosumption," *Social Compass* 2, no. 3(2008): 963–980; and, in the case of Henry Jenkins, "transmedia," see Henry Jenkins, *Convergence Culture: Where Old and New Media Collide* (New York: New York University Press, 2008); "participatory media," see Henry Jenkins, *Textual Poachers: Television Fans and Participatory*

Culture (New York: Routledge, 2012); and "spreadable media" (Henry Jenkins, Sam Ford, and Joshua Green, *Spreadable Media: Creating Value and Meaning in a Networked Culture* (New York: New York University Press, 2013).

11 Alex Wipperfurth, *Brand Hijack: Marketing Without Marketing* (New York: Portfolio, 2005), 17.

12 Ibid, 61.

13 Benjamin Lawrence, Susan Fournier, and Frederick Brunel, "When Companies Don't Make the Ad: A Multimethod Inquiry into the Differential Effectiveness of Consumer-Generated Advertising," *Journal of Advertising*, 42, no. 4 (2013): 292–307.

14 When this campaign was first run, the winner got 1 percent of the profits from the sales. It has since changed to be a million dollar prize.

15 *Despicable Me* website: http://despicableme.com.

16 The Coca-Cola ad can be viewed at http://www.youtube.com/watch?v= 6r_9HPzMZTU, and "Honest Coca-Cola Ad" can be viewed at http://www .youtube.com/watch?v=bHhCP5ad-zM.

17 Mike Wolfsohn, "The Consumer Isn't Really in Control," *Ad Age*, 2011, http://adage. com/article/agency-news/consumer-control/149561/ (accessed October 24, 2015).

18 Bob Jeffrey, "JWT CEO Bob Jeffrey Says the Consumer Is Still in Control: The revolution isn't about tech—it's about people expecting more from brands," *Adweek*, November 10, 2013, http://www.adweek.com/news/advertising-branding/jwt-ceo-bob-jeffrey-says-consumer-still-control-153724 (accessed October 24, 2015).

19 Mitch Joel, "Consumers Control the Brand (And Other New Media Myths)," 2011, http://www.twistimage.com/blog/archives/consumers-control-the-brand-and-other-new-media-myths/ (accessed October 24, 2015).

20 Angela Doland, "In China, People Cover Brands' Online Videos With Snark," *Advertising Age*, October 1, 2015, http://adage.com/article/global-news/china-people-cover-brands-onlilne-videos-snark/300560/ (accessed October 24, 2015).

21 Ken Wheaton, "So Which Ad-blocking Parasite Are You Going to Go After, The Consumer or the Tech Company?" *Advertising Age*, September 14, 2015; see also "The Rise of the Empowered Consumer," Mediacom, 2012, http://www .mediacomusa.com/media/2088012/mediacom%20the%20insider_the%20 empowered%20consumer_whitepaper.pdf (accessed October 13, 2015).

22 Brooke Erin Duffy and Emily Hund, "The Invisible Labor of Fashion Blogging," *Atlantic*, September 25, 2015, http://www.theatlantic.com/entertainment/archive/ 2015/09/fashion-blogging-labor-myths/405817/ (accessed October 23, 2015).

23 David Edelman and Brian Salsberg, "Beyond paid media: Marketing's New Vocabulary," McKinsey & Company, 2010, http://www.mckinsey.com/insights/ marketing_sales/beyond_paid_media_marketings_new_ vocabulary (accessed October 24, 2015).

24 I did not create this term, though I used it as far back as 2007. See Mara Einstein, *Brands of Faith: Marketing Religion in a Commercial Age*. Some have credited former Apple chief evangelist Guy Kawasaki with coining the term, but I have

not found hard evidence of this. Brand evangelism is, however, a widely used term within the marketing field.

25 James H. McAlexander, John W. Schouten, and Harold F. Koening, "Building brand community," *Journal of Marketing* 66 (January 2002): 38–54; John W. Schouten and James H. McAlexander, "Subcultures of Consumption: An Ethnography of the New Bikers," *Journal of Consumer Research* 22 (June 1995): 43–61.

26 Albert M. Muniz and Thomas C. O'Guinn, "Brand community," *Journal of Consumer Research* 27 (4) (2001): 412–32.

27 Douglas Atkin, *The Culting of Brands: When Customers Become True Believers* (New York: Portfolio Trade, 2004); Matthew W. Ragas and Bolivar J. Bueno, *The Power of Cult Branding: How 9 Magnetic Brands Turned Customers into Loyal Followers (And Yours Can, Too)* (New York: Crown Business, 2002).

28 "Tesla Motors Club—Enthusiasts & Owners Forum," http://www.teslamotorsclub .com/forum.php.

29 "BMW Driving Experience," http://www.bmw-drivingexperience.com/en/ index.html.

30 "Uber—What's Fueling Uber's Growth Engine?" Growth Hackers (n.d.), https:// growthhackers.com/growth-studies/uber (accessed October 24, 2015); Jason Abbruzzese, "Report: Snapchat Valued at $10 Billion in Latest Investment," Mashable, August 26, 2014, http://mashable.com/2014/08/26/snapchat-10-billion-valuation/ (accessed October 24, 2015); "Netflix Shareholder letter," http://files. shareholder.com/downloads/NFLX/47469957x0x821407/DB785B50-90FE-44DA-9F5B-37DBF0DCD0E1/Q1_15_Earnings_Letter_final_tables.pdf (accessed October 24, 2015).

31 The last posting was from 2014.

32 "About lululemon," https://www.heylululemon.com/about (accessed October 24, 2015).

33 "Awaken Your Potential Chakra Mediation: Clarity," podcast, https://soundcloud. com/lululemon-athletica-1/awaken-your-potential-chakra-meditation-clarity (accessed October 24, 2015).

34 Einstein, *Brands of Faith.*

35 Josh Barro, "SoulCycle: You Say 'Cult.' I Say 'Loyal Customer Base,'" *New York Times*, August 7, 2015, http://www.nytimes.com/2015/08/09/upshot/soulcycle-you-say-cult-i-say-loyal-customer-base.html (accessed October 24, 2015).

36 Mara Einstein, *Compassion, Inc.: How Corporate America Blurs the Line Between What We Buy, Who We Are, and Those We Help* (Berkeley: CA: University of California Press, 2012).

37 "Fans Pick Favorite Starbucks Frappuccino from Six New Flavors," Starbucks, July 3, 2015, https://news.starbucks.com/news/frappuccino-fan-favorite-winner (accessed October 24, 2015).

38 "10 Trends for 2015," Trendwatching, December 2014/January 2015, http:// trendwatching.com/x/wp-content/uploads/2014/11/2014-12-10-TRENDS-FOR-2015.pdf (accessed July 17, 2015).

CHAPTER 7

1   Thomas H. Davenport and John C. Beck, *The Attention Economy: Understanding the New Currency of Business*, Cambridge (MA: Harvard Business Review Press, 2002).

2   Ashlee Vance, "This Tech Bubble is Different," Bloomberg Business, April 14, 2011, http://www.bloomberg.com/bw/magazine/content/11_17/b4225060960537.htm (accessed October 28, 2015).

3   "BJ Fogg's Behavior Model," http://www.behaviormodel.org/motivation.html (accessed October 28, 2015).

4   Scholars, including me, have roundly criticized an overcommercialized culture. Notable among these are Sut Jhally, Naomi Klein, Susan Linn, Juliet Schor, Susan Douglas, Jean Kilborne, and James Twitchell. Here I delineate between a society that uses advertising to support media and a society where advertising pervasively covers the landscape.

5   Joseph Turow, Michael Hennessy, and Nora Draper.

6   Peter S. Green, "The Syndicate," Wall Street Journal Custom Studios (n.d.), http://www.wsj.com/ad/cocainenomics (accessed October 28, 2015).

7   Maureen Morrison and Tim Peterson, "The War on Advertising?" *Advertising Age*, September 14, 2015, 10–12.

8   Farhad Manjoo, "Ad Blockers and the Nuisance at the Heart of the Modern Web," *New York Times*, August 19, 2015, http://www.nytimes.com/2015/08/20/technology/personaltech/ad-blockers-and-the-nuisance-at-the-heart-of-the-modern-web.html (accessed September 1, 2015).

9   Simon Dumenco, "Imagine a World Without Ads," *Advertising Age*, September 28, 2015, 28–32. *Emmy* Magazine from the Academy of Television Arts and Science came up with a similar analysis, and they concluded that for single person households, cutting the cord might make sense. But with families, the costs quickly become more expensive, especially since ESPN is the most expensive cable channel and the model assumes that most men will want that network. Daniel Frankel, "Cutting Corners," Emmy, 2015, 159–161.

10 For a thoughtful op-ed, see Zeynep Tufekci, "Mark Zuckerberg, Let Me Pay for Facebook," *New York Times*, June 4, 2015, http://www.nytimes.com/2015/06/04/opinion/zeynep-tufekci-mark-zuckerberg-let-me-pay-for-facebook.html (accessed October 27, 2015).

11 Lara O'Reilly, "A bunch of big companies are about to get punished by Google's latest search algorithm update," *Business Insider*, April 15, 2015, http://www.businessinsider.com/brands-affected-by-googles-mobile-friendly-algorithm-search-update-2015-4 (accessed July 30, 2015). One of the big concerns for the marketers I talked with was the fact that many ads that are bought don't get seen, or are only "viewed" by bots. But this issue is beyond the scope of this work. For information on viewability, see Ginny Marvin, "Google's Report That 56% Of Ads Aren't Seen Isn't Shocking & Here's Why," *Marketing Land*, December 8, 2014,

http://marketingland.com/googles-report-56-percent-ads-arent-seen-isnt-shocking-heres-110433 (accessed June 15, 2015). For bots, see the website whiteops.com.

12   Robinson Meyer, "72 Hours with Facebook Instant Articles," October 23, 2015, http://www.theatlantic.com/technology/archive/2015/10/72-hours-with-facebook-instant-articles/412171/ (accessed October 26, 2015).

13   Michael Sebastian and Tim Peterson, "Facebook Instant Articles Open Window to Mobile Ads," *Advertising Age*, May 18, 2015, 4. Facebook has also been implementing a number of objectives that turn the social site into a sales platform. Others include immersive ads that take over the entire screen, adding buttons to posts that say "call now" or "contact us," making selling easier through groups, and testing new and improved video services for the inevitable video-based content marketing. See Lauren Johnson, "Facebook's Immersive Mobile Ads Finally Give Brands the Creative They Want," *Adweek*, June 25, 2015, http://www.adweek.com/news/technology/facebooks-immersive-mobile-ads-finally-give-brands-creative-they-want-165591 (accessed October 28, 2015); Karissa Bell, "Facebook is turning Pages into an online mall," Mashable, September 8, 2015, http://mashable.com/2015/09/08/facebook-shopping-and-services/ (accessed October 28, 2015); Angela Moscaritolo, "Facebook Wants to Help You Sell Your Stuff Within Groups," *PC Magazine*, February 11, 2015, http://www.pcmag.com/article2/0,2817,2476619,00.asp (accessed October 28, 2015); Napier Lopez, "Facebook is testing a video-only tab to take on YouTube," *The Next Web*, 2015, http://thenextweb.com/facebook/2015/10/13/facebok-is-testing-a-video-only-tab-to-take-on-youtube/ (accessed October 15, 2015).

14   David Cohen, "No Dislike Button, But Facebook Begins Testing Reactions," *Social Times*, October 8, 2015, http://www.adweek.com/socialtimes/reactions/627964 (accessed October 15, 2015); For a history of the "Like" button see: "What's the history of the Awesome Button (that eventually became the Like button) on Facebook?" *Quora*, http://www.quora.com/Whats-the-history-of-the-Awesome-Button-that-eventually-became-the-Like-button-on-Facebook (accessed February 10, 2015).

15   Jacob Silverman, 31.

16   Ginny Marvin, "Amazon Is the Starting Point for 44 Percent of Consumers Searching for Products. Is Google Losing, Then?" *Marketing Land*, October 8, 2015, http://marketingland.com/amazon-is-the-starting-point-for-44-percent-of-consumers-searching-for-products-is-search-losing-then-145647 (accessed October 15, 2015).

17   Simon Dumenco, "Living with my fear of Amazon, destroyer of worlds," *Advertising Age*, January 26, 2015, 38; Spencer Soper, "Amazon to Ban Sale of Apple, Google Video-Streaming Devices," *Bloomberg Business*, October 1, 2015, http://www.bloomberg.com/news/articles/2015-10-01/amazon-will-ban-sale-of-apple-google-video-streaming-devices (accessed October 15, 2015).

18　Lydia DePillis, "Amazon's Drones and the Rise of Ostentatious R&D," *Washington Post*, December 2, 2013, http://www.washingtonpost.com/news/wonkblog/wp/2013/12/02/amazons-drones-and-the-rise-of-ostentatious-rd/(accessed October 28, 2015).

19　Dave Jamieson, "The Life and Death of an Amazon Warehouse Temp," Medium, October 23, 2015, https://medium.com/the-wtf-economy/the-life-and-death-of-an-amazon-warehouse-temp-8168c4702049# (accessed October 27, 2015); Jodi Kantor and David Streitfeld, "Inside Amazon: Wrestling Big Ideas in a Bruising Workplace," *New York Times*, August 15, 2015, http://www.nytimes.com/2015/08/16/technology/inside-amazon-wrestling-big-ideas-in-a-bruising-workplace.html (accessed October 15, 2015).

20　Amazon recently introduced what they are calling native sales advertising. This system allows associates who sell products on their websites (like books) to sell other products that relate to their content. So if a blog is about camera equipment, Amazon will post cameras on the site, and the associate can receive a percentage of the sales. This is more content-relevant than native, as it is glaringly a sales message. Accessed October 27, 2015 from https://affiliate-program.amazon.com/gp/associates/network/nativeshoppingads/main.html

21　Natasha Lomas, "Facebook's Creepy Data-Grabbing Ways Make it the Borg of the Digital World," *Tech Crunch*, June 24, 2013, http://techcrunch.com/2013/06/24/creepy-facebook/ (accessed October 28, 2015).

22　"Have you been flying BLAH Airlines?" Available at: https://www.youtube.com/watch?v=UsMZRl71Zo4.

23　Marianne Garvey, Brian Niemietz, and Oli Coleman, "NBC News fooled by E! show filming nearly naked man sneaking out of Buckingham Palace," *Daily News*, April 2, 2015, http://www.nydailynews.com/entertainment/gossip/confidential/nbc-news-fooled-e-filming-naked-man-buckingham-article-1.2170427 (accessed September 9, 2015).

24　Alan Charlesworth, *Digital Marketing: A Practical Approach* (London: Routledge, 2014), 8.

25　Silverman, 22.

26　Maureen Callahan, "Our double lives: Dark realities behind 'perfect' online profiles," *New York Post*, October 11, 2015, http://nypost.com/2015/10/11/our-double-lives-dark-realities-behind-perfect-online-profiles/ (accessed October 12, 2015).

27　Claire Cain Miller, "When algorithms discriminate," *New York Times*, July 9, 2015, http://www.nytimes.com/2015/07/10/upshot/when-algorithms-discriminate.html (accessed October 27, 2015).

28　Andrew K. Przybylski and Netta Weinstein, "Can you connect with me now? How the presence of mobile communication technology influences face-to-face conversation quality," *Journal of Social and Personal Relationships* 30, no. 3 (2013): 237–246.

29　Sherry Turkle, "Stop Googling. Let's Talk," *New York Times*, September 26, 2015, http://www.nytimes.com/2015/09/27/opinion/sunday/stop-googling-lets-talk.html (accessed October 1, 2015).

30   Brigid Schulte, "Why being too busy makes us feel so good," *Washington Post*, March 14, 2014, https://www.washingtonpost.com/opinions/why-being-too-busy-makes-us-feel-so-good/2014/03/14/c098f6c8-9e81-11e3-a050-dc3322a94fa7_story.html (accessed October 15, 2015).

31   Peter Roesler, "FTC Says Advertorial Native Ads May Be Illegal," Web Marketing Pros Blog, January 1, 2014, http://www.webmarketingpros.com/blog/ftc-says-advertorial-native-ads-may-be-illegal/ (accessed October 27, 2015).

32   "How the Marine Corps Enlists Big Data for Recruitment Efforts," *Advertising Age*, January 13, 2014, http://adage.com/article/datadriven-marketing/marine-corps-enlists-big-data-recruitment/291009/ (accessed January 20, 2014).

33   Viktor Mayer-Schonberger and Kenneth Cukier, *Big Data: A Revolution That Will Transform How We Live, Work, and Think* (Boston: Houghton Mifflin Harcourt, 2013).

34   Alex Morris, "How Crisis Text Line Founder Nancy Lublin is Saving Lives, Text by Text," *Glamour*, July 19, 2015, http://www.glamour.com/inspired/2015/06/crisis-text-line-founder-nancy-lublin (accessed October 27, 2015).

35   Lena Groeger, Charles Ornstein, Mike Tigas, and Ryann Grochowski Jones, "Dollars for Docs: How Industry Dollars Reach Your Doctors," July 1, 2015, https://projects.propublica.org/docdollars/ (accessed October 27, 2015).

36   Ben Hubbard, "Young Saudis, Bound by Conservative Strictures, Find Freedom on Their Phones," *New York Times*, May 22, 2015, http://www.nytimes.com/2015/05/23/world/middleeast/saudi-arabia-youths-cellphone-apps-freedom.html (accessed May 28, 2015).

37   Lee Rainie, Aaron Smith, and Maeve Duggan, "Coming and Going on Facebook," Pew Research Center, 2013, http://www.pewInternet.org/2013/02/05/coming-and-going-on-facebook/ (accessed October 27, 2015).

38   Oliver Burkeman, "Conscious computing: how to take control of your life online," *The Guardian*, May 10, 2013, http://www.theguardian.com/technology/2013/may/10/conscious-computing-twitter-facebook-google (accessed October 27, 2015).

39   Alexis C. Madrigal, "'Camp Grounded,' 'Digital Detox,' and the Age of Techno-Anxiety," *The Atlantic*, July 9, 2013, http://www.theatlantic.com/technology/archive/2013/07/camp-grounded-digital-detox-and-the-age-of-techno-anxiety/277600/(accessed October 27, 2015).

40   Richard Sennett, "Real progressives believe in breaking up Google," *Financial Times*, June 28, 2013, http://www.ft.com/intl/cms/s/0/06512782-de6e-11e2-9b47-00144feab7de.html (accessed October 27, 2015).

41   Farhad Manjoo, "'Right to be Forgotten' Online Could Spread." *New York Times*, August 6, 2015, http://www.nytimes.com/2015/08/06/technology/personaltech/right-to-be-forgotten-online-is-poised-to-spread.html.

42   Finn Brunton and Helen Nissenbaum, *Obfuscation: A User's Guide for Privacy and Protest* (Cambridge, MA: MIT Press, 2015).